A Voice from Waterloo

A Voice from Waterloo

The Personal Experiences of a
British Cavalryman Who Became
a Battlefield Guide and Authority
on the Campaign of 1815

Sergeant-Major
Edward Cotton

LEONAUR

*A Voice from Waterloo: the Personal Experiences of a British Cavalryman
Who Became a Battlefield Guide and Authority on the Campaign of 1815*
by Edward Cotton

Published by Leonaur Ltd

ISBN: 978-1-84677-346-8 (hardcover)
ISBN: 978-1-84677-347-1 (softcover)

http://www.leonaur.com

Publisher's Note

The opinions expressed in this book are those of the author
and are not necessarily those of the publisher.

Contents

Preface   7

Napoleon's Return   13

The Eve of Waterloo   32

The Battle Commences   61

The Great Charges   86

The Prussians Arrive   99

The Struggle for the Centre   113

The Imperial Guard Attacks   126

The Advance   139

The Pursuit to Paris   154

Official Accounts   162

Afterword   197

Appendices   233

Sergeant-Major Cotton's Waterloo Cabinet   311

Preface

A Voice from Waterloo is the unassuming tale of an old soldier who was an eyewitness of and actor in many of the scenes he attempts to describe. His having resided more than fourteen years on the field, as Guide, and Describer of the battle, may be considered as the parent of the present memoirs[1].

No one can be more convinced than I am, of my inability to do justice to the subject, but I have had great advantages in communicating personally on the spot with "Waterloo men" of every nation; all of whom, from the General to the private, have evidently considered it, at once, a duty and a pleasure to assist an old companion in arms. The inquiries and comments made by those gallant men, have afforded me opportunities of gleaning much information which no other person has obtained; this has enabled me to give a fuller and truer history of the battle, than a more talented man could have done, unless he had enjoyed the same privi-

---

1. In the first instance this little volume was only intended for sale on the battlefield and in Belgium, but, from the quick sale of the first and second editions, I have been induced to put it into the hands of a London publisher.

lege. I have also read the *whole* of the numerous accounts of the military operations of 1815, which have been published in French, English, and German.

General Jomini observes, that a soldier writes well enough if he can make himself understood. To write on military operations requires a soldier's pen, as no other can properly treat of military matters.

The reader will here find many new facts, and meet with several interesting and pertinent documents that have never before appeared in the English language; given with an accuracy and detail which I regard as quite my own.

One of my objects in writing is to correct opinions which have gone forth, and which are greatly at variance with facts: opinions so erroneous as to warrant the remark of the highly talented General already referred to, that "Never was a battle so confusedly described as that of Waterloo." It is certain that the hour of many occurrences on the field has been erroneously stated; such as of the arrival, or rather becoming engaged, of the different Prussian corps; the foil of La Haye Sainte, defeat of the Imperial Guards, etc.[2]

Notwithstanding this, after the publication of so many accounts of the battle of the 18th of June, it may be fairly asked, upon what grounds I expect to awaken fresh interest in a subject so long before the public. Can I reconcile the conflicting statements which have already appeared in print? Can I add to the information which most of my countrymen already possess concerning this memorable epoch? Or can I present that information in a compendious and lucid form, such as the General reader may still want? Something in all these ways, I hope I have accomplished.

Putting aside some of the French and English accounts as not only irreconcilable with facts, but as self-refuted by their

---

2. It was near half-past five o'clock before Büllow's advanced troops became engaged; and the sun was setting (a quarter past eight) when the Imperial Guards were repulsed.

inconsistencies and mutual contradictions—using such of the French narratives as agree with those of their opponents, which, as Wellington observed of Napoleon's bulletins, may be safely relied upon as far as they tell against themselves—I have cleared up a great number of the points disputed by our own writers, who agree in the main, but differ in some circumstances involving not merely questions of time and locality of certain events, but even the claims of individuals, regiments and brigades to the honour attached to their deeds on that day. By my long residence at Mont St. Jean, constant study of the surface of the battlefield, knowledge of the composition and even *dress* of the different bodies of the French troops which stood before us, and my close attention to the remarks made by many a gallant comrade revisiting the spot, I have in a great measure succeeded in reconciling discrepancies which perhaps no other person could explain.

I am also emboldened to think that my *Voice from Waterloo* presents to the General reader all the leading facts of this eventful struggle, in so concise a manner, and at so moderate a cost, as to secure it a preference over every other narration of the battle. I feel confident that this work will furnish the visitor to the field, with a local guide not to be found in any description hitherto published.

In the Appendix to this work, No. VII, are testimonials of my more than common acquaintance with the incidents of the battle, testimonials left in my hands by some of the most distinguished officers who took part in the fight. Other documents of similar import I am proud to possess, and am ready to show to all who visit Waterloo.

Although not strictly belonging to *A Voice from Waterloo*, I have added, as a connecting link in the narrative, an outline map, and a sketch of the military operations of the campaign of 1815.

Most anxious to avoid the imputation of having employed the materials of others without acknowledgment, I beg to state that, besides the various military periodicals, I have made use of Captain Siborne's *History of the War in France and Belgium*[3]; *The Military Life of the Duke of Wellington*, by Major Basil Jackson[4] and Captain R. Scott; *The Wellington Despatches and General Orders*, by Colonel Gurwood; *Fall of Napoleon*, by Colonel Mitchel; *Political and Military Life of Napoleon* and *The Art of War* by General Jomini; *History of the King's German Legion*, by Major Beamish; *Prussian History of the Campaign of 1815*, by General Grollman, etc., etc.

As to the manner in which I have executed my task, I know I am open to criticism. No doubt many of my remarks will be considered too digressive. Some persons will think I am too hard upon Napoleon: my authorities in this are more frequently French than English. Others will judge me too partial to the immortal Wellington. Be it so: for I confess that I think it impossible to estimate his services too highly as a soldier, or as a statesman. Let no man contradict me until he has read the *Despatches*, etc. Is there another man on the records of history in whom we see such a combination of talent, patriotism, firmness, and perseverance? Even Napoleon confessed of him what he said of no other man: "In the management of an army he is fully my equal, and in prudence my superior." General Bertrand attested this, (see Scott's *Napoleon*, chap. 109.) Britons take a larger view, and appreciate his varied qualifications much more highly.

Waterloo was termed by Napoleon, "a concurrence of unexampled fatalities, a day not to be comprehended. Was there treason? or was there only misfortune?"

Wellington said, that "he had never before fought so hard

---

3. Captain Siborne's work may, beyond a doubt, be considered the standard history of the Waterloo campaign.

4. To Major Basil Jackson's able pen, through the pages of the United Service Magazine, I am most particularly indebted for information on various occasions.

a battle, nor won so great a victory." If the reader derive the same impression from his attention to *A Voice from Waterloo*, I shall be satisfied, because I shall have succeeded.

Edward Cotton
Mont St. Jean
February, 1840

CHAPTER 1

Napoleon's Return

On the 26th of February 1815, Napoleon, accompanied by twelve hundred of his guards, and all his civil and military officers, secretly left the isle of Elba, and landed the 1st of March, near Cannes, on the coast of France. The Emperor immediately marched towards the French capital; and arrived in Paris on the evening of the 20th; the same day that Louis XVIII set out for Ghent. Joined by all the troops which had been sent to oppose him, Napoleon was enabled to re-establish his authority in France. Amongst those who rejoined him, was Marshal Ney, "*le brave des braves;*" he who had so warmly expressed himself in favour of the restoration of the Bourbons, and who, when appointed to the command of a body of troops to oppose his former master, declared, whilst kissing the King's hand, that "he would bring back Napoleon *in an iron cage.*" And Ney and the iron cage was the chief topic of conversation in Paris, when the news of his having joined Napoleon with his *corps d'armée* reached that capital[1].

---

1. "I did in truth," said Ney at his trial, "kiss the hand of the King, His Majesty having presented it to me when he wished me a good journey. I spoke of the descent of Napoleon with indignation, and made use of the expression, *the iron cage.* During the night of the 13th of March, (down to which time I protest my fidelity,) I received a proclamation from Napoleon, which I signed." On the following day he published the fatal proclamation to his troops, which afterwards cost him his life. See Appendix.

The great powers of Europe, then assembled in congress at Vienna, instantly declared, that Napoleon, by breaking the convention which established him as an independent sovereign at Elba, had destroyed the only legal title on which his political existence depended; placed himself without the pale of the law, and had proved to the world, that there could neither be truce nor peace with him. The allied powers, in consequence, denounced Napoleon, as the enemy and disturber of the tranquillity of Europe, and resolved immediately upon uniting their forces against him and his faction, to preserve, if possible, the General peace.

Notwithstanding the hostile declaration of the allied sovereigns, they were utterly unable to put their armies in motion without that most powerful lever, *English gold,* the real sinews of war. Britain's expenditure in 1815, was no less than 110,000,000*l.*

Menacing, however, as the position of the allies towards Napoleon appeared to be, and imposing as were their armies assembling to oppose him, he assumed a bold and resolute posture of defence.

The general aspect of France at that time was singularly warlike; nearly the whole nation appeared to he electrified, and buckled on its armour to join the messenger of war. The exaltation of Napoleon was soon however sobered down by the arrival in Paris of the declaration of the allied powers, which was little calculated to produce a favourable impression, as to the ultimate success of the Emperor's enterprise. The war-cry of Europe was now, *Draw the sword, throw away the scabbard,* until the usurper, with whom all treaty or truce had become impossible, should be entirely subjugated and his adherents put down.

Napoleon, however, appeared undismayed, and endeavoured, by every means, to conceal the determined resolution of Europe from the French nation, who, for the most part, cheerfully responded to their leader's call. Troops were quickly organized all over the country, as if by magic. The scarred veterans of a hundred battles, they who had followed their *petit caporal* through many a gory fight, heard with joy the voice of their idolized Emperor, summoning them again to glorious war and the battlefield. There was a generation of fierce daring, war-breathing men, ever ready to range themselves under the Imperial banners. Davoust states that France, on Napoleon's return, was overrun with soldiers, just released from the prisons of Europe, most of whom counted as many battles as years, and who quickly flocked round the Imperial eagles. France, in a short time, bore the appearance of a vast camp.

To surround Paris completely with fortifications, which has been since done by Louis-Philippe, was also desired by Napoleon, who inquired of Carnot, how much time and money it would require. "Three years and two hundred millions," replied the minister, "and when finished, I would only ask for sixty thousand men and twenty-four hours to demolish the whole."

Early in April 1815, the allied troops began to assemble in Belgium. The Anglo-Hanoverian army, commanded by the Prince of Orange, (now King of Holland,) had occupied the Low Countries for the protection of Belgium and Holland, lately constituted by the congress of Vienna into a new monarchy, under the name of the Kingdom of the Netherlands. This army comprised about 28,000 men, 10,000 being composed of British and German troops, a part of them the remains of Lord Lynedoch's army, and the rest made up of young Hanoverians. 20,000 Dutch-Belgians were raised to act in concert with these troops. The General appearance of the army is thus described by Sir Henry, now Lord Hardinge, in a letter to Lord Stewart:

> This army is not unlike Lord Handcliff's description of
> a French pack of hounds, pointers, poodles, turnspits, all
> mixed up together and running in sad confusion.

15

The Duke of Wellington arrived in Brussels from the congress of Vienna on the night of April 4th, and took from the Prince of Orange the command of the allied army; but the Dutch-Belgian army had not been placed immediately under the Duke's command. His Grace being strongly convinced that his power of regulating the movements of the Dutch-Belgian troops ought not to be left open to any cavil or dispute, demanded the most unequivocal statement upon this matter from the King of the Netherlands, who wisely placed all his forces at the absolute disposal of the Duke. Nothing less than this measure could have made those troops serviceable to the cause of their country; such was still the fascinating power of Napoleon's name over countries in which his rule and conscriptions had subdued and enervated the minds of men.

On the 4th of May, Wellington received copies of the King's decrees, making him Field-Marshal in his service, and placing the Dutch-Belgian army entirely under his command. The Duke immediately put matters in a better condition[2], and instructed the Prince of Orange how to keep up the necessary communications[3]. He transferred Prince Frederick's corps to Lord Hill[4], warned the Duke of Berry, the Prussian commandant at Charleroy, and all others concerned, to be on the alert; he also gave them exact accounts of the movements and strength of the enemy between Valenciennes and Maubeuge. All this was accomplished by the Duke before the 10th of May.

On the 11th, he wrote to Sir Henry Hardinge, then at the Prussian headquarters, that he reckoned the enemy's strength on the frontiers at 110,000 men; and was glad that Blücher was drawing his forces nearer to the British. His Grace adopted the most effective measures for placing all the fortified

---

2. See Gurwood, *Despatches,* vol. XII, page 356.
3. *Ibid.,* page 363.
4. *Ibid.,* page 365.

towns and strong places in a condition to embarrass the enemy; and notwithstanding the objections made, by interested parties, to the necessary inundations, he was firm in ordering them, wherever the General security required it.

The Duke sent able engineers to limit, as much as possible, the injury arising from letting out the waters, and to inundate with fresh instead of salt water, when practicable. For this timely care of the General interests, and even, as far as it was possible, of private property, the return he met with was unceasing complaints from the authorities of the several towns, where these measures had been applied. But the Duke did his duty firmly, and, after some expostulation with unreasonable grumblers, compelled them to do theirs.

On the 7th of June, he issued his orders for the defence of the towns of Antwerp, Ostend, Nieuport, Ypres, Tournay, Ath, Mons and Ghent. The governors of these respective towns were required to declare them in a state of siege, the moment the enemy should put his foot on the Belgian territory: the towns were to be defended to the utmost; and if any governor surrendered before sustaining at least one assault, and without the consent of his council, he should be deemed guilty, not only of military disobedience, but of high treason. Such decisive measures were rendered necessary, in consequence of the equivocal loyalty of many who held municipal and military rank in the Netherlands. The King had prudently invested Wellington with these important powers, and no man could have exercised them more effectively.

The French court (Louis XVIII and his suite) received advice how to save themselves by retiring to Antwerp, in case the enemy should succeed in turning the British right: they were desired to be in no alarm, nor to be startled by mere rumours, but to await positive information. Having thus provided for the military wants, and even for the *fears* of those behind him, the Duke devoted his whole attention to the army; and in proportion as the storm approached, repeated his warnings to the Prussians, by incessant despatches to Sir Henry Hardinge. He also sent frequent instructions to his own officers who were the nearest to the enemy, to keep on the alert.

The regiment I belonged to disembarked at Ostend on the 21st of April, and we soon found there was work in hand. Swords were to be ground and well-pointed, and the frequent inspections of arms, ammunition, camp equipage, etc., plainly announced that we were shortly about to take the field. The army, soon after our arrival, had, in consequence of a secret memorandum[5] issued by the Duke of Wellington to the chief officers in command, drawn closer together, in the probable expectation of its being attacked, and our great antagonist was not the sort of man to send us word of the when and the where. Louis XVIII, with his suite and a train of followers, being with us at Ghent, we were not destitute of information. Napoleon was as well informed of all that transpired in Belgium as if it had taken place at the Tuileries.

Things continued in this state until June, when, from various rumours, we began to be more on the alert.

At the commencement of operations, the Duke of Wellington's army comprised about 100,000 men, including the troops in garrison, and composed of about 35,000 British, 6,000 King's German Legion, 24,000 Hanoverians, 7,000 Brunswickers, and 32,000 Dutch-Belgian and Nassau-men, with a hundred and ninety-six guns. Many in the ranks of the last-named troops had served under Napoleon, and there still prevailed amongst them a most powerful prejudice in his favour; it was natural, therefore, that we should not place too strong a reliance upon them, whenever they might become opposed to their old companions in arms.

The Anglo-allied army was divided into two corps, of five divisions each. The first was commanded by the Prince of Orange, and its headquarters, Braine-le-Comte. The headquarters of the second corps, under Lord Hill, were at Grammont.

5. See Appendix, No. 1.

The cavalry, divided into eleven brigades, was commanded by the Earl of Uxbridge, now Marquis of Anglesey; its headquarters were at Ninove. His Grace's headquarters were at Brussels, in and around which place was our reserve of all arms, ready to be thrown into whatever point of our line on the frontier the enemy might attack, so as to hold the ground until the rest of the army could be united.

The Prussian army, under the veteran Prince Blücher, consisted of about 115,000 men, divided into four corps, each composed of four brigades. The headquarters of the 1st, or Zieten's corps, were at Charleroy; the 2nd, Pirch's, at Namur, which was also Blücher's headquarters; the 3rd, Thielmann's, at Ciney; and the 4th, Bülow's, at Liege.

Each corps had a reserve cavalry attached, and was respectively commanded by Generals Roder, Jurgass, Hobe, and Prince William. Their artillery comprised three hundred and twelve guns.

A large proportion of the British troops was weak; second and third battalions made up of militia and recruits, who had never been under fire; most of our best-tried Spanish infantry, the victors of many a hard-fought field, were on their way from America. The foreign troops, with the exception of the old gallant Peninsular German Legion, were chiefly composed of raw levies, hastily embodied, and very imperfectly drilled; quite inexperienced in war, and wholly strangers to the British troops and to each other. Nor was the Prussian army what it had been; it was no longer the old Silesian one: many had just been embodied, and thousands had fought under the Imperial eagles.

The French army of the North, commanded by the Emperor in person, and destined to act against Belgium, early in June, was divided into seven corps, and cantoned: the 1st, or D'Erlon's, at Lille; the 2nd, or Reille's, at Valenciennes; the 3rd, or Vandamme's, at Mézières; the 4th, or Gerard's, at Metz; and the 6th, or Lobau's, at Laon. The Imperial Guards were at Paris. The reserve cavalry, commanded by Generals Pajol, Excelmans, Milhaud, and Kellermann, cantoned between the Aisne, the Meuse and the Sambre. These, with three hundred and fifty pieces of artillery, constituted the Grand Army with which Napoleon made his eruption into Belgium.

The principal towns of Belgium, as we have previously mentioned, were prepared for defence, and orders were given to declare them to be in a state of siege, as soon as the French should have crossed the frontiers and entered the Belgian territory.

The Prussian army, under the veteran Prince Blücher, and most eager for revenge, was posted on the frontier upon our left, from Charleroy to Maestricht. Our left, communicating with Blücher's right, was at Binche; and our right stretched to the sea.

On the 16th of May, we received intelligence of there being 110,000 French troops in our front; on the 1st of June it was rumoured, we should be attacked. Napoleon was expected at Laon on the 6th, and extraordinary preparations were being made for the conveyance of troops in carriages from Paris to the frontiers.

Intelligence reached the Duke, on the 10th of the same month, that Napoleon had arrived at Maubeuge, and was passing along the frontier. On the 12th it was ascertained, for certain, that the French army had assembled, and was about to cross the frontiers[6]; but the Duke, for reasons we shall hereafter give, did not think proper to move his troops until quite satisfied as to the point where Napoleon would make his attack; the point proved to be Charleroy, on the highroad to Brussels, on the left of the allied and right of the Prussian armies, said to be the most favourable for defeating the two armies in detail; which I am inclined to doubt.

---

6. Colonel De Wissel, of the 1st German hussars, reported the fact to General Vivian, who went to the outposts next day, and, finding the enemy ready to attack, informed the Duke.

Brussels, the capital of Belgium, is situated in the very centre of that country, which was declared by that able officer General Gneisenau, chief of the Prussian staff, to be a formidable bastion, flanking efficaciously any invasion meditated by France against Germany, and serving at the same time as a *tête de pont* to England.

In Belgium Napoleon had numerous partisans and friends who secretly espoused his cause, and who, no doubt, would have seconded him in his attempt to again annex this country to the French Empire. The people also were by no means reconciled to the union forced upon them by the congress of Vienna, a union with a country differing from them in religion and customs; and the dense population and troops of Belgium might probably have made a movement in favour of the French, had Napoleon obtained possession of the capital. From the tenor of Napoleon's letter to Ney, and his proclamations to the army and to the Belgians, given further on, it is quite evident that the Emperor expected a manifestation of this kind, which would certainly have added that moral force to his cause, of which it stood so much in need, and have induced thousands to rally round the Imperial eagles.

Brussels was our main line of operations and the line of communication with Ostend and Antwerp, the depots where our reinforcements and supplies were landed. The Duke, in consequence, saw clearly, it was of the utmost importance, both in a military and political point of view, that the enemy should not, even for a moment, obtain possession of Brussels[7].

Napoleon's intention of taking the two armies by surprise, was defeated, on the night of the 13th, by the circumstance of the Prussian outposts, in advance of Charleroy, having observed the horizon illumined by the reflection of numerous bivouac fires in the direction of Beaumont, which announced that a numerous enemy had assembled in their immediate

---

7. See Gurwood, *Despatches*, vol. XII, p. 390.

front; the intelligence of which was forthwith transmitted to each of the commanders.

Zieten, the Prussian commander in front of Charleroy, received intelligence, on the afternoon of the 14th, that the enemy's columns were assembling in his front, the certain prelude to an attack, probably the next day. Blücher, apprized of this about ten o'clock the same evening, immediately sent off orders for the concentration of the Prussian army at Fleurus, a preconcerted plan between the two commanders. When the order was first sent to Bülow at Liege, to move to Hannut, had the most trifling hint been given him of the French being about to attack, he would have been up in time to share in the battle of Ligny, which probably would have changed the aspect of affairs.

After despatching orders for the concentration of the Grand Army, Napoleon left Paris on the 12th, as he himself states, under a great depression of spirits, aware he was leaving a host of enemies behind, more formidable to his authority than those he was going to confront. He slept at Laon, and arrived at Avesnes on the 13th, near which place he found his army assembled, and amounting, according to his own account, to 122,400 men and three hundred and fifty guns. Their bivouacs were behind small hills, about a league from the frontier, situated so as to be concealed, in a great measure, from the view of their opponents.

The Emperor's arrival amongst his devoted soldiers raised their spirits to the highest degree of enthusiasm, and on the 14th he issued the following soul-stirring order:

Imperial Headquarters
14th June, 1815
Napoleon, by the grace of God and the constitution of the Empire, Emperor of the French, etc., to the Grand Army.

Soldiers! this day is the anniversary of Marengo and of Friedland, which twice decided the fate of Europe. Then, as after Austerlitz, as after Wagram, we were too generous: we believed in the protestations and in the oaths of

Princes, whom we left on their thrones. Now, however, leagued together, they aim at the independence and most sacred rights of France. They have commenced the most unjust of aggressions. Let us then march to meet them: are they, and we, no longer the same men?

Soldiers! at Jena, against those same Prussians, now so arrogant, you were one to three, and at Montmirail one to six. Let those amongst you, who have been captives to the English, describe the nature of their prison ships, and the frightful miseries they endured.

The Saxons, the Belgians, the Hanoverians, the soldiers of the Confederation of the Rhine, lament that they are compelled to use their arms in the cause of Princes, the enemies of justice, and of the rights of nations. They know that this coalition is insatiable: after having devoured twelve millions of Italians, one million of Saxons, and six millions of Belgians, it now wishes to devour the States of the second rank in Germany. Madmen! one moment of prosperity has bewildered them: the oppression and humiliation of the French people are beyond their power: if they enter France, they will find their grave.

Soldiers! we have forced marches to make, battles to fight, dangers to encounter; but with firmness, victory will be ours.

The rights, the honour and the happiness of the country will be recovered.

To every Frenchman who has a heart, the moment is now arrived to conquer or to die.[8]

---

8. One would say, after such language as this to his devoted and enthusiastic followers, and maintaining as Napoleon did, that Frederick the Great was right in carrying poison about his person to put an end to his existence in case of a great reverse of fortune, "He was right, he was right, it would have been dastardly indeed to live like a wretch *(pleutre)* after having once attained to the highest pinnacle of fame;" the Emperor would have brought his actions more in unison with his words, if, when on finding the day of Waterloo going against him, he had led his Imperial Guards, in person, to attack our position.

About four o'clock in the morning of the 15th of June, Napoleon attacked the Prussian outposts in front of Charleroy, at Thuin and Lobbes[9]. The Prussians fell back, slowly and with great caution, on their supports. By some unaccountable neglect Wellington was not informed of the attack until after three o'clock in the afternoon, although the distance from Thuin and Lobbes to Brussels is under forty miles[10]. Had a well arranged communication been kept up, the Duke should have been informed of the first advance of the French by nine o'clock a. m., and of the real line of attack by three p. m.

The French were in possession of Charleroy by eleven o'clock. The Prussians retired to a position between Ligny and St. Amand, nearly twenty miles from the outposts. At three o'clock in the afternoon, the 2nd Prussian corps had taken position not far from Ligny; Blücher had established his headquarters at Sombreffe. The advanced posts of the French left column were at Frasnes, three miles beyond Quatre-Bras, from which the advanced posts of the allies had been driven. Ney's headquarters were at Gosselies, with a part of his troops only, whilst D'Erlon's corps and the cavalry of Kellermann were on the Sambre. The centre column of the French army lay near Fleurus, the right column near Châtelet, and the reserve, composed of the Imperial Guards and the 6th corps, between Charleroy and Fleurus.

The Duke of Wellington, although apprized of the advance of Napoleon and his attack on the Prussian outposts, would, notwithstanding, make no movement to leave Brussels uncovered, until certain of the real line of attack, as such attacks are often made to mask the real direction of the main body of the enemy. But orders were immediately

---

9. See outline Map of the campaign.
10. Had General Zieten been equally alert in making the Duke of Wellington acquainted with the attack of the French, as he was in communicating the intelligence to Blücher, the battle of Ligny might have either not been fought at all, or would have terminated less disastrously to his countrymen. (Gleig's *Story of the Battle of Waterloo*.)

transmitted to the different divisions to assemble and hold themselves in readiness to march, *some at a moment's notice, and some at daylight in the morning*[11].

Lord Uxbridge was ordered to get the cavalry together at the headquarters (Ninove) that night, leaving the 2nd hussars of the King's German Legion, on the look-out between the Scheldt and the Lys.

The troops in Brussels, composed of the 6th, or Picton's division, the 81st regiment, and the Hanoverian brigade of the 6th division, called the reserve, were to be in readiness to march at a moment's notice.

After the Duke had completed his arrangements for the concentration of the army, His Grace, with many of our officers, went to the celebrated ball, given on the eve of the memorable engagement at Quatre-Bras, by the Duchess of Richmond, at her residence. The saloons of the Duchess were filled with a brilliant company of distinguished guests. The officers in their magnificent uniforms threading the mazy dance with the most lovely and beautiful women. The ball was at its height, when the Duke of Wellington first received *positive* intelligence that Napoleon had crossed the Sambre with his whole army and taken possession of Charleroy.

The excitement which ensued, on the company being made acquainted with Napoleon's advance, was most extraordinary. The countenances, which, a moment before, were lighted up with pleasure and gaiety, now wore a more solemn aspect. The Duke of Brunswick, sitting with a child on his knees, was so affected, that in rising he let the child fall on the floor. Little imagined the guests, that the music which accompanied the gay and lively dances at Her Grace's ball, would so shortly re-echo more martial airs on the battlefield, or that some of the officers present at the fete might be afterwards seen fighting in their ball dresses, and in that costume found amongst the slain.

---

11. See Appendix, No. I.

At about the same time, His Grace also received information from his outposts in front of Mons, and from other sources, which proved that the enemy's movement upon Charleroy was the real point of attack, and he immediately issued the following orders:

Brussels
15th June, 1815
After-orders.—10 o'clock, p. m.
Picton's division, to march on Waterloo at two o'clock tomorrow morning.

The 3rd, or Alten's division of infantry, to continue its movement from Braine-le-Comte upon Nivelles.

The 1st, or Cooke's division of infantry, to move from Enghien upon Braine-le-Comte.

The 2nd, or Clinton's, and 4th, or Colville's division of infantry, to move from Ath and Grammont, also from Audenaerde, and to continue their movement upon Enghien.

The cavalry, to continue its movement from Ninove upon Enghien.

The above movements to take place with as little delay as possible.
Wellington

Picton's division and the Hanoverian brigade marched from Brussels about two o'clock a. m., on the 16th, taking the road to Waterloo by the forest of Soigne; near which they halted, and shortly after they were joined by the Brunswickers.

And Ardennes[12] *waves above them her green leaves,*
Dewy with nature's tear-drops, as they pass,
Grieving, if aught inanimate e'er grieves,
Over the unreturning brave—alas I
Ere evening to be trodden like the grass,
Which now beneath them, but above shall grow,

---

12. A pity the poet did not put, *Soigne.*

In its next verdure, when this fiery mass,
Of living valour, rolling on the foe
And burning with high hope, shall moulder cold and low.

While halted, the Duke of Wellington passed and gave strict orders to keep the road clear of baggage, and everything that might obstruct the movements of the troops. The Duke of Brunswick dismounted, and seated himself on a bank on the roadside, in company of his adjutant-General, Colonel Olferman. How little idea had many who observed this incident relative to the illustrious Duke, that in a few hours he would be laid low with many of themselves! and numbers truly there were amongst the slain ere the sun set.

The troops were halted to refresh, and to await orders, to march either on Nivelles or Quatre-Bras, (the roads branching off at Mont St. Jean,) according as the Duke might direct, upon his becoming acquainted with the real state of affairs in front. About twelve o'clock, orders arrived for the troops to proceed on to Quatre-Bras, leaving the baggage behind; this looked rather warlike, but as yet nothing was known for certain. The Duke galloped on, and, after a hasty glance at the Waterloo position, spurred on to Quatre-Bras, where he conversed with the Prince of Orange, and well reconnoitred the enemy's position. Finding the latter not in great force, he rode on to hold a conference with Blücher, whom he found about half past one o'clock p. m. at the windmill at Bussy, between Ligny and Bry, where about noon three corps of the Prussian army, about 85,000 men, were in position. After the conference, during which His Grace saw that the enemy were in great force in Blücher's front, the Duke promising to support his gallant and venerable colleague, shook hands and pushed back to Quatre-Bras, where he arrived a little before three o'clock, soon after which time Napoleon began his attack upon Blücher.

Marshal Ney, who commanded the French troops at Quatre-Bras, commenced his attack upon Perponcher's Dutch-

Belgian division under the Prince of Orange. About two o'clock, shortly after the Duke arrived, Picton's division, composed of Kempt's brigade, the 28th, 32nd, 79th Highlanders, and 1st battalion 95th rifles, and of Pack's brigade, the 1st Royal, 44th, 42nd and 92nd Highlanders, with Best's Hanoverian brigade, came up; soon after the Brunswickers arrived. Towards six o'clock, Sir Colin Halkett's brigade, the 30th, 33rd, 69th, and 73rd regiments, also Kielmansegge's Hanoverian brigade, most opportunely arrived at the scene of action.

At this time Pack's noble fellows were so hard pressed, and so much exhausted, together with their ammunition being all but expended, that Sir Denis Pack applied for a fresh supply of cartridges, or assistance, to Sir Colin Halkett, who immediately ordered the 69th to push on and obey any orders given by Pack; the latter then galloped forward to a commanding point, and soon discovered the formation of a large force of cuirassiers preparing for attack. He spurred off to his brigade to prepare them for the coming storm, and in passing by the 69th, ordered Colonel Morice to form square, as the enemy's cavalry was at hand. The formation was nearly completed, when the Prince of Orange rode up, and, by a decided misconception, most indiscreetly directed them to reform line, which they were in the act of doing, when the rushing noise in the high corn announced the arrival of the enemy's cuirassiers, who charged them in flank, rode right along them, regularly rolling them up. A cuirassier carried off the 69th's colour, in defence of which cadet Clarke, afterwards Lieutenant in the 42nd, received twenty-three wounds, one of which deprived him of the use of an arm for life.

The Duke of Wellington was nearly taken prisoner, and owed his escape to an order which he promptly gave to a part of the 92nd, who were lining a ditch, to lie down whilst he galloped over them.

A little before seven o'clock, Sir G. Cooke's division, composed of the 1st brigade, under Major-General Maitland, (the second and third battalions of the 1st foot-guards,) and of the 2nd brigade, under Sir J. Byng, (now Lord Strafford,) composed of the 2nd battalions of the Coldstream and the 3rd foot-guards, came up, and soon drove the enemy back. Ney's attacks were maintained with the greatest impetuosity during the first hours, but as our reinforcements arrived, became fewer and feebler, and towards the close of the day conducted with greater caution, and, soon after sunset, Ney fell back upon Frasnes, and the desperate struggle terminated. The Duke of Wellington then advanced his victorious troops to the foot of the French position, when piquets were thrown forward for the night by both sides.

Thus the action of Quatre-Bras terminated, during which our troops were fully employed, and the Duke was unable to render his promised aid to the Prussians. It was only through the greatest personal exertions of our gallant chief and the most determined resistance on the part of his troops, that the enemy's attacks were repulsed, and our communication with Blücher at Ligny by the Namur road kept open. The Emperor's instructions to Ney to drive back the English, whom he supposed to be at that point in no great force, and afterwards to turn round and envelop the Prussian right flank, were thus completely frustrated. Our force in the field towards the close of the day was about 29,000 infantry, 2,000 cavalry, and sixty-eight guns; that of the enemy about 16,000 infantry, 6,000 cavalry, with fifty guns.

To the fortunate circumstance of the marching and countermarching of D'Erlon's corps (Ney's reserve) between Frasnes, Ligny and Quatre-Bras, without pulling a trigger, we may probably attribute our success on the 16th. An additional force of 25,000 men, either at Ligny or Quatre-Bras, might have gained Napoleon a decisive victory.

The action at Quatre-Bras possessed its own separate merits, of the greatest importance, and with our masterly retreat to the Waterloo position would have been sounded by the trumpet of fame, but for the glorious achievement that followed on the field of Waterloo, which eclipsed all.

In no battle did the British infantry display more valour or more cool determined courage than at Quatre-Bras. Cavalry we had none that could stand the shock of the French; the Brunswick and Belgian cavalry, it is true, made an attempt, but were scattered like chaff before the wind by the veteran cuirassiers, who, to render them the more effective, had been mounted on horses taken from the gendarmes throughout France. The British cavalry had had a long march, some nearly forty miles, and consequently did not arrive until the battle was over. The gallant Picton, seeing the cavalry driven back, led on our infantry in squares into the centre of the enemy's masses of cavalry, facing charging squadrons with squares, and in line against heavy columns of infantry. What may not be effected by such troops, led by such a General? The Duke of Brunswick, Colonel Sir Robert Macara of the 42nd, and Colonel Cameron of the 92nd, were killed.

During our struggle at Quatre-Bras, Napoleon had attacked the Prussians at Ligny, and between nine and ten o'clock in the evening, their centre was broken, and they began a retreat upon Wavre[13]. The horse of Marshal Blücher, a beautiful grey charger, presented to him by our Prince Regent in 1814, was shot under him, and, while lying on the ground, the Field-Marshal was twice charged over by the enemy's cavalry. Sir Henry Hardinge, attached to the Prussian headquarters, lost his left hand at Ligny; and about eight thousand Prussians deserted and returned home.

The battle of Ligny may be considered a series of village fights, and probably, had the impetuous old hussar, the gallant Blücher, then seventy-three years of age, not drawn troops

---

13. What appears most astonishing is, that the real line of retreat of the Prussian columns was not discovered by the victorious French until the afternoon of the 17th

from his centre, to strengthen his right, and to enable him to attack the enemy's left, he might probably have maintained his position; but immediately Napoleon perceived that Blücher drew his troops from his centre, he made a dash at it, forced it, and thus gained the victory. Notwithstanding the Prussians were defeated, they highly distinguished themselves by their valour and audacity.

The battle of Ligny was a fierce and sanguinary contest, and little or no quarter given by either side. Both were excited by deadly animosity, and the helpless wounded became the victims. The Prussian loss was about fifteen thousand men and twenty-five guns, exclusive of the eight thousand men that disbanded themselves. The French loss rather less.

CHAPTER 2

The Eve of Waterloo

Our bivouac was quiet during the night, except that the arrival of cavalry and artillery caused an occasional movement.

About two o'clock in the morning, a cavalry patrol got between the piquets, and a rattling fire of musketry began, which brought some of our Generals to the spot; Picton was the first that arrived, when it was found that no attempt to advance had been made, and all was soon quiet again. After which the stillness of the enemy quite surprised His Grace, and drew the remark, "They are possibly retreating."

The Duke, who had slept at Genappe, came up early. Up to this time we had no satisfactory intelligence of the Prussians. His Grace consequently sent a patrol along the Namur road to gain intelligence; Captain Gray's troop of the 10th hussars was sent on this duty, accompanied by Lieutenant-Colonel the Hon. Sir Alexander Gordon, one of the Duke's aids-de-camp. Shortly afterwards, Captain Wood, of the 10th, who had been patrolling, informed the Duke that the Prussians had retreated. Gordon's patrol discovered, on the right of the road, some of the enemy's videttes and a piquet; they fell back hurriedly before the patrol, who turned off the highroad to their left, about five miles from Quatre-Bras, and about an hour afterwards came up with the Prussian rear. After obtaining the required information, the patrol returned to headquarters at Quatre-Bras, where they arrived about seven o'clock a. m., reporting that the Prussians were retreating upon Wavre[1]. The Duke immediately issued the following orders:

To General Lord Hill
Quatre-Bras
17th June, 1815
The brigades of the 4th division, now at Nivelles, to march from that place on Waterloo, at ten o'clock.

The brigades of the 4th division, at Braine-le-Comte and on the road from Braine-le-Comte to Nivelles, to collect and halt at Braine-le-Comte this day.

The 2nd division of British infantry, to march from Nivelles upon Waterloo, at ten o'clock.

All the baggage on the road from Braine-le-Comte to Nivelles, to return to Braine-le-Comte, and to proceed immediately from thence to Hal and Brussels.

The spare musket ammunition to be immediately parked behind Genappe.

The corps under the command of Prince Frederick of Orange will move from Enghien this evening, and take up position in front of Hal, occupying Braine-le-Château with two battalions.

Colonel Estorff will fall back with his brigade on Hal, and place himself under the orders of Prince Frederick.

An officer from the Prussian headquarters, bearing despatches, written, no doubt, in secret characters, or the French would have immediately discovered the direction in which

---

1. The road by which the Prussians retreated upon Wavre, was examined by Lieutenant-Colonel Jackson, of the Royal staff corps, and a report thereof sent to the Prussian headquarters, before the campaign opened.

the Prussians retreated, had been waylaid and made prisoner in the night. But a second officer afterwards arrived at our headquarters, and confirmed Colonel Gordon's statement that the Prussians had fallen back upon Wavre. The Duke immediately wrote to Blücher, informing him of his intention to retreat upon the position in front of Waterloo, and proposing to accept battle on the following day, provided the Prince would support him with two corps of his army.

The first hint to Picton of the Duke's intention to retreat, was an order conveyed to him, to collect his wounded; when he growled out, with his Stentorian voice, "Very well, Sir," in a tone that showed his reluctance to quit the ground his troops had so bravely maintained the day before.

The Duke commenced the retrograde movement, masked as much as possible from the enemy, who followed us with a large force of cavalry, shouting, *Vive l'Empereur!*

The first part of the day (the 17th) was sultry, not a breath of air to be felt, and the sky covered with dark heavy clouds. Shortly after the guns came into play, it began to thunder, lightning and rain in torrents, and the ground in a short time became so soaked, that it was difficult for the cavalry to move, except on the paved road: this, in some measure, checked the advance of the French cavalry, who pressed us very much.

The regiment to which I belonged covered the retreat of the main columns. As we neared Genappe, our right squadron, under Major Hodge, was skirmishing. By this time the ploughed fields were so completely saturated with rain, that the horses sunk up to the knees, and at times nearly up to the girths, which made this part of the service very severe. Our other two squadrons cleared the town of Genappe, and formed on the rising ground on the Brussels side.

Shortly after, the right squadron retired through the town, and drew up on the highroad in column, when a few straggling French lancers, half tipsy, came up and dashed into the head of the column; some were cut down, and some made prisoners. The head of the French column now appeared debouching from the town, and Lord Uxbridge being present, he ordered the 7th hussars to charge.

The charge was gallantly led by the officers, and followed by the men, who cut aside the lances, and did all in their power to break the enemy: but they being chiefly lancers, backed by cuirassiers, were rather awkward customers to deal with, particularly so, as it was an arm with which we were quite unacquainted. When our charge first commenced, their lances were erect, but upon our coming within two or three horses' length of them, they lowered the points and waved the flags, which made some of our horses shy. Upon seeing we could make no impression on them, Lord Uxbridge ordered us about: we retired, pursued by the lancers and the cuirassiers intermixed.

We rode away from them, reformed and again attacked them, but with little more effect than at first. Upon this, Lord Uxbridge brought forward the 1st Lifeguards, who made a splendid charge and drove the cuirassiers and lancers pell-mell back into Genappe; the Lifeguards charging down hill, with their weight of men and horses, literally rode the enemy down, cutting and thrusting at them as they were falling. In this affair my old regiment had to experience the loss of Major Hodge and Lieutenant Myer, killed; Captain Elphinstone[2], Lieutenants Gordon and Peters, wounded; and forty-two men, with thirty-seven horses, killed and wounded. We were well nigh getting a bad name into the bargain.

Reports, as false as they were invidious, having been propagated by some secret enemy of the 7th hussars, it may not be uninteresting to the military world to be made acquainted with the opinion of their Colonel and General, the Marquis of Anglesey[3], as conveyed in the following letter:

---

2. See anecdote, Appendix, No. VI.
3. Lord Uxbridge was created Marquis of Anglesey, for his distinguished conduct on the field of Waterloo.

Brussels

28th June, 1815

My Dear Brother Officers

It has been stated to me, that a report injurious to the reputation of our regiment has gone abroad, and I do not therefore lose an instant in addressing you on the subject. The report must take its origin from the affair which took place with the advance-guard of the French cavalry, near Genappe, on the 17th inst., when I ordered the 7th to cover the retreat. As I was with you and saw the conduct of every individual, there is no one more capable of speaking to the fact than I am. As the lancers pressed us hard, I ordered you, (upon a principle I ever did, and shall act upon,) not to wait to be attacked, but to fall upon them.

The attack was most gallantly led by the officers, but it failed. It failed because the lancers stood firm, had their flanks completely secured, and were backed by a large mass of cavalry.

The regiment was repulsed, but it did not run away: no, it rallied immediately. I renewed the attack; it again foiled, from the same cause. It retired in perfect order, although it had sustained so severe a loss; but you had thrown the lancers into disorder, who being in motion, I then made an attack upon them with the 1st Lifeguards, who certainly made a very handsome charge, and completely succeeded. This is the plain honest truth. However lightly I think of lancers under ordinary circumstances, I think, posted as they were, they had a decided advantage over the hussars. The impetuosity however and weight of the Lifeguards carried all before them, and whilst I exculpate my own regiment, I am delighted in being able to bear testimony to the gallant conduct of the former. Be not uneasy, my brother officers; you had ample opportunity, of which you gallantly availed yourselves, of avenging yourselves on the 18th for the failure on the 17th; and after all, what regiment, or which of us is certain of success?

Be assured that I am proud of being your Colonel, and that you possess my utmost confidence.

Your sincere friend,

Anglesey

Lieutenant-General

After this, the 23rd light dragoons, supported by the life-guards, covered the retreat, and we arrived at a position on which was exhibited as noble a display of valour and discipline, as are to be found either in our own military annals or in those of any other nation. This position was in front of and about two miles and a half from Waterloo, where most of our army was then drawn up.

The French advanced guard halted on the heights near La Belle-Alliance, when Napoleon said, he wished he had the power of Joshua to stop the sun, that he might attack us that day.

They opened a cannonade upon our line, but principally upon our centre behind the farm of La Haye Sainte: our guns soon answered them to their cost, and caused great havoc amongst the enemy's columns, as they arrived on the opposite heights between La Belle-Alliance and the orchard of La Haye Sainte. It was now getting dusk, and orders were given to throw out piquets along the front and flanks of the army.

Our left squadron, under Captain Verner, was thrown into the valley in front of the left wing; the rest of my regiment bivouacked near where Picton fell the next day.

The mutual spirit of defiance was such, that in posting the piquets, there were many little cavalry affairs, which, although of no useful result to either side, were conducted with great bravery and earned to such a pitch, that restraint was absolutely necessary. Captain Heyliger of the 7th hussars, (part of our piquet,) with his troop, made a spirited charge upon the enemy's cavalry, and when the Duke sent to check him, His Grace desired to be made acquainted with the name of the officer who had shown so much gallantly. A better or more gallant officer, than Captain Heyliger, never drew a sword; but he was truly unfortunate: if there was a ball flying about, he was usually the target. I was three times engaged with the enemy, serving with the Captain, and he was wounded on each of those occasions: the first time, foraging at Haspereen; next, at the battle of Orthez; and thirdly, at Waterloo. The ball he received on the last occasion was extracted at Bruges, in 1831.

Our bivouac was dismal in the extreme; what with the thunder, lightning and rain, it was as bad a night as I ever witnessed, a regular soaker; torrents burst forth from the well charged clouds upon our comfortless bivouacs, and the uproar of the elements, during the night preceding Waterloo, seemed to have been the harbinger of the bloody contest. We cloaked, throwing a part over the saddle, holding by the stirrup leather, to steady us if sleepy: to lie down with water running in streams under us, was not desirable, and to lie amongst the horses not altogether safe. A comrade of mine, Robert Fisher, a tailor by trade, proposed that one of us should go in search of something to sit on. I moved off for that purpose and obtained two bundles of bean-stalks from a place that I now know as Mont St. Jean farm. This put us, I may say, quite in clover. The poor tailor had his thread of life snapped short on, the following day.

The Duke of Wellington established his headquarters opposite the church at Waterloo, (now the post-house and post-office;) while his Imperial antagonist Napoleon pitched his tent near the farm of Caillou, about five miles from Waterloo, on the left of the Genappe road, in the parish of Old Genappe. The Imperial baggage was also at this farm.

Most of the houses in the villages adjacent Waterloo were occupied by our Generals, their staff, and the superior officers.

Their names and rank were chalked on the doors, and legible long after a soldier's death had snatched many of them from the field of their prowess and glory.

In the course of the evening the Duke received a despatch from Blücher, in answer to his letter sent from Quatre-Bras, requesting the support of two corps of the Prussian army. The officer bearing this despatch was escorted from Smohain, to Waterloo, by a party of the 1st King's German hussars. Blücher's reply was:

> I shall not come with two corps only, but with my whole army, upon this condition, that should the French not attack us on the 18th, we shall attack them on the 19th.

The Duke therefore accepted battle only under these circumstances; Napoleon's lauded plan of operations enabling His Grace to ultimately place the author of those brilliant conceptions between two fires. Blücher appeared most anxious to fight side by side with the allies and their chief, deeming an Anglo-Prussian army invincible; while Wellington, after having defeated most of Napoleon's best Marshals, was no doubt desirous of measuring swords with their mighty master himself, the hero of a hundred fights.

There is every reason to believe that the Duke was more apprehensive of being turned by Hal on his right, and of Brussels being consequently taken by a *coup de main* than about any other part of his position. This fact is confirmed by the following orders:

Waterloo
17th June, 1815
The army retired from its position at Quatre-Bras, and took up its present position in front of Waterloo.

The brigades of the 4th division at Braine-le-Comte are to retire tomorrow morning at daylight upon Hal. Major-General Colville must be guided by the intelligence he receives of the enemy's movements, in his march to Hal, whether he move by the direct route, or by Enghien.

Prince Frederick of Orange is to occupy with his corps the position between Hal and Enghien, and is to defend it as long as possible.

Lieutenant-Colonel Torrens will inform Lieutenant-General Sir C. Colville of the position and situation of the armies.

The field of Waterloo is an open undulating plain; and, on the day of the battle, was covered with splendid crops of rye, wheat, barley, oats, beans, peas, potatoes, tares and clover; some of the grains were of great height. There were a few patches of ploughed ground. The field is intersected by two highroads which branch off at Mont St. Jean: these are very wide; the one on the right, leading to Nivelles and Binche, since planted with trees, is straight as an arrow for miles; that on the left, lying in the centre of both armies, leading south to Genappe, Charleroy and Namur, is not so straight as the former: about eleven hundred yards in advance of the junction, is a gently elevated ridge which formed a good natural position.

The Duke, nearly a year before these events, had written to Lord Bathurst, enclosing a Memorandum on the defence of the Netherlands, in which he says:

> About Nivelles, and between that and Binche, there are many advantageous positions; and the entrance to the Forêt de Soigne by the highroad, which leads to Brussels from Binche, Charleroy and Namur, would, if worked upon, afford others[5].

The great advantage was that the troops could rest in rear of the crest of the ridge, screened in a great measure from the enemy's artillery and observation, whilst our guns were placed at points, from whence they could sweep (they are

---

4. See Gurwood, *Despatches,* vol. XII, page 129.

wonderful brooms) the slope that descends to the valley in front. Upon the crest is a crossroad running east and west, intersecting the Genappe road at right angles, about two hundred and fifty yards on this side of the farm of La Haye Sainte. The crossroad marks nearly the front of the allied position. Near where the lion now stands, the crossroad or line runs curving forward a little, and joins the Nivelles road near the abrupt termination of the ridge.

This point was at first our right centre, but became our right when Lord Hill's troops were brought forward into the front line, between four and five o'clock p. m.

About four hundred and fifty yards south of this point, is the important post of Hougoumont, destined to become so celebrated in the annals of history, and which even now stands a noble monument of the determined valour of both the assailed and assailants.

It was then a gentleman's seat, with farm, out-buildings, walled garden, orchard and wood. The latter has been since cleared, in consequence of the injury the trees sustained in the battle. The buildings are more than two hundred years old, and were erected for defence. Many of the stone loopholes made in the garden walls when first built, are still quite perfect, as are also those made by our troops at the spur of the moment. The hedges are all banked up, and with the ditches on the inner side form excellent breastworks.

A ravine or hollow-way, called by Colonel Hepburn "our friendly hollow-way," runs along the northern boundary of the premises, which during the battle frequently served as a covered communication with the walled enclosures and buildings, as also for a rallying point and cover.

Hougoumont was formerly the property of Arrazola Deonate, who had been viceroy of Naples, and in 1815 was in the occupation of M. De Luneville, a descendant of the above family; it is now the property of the Count Robiano. This post is situated about midway between the positions of

41

the two hostile armies. The chateau, farm, walls, etc., were at the time of the battle of a substantial nature. The garden or park was walled on the east and south sides, where our troops made additional loop-holes; and in the inside of the front or south wall, they cut down a portion of the buttresses, for the purpose of erecting a scaffolding to enable them to fire over the top of the wall, or to bayonet intruders.

At the east wall, an embankment with the loop-holes, and scaffolds erected with some farming utensils, enabled the Coldstream from the inside to throw such a fire upon the enemy's left flank when in the large orchard, that Colonel Hepburn, who commanded there from about two o'clock, considered the east wall as the strength of his position. Loop-holes were also made in the stables joining the south gate, and a scaffold was erected against the west wall that ran from the south to the barn. The flooring over the south gateway was partly torn up, to enable our men to fire down upon the enemy, should they force the gate which had been blocked up, and was not opened during the action.

The little chapel and crucifix still remain; but the interesting autographs are all cut down, and the walls have been fresh plastered. The front or north gateway facing our position, by which the enemy entered, with its burnt beams; the small barn where many of the wounded were burnt, the cannon ball hole in the east gable of the building attached to the present farmhouse[5], the well perforated top part of the south gate, the battered front of the house, stables, and the loop-holed walls with the banked-up hedges, hollow-way, and some perforated trees in front of the walls, are now the most interesting objects at Hougoumont, for visitors to behold. In the garden is a tomb, beneath which lie the remains of Captain Blackman of the Coldstream, (brother to Sir George Harnage,) who

---

5. The cannon ball entered the west end of the large building still in existence; consequently must have passed through four, if not five walls, before it came out at the east end looking into the garden or park.

fell on that spot. Hougoumont presents even at this moment a scene of shattered ruins, which cannot be viewed without exciting feelings of the deepest interest.

On the troops being thrown into Hougoumont on the 17th, all means were employed to strengthen it as much as possible, and there are still to be seen many of the intended loop-holes in an incomplete state, from which it may be inferred that the troops were called off to defend the post, whilst in the act of making them.

Hougoumont was first occupied on the afternoon of the 17th by the light companies of the 1st division of British guards: the light troops of the 1st regiment, under Colonel Lord Saltoun, held the orchard and wood; those of the Coldstream and 3rd guards held the buildings and garden, under Colonel Macdonnell: there were also in the out-grounds and wood a battalion of Nassau troops, a company of field riflemen, and a hundred men from the Lunenburg battalion; and the supernumerary light companies of the guards were thrown into the valley on our side of the enclosures, as a support and to keep up a communication with the main line.

On the east side of the Genappe road, the crossroad was lined by two broken banked-up hedges, extending about half a mile; near the termination of which is a knoll, with a bit of copse or brushwood on the rear slope: this mound, or knoll, overlooks the farms of Papelotte, La Haye, Frischermont, and the hamlet of Smohain in the valley.

The undulation in rear of the ridge afforded excellent protection to the second line, cavalry and reserves, which were quite concealed from the enemy's view. Beyond the right of the main ridge, on the right of the Nivelles road, is a deep valley which runs round Hougoumont in the direction of Merbe-Braine, and from the valley cutting through the ridge to the little white chapel on the Nivelles road, runs a deep ravine, which is the one mentioned by the Duke in his despatch, and intersects the second ridge or plateau, that was occupied by part of the 2nd corps, under Lieutenant-General Lord Hill, who were to act as a right wing, *en potence*[7], or as a reserve, as circumstances might require.

The principal part of the troops occupying this plateau and valley, belonged to the 2nd British division under Lieutenant-General Sir H. Clinton: it was composed of the 3rd light brigade, under Major-General F. Adam; the 52nd, under Colonel Sir John Colborne (now Lord Seaton); the 71st, under Colonel T. Reynell; the 2nd battalion 95th rifles, under Colonel Norcott, with two companies of the 3rd battalion 95th, under Lieutenant-Colonel Ross, who were posted near Merbe-Braine.

The 1st brigade, King's German Legion, under Colonel Duplat, was composed of the 1st, 2nd, 3rd, and 4th line battalions. The 3rd, Hanoverian brigade, under Colonel Hugh Halkett, consisted of the militia battalions, Osnabruck, Salzgitter, Bremeverden, and Quakenbruck.

The Brunswick corps, after their Duke had fallen, were under Colonel Olferman, also near Merbe-Braine. Along the Hougoumont avenue and the road leading from it to Braine-Lalleud, were some light troops, who, in conjunction with the hussars posted on their right, had a sharp skirmish with the enemy, in the morning, before the battle began. They were part of the fourth brigade of the 4th division, under Colonel Mitchell, and attached to the 2nd division, composed of the 51st regiment, under Lieutenant-Colonel Rice, the 14th regiment, under Lieutenant-Colonel Tidy, and of the 23rd fusiliers, under Colonel Sir H. Ellis; the latter came into front line during the afternoon.

On the right of the former, was a squadron of the 15th hussars, under Captain Wodehouse, who threw out videttes and kept a look-out upon our extreme right. Upon the Nivelles road, opposite the Hougoumont avenue, was an *abattis,* or barricade. Near

---

6. *En potence,* is a military phrase which expresses a bending or throwing back of either flank or wing of an army.

Mitchell's brigade were posted, about two o'clock, two companies of the Coldstream guards, with their colours, in reserve.

Upon the ridge above and overlooking Hougoumont was posted the 1st division of British guards, composed of the 2nd battalion of the Coldstream guards, under Colonel Woodford, who was a little in advance; the 2nd battalion of the 3rd guards, under Colonel Hepburn, posted a little in rear of the crest of the ridge. The whole were in battalion columns, with deploying intervals, and in chequer.

On their left was the first brigade, composed of the 2nd battalion of the 1st guards[7], under Colonel Askew, and posted in rear, and of the 3rd battalion, under Colonel the Hon. W. Stuart, posted a little in advance of the crest.

On the left of Maitland, was the 3rd division, under Lieutenant-General Count Alten; the 5th British brigade, composed of the 30th, under Colonel Hamilton, and the 73rd, under Colonel G. Hands, posted in advance; and of the 33rd, under Colonel Elphinstone, with the 69th, under Colonel Morice, posted upon the right rear of the 30th and 73rd. The four regiments formed and acted as two.

On their left was the 1st Hanoverian brigade, under Major-General Count Kielmansegge. The field battalions of Bremen, Verden, York, Grubenhagen and Lüneburg were posted three in front and two in second line.

On Kielmansegge's left, was the 2nd brigade of the King's German Legion, under Colonel Ompteda, which formed Alten's left and rested upon the Genappe highroad: it was composed of the 1st light battalion, under Major Bussche, and the 2nd, under Colonel Baring; of the 5th line, under Colonel Linsingen, and the 8th, under Colonel Schroder: the 1st and 5th were a little in rear of the crossroad upon the ridge; the 8th in reserve.

The 2nd light, under Colonel Baring, held La Haye Sainte,

---

7. Since named Grenadier guards, on account of their gallant conduct when opposed to the Imperial grenadiers of France, at the close of the day of Waterloo.

a post far from being so commodious as Hougoumont, but considerably nearer our position, consequently easier of access, although more exposed to the enemy's attacks and cannonade. It was a strong stone and brick building, with a narrow orchard in front, and a small garden in the rear, both of which were hedged round, except the east side of the garden, on which there was a strong wall running along the highroad side, then taking a western direction terminated upon the east end of the barn; a large and small gate opened on the road; a yard and barn door led to the orchard and fields which now nice the lion. At this point was the chief tug of war.

A passage led through the house from the farmyard into the garden, which lies on the north or allied side of the buildings, the door of which was four feet wide; there were also on the same side four windows and ten loop or air-holes, by which any quantity of ammunition might have been thrown in; consequently, the oft-told tale that a breach should have been made on that side but was forgotten, like many other raise reports, rails to the ground. A dozen loop-holes in the west or Lion side of the buildings would have added considerably to the strength of the post. Loop-holes were made in the south and east walls as well as in the roofs, and the post strengthened on being occupied by our troops.

A barricade was thrown across the highroad, near the south-east angle of the wall; but it appears there were several drawbacks to the strengthening of this post. The working tools had been lost, the carpenters had been sent to assist at Hougoumont; half of the large barn door was wanting, and in addition, the post was exposed to a line of batteries, that had been pushed forward upon the inner ridge of the French right wing, at a range of from six to eight hundred yards.

In rear of the interval between Halkett's and Kielmansegge's brigades, stood the Nassau brigade, three battalions of the 1st regiment of Nassau, under General Kruse. Upon the left of the Genappe road was the 6th division: the 8th brigade, composed of the 28th, under Colonel Sir P. Belson; the 32nd, under Colonel Hicks; the 79th Highlanders, under Colonel Douglas, and of the 1st battalion 95th rifles, under Colonel Sir A. Barnard, in columns just under the crest of the ridge. In front of the right of the brigade, and about a hundred and forty yards from the crossroad stood a knoll, in front of which was a sand-hole, (where the Hanoverian monument now stands;) on our side of the knoll and parallel with our front, was a hedge slightly studded with trees, about a hundred and forty yards long. The whole of this ground was occupied by three companies of riflemen, under Major Leach, who made a barricade across the road: more of the rifles lined the straggling hedge along the crossroad; their reserve was at the junction of the roads.

On their left was the 9th brigade, consisting of the 1st or Royal Scots, under Colonel Campbell; the 42nd Royal Highlanders, under Colonel Sir R. Macara; the 44th, under Colonel Hamerton; and the 92nd Highlanders, under Colonel Cameron; their left near the brushwood, upon the rear face of the knoll upon our left. From this to Wavre, which is concealed by woods and high ground, and from whence the Prussians had to march, the distance is about twelve miles.

In Pack's left front was the 4th Hanoverian brigade, under Colonel Best, composed of the militia battalions, Lüneburg, Verden and Osterode, the Munden in reserve.

In Best's left rear was the 5th Hanoverian brigade, 5th division, under Colonel Vincke, in columns of battalions: namely, those of Hameln and Hildersham, Peine and Gifhorn, posted a little under the crest of the ridge.

The hamlet of Smohain, with the farms of Papelotte and La Haye, and the houses and enclosures in the valley, were occupied by the second brigade of the 2nd Dutch-Belgian division, under General Perponcher. This brigade, under the Duke of Saxe-Weimar, was composed of the two battalions of Orange-

Nassau, and the 2nd and 3rd battalions of the regiment of Nassau, the 1st battalion of which was at Hougoumont.

Upon our extreme left was the 6th cavalry brigade, under Major-General Sir Hussey Vivian, composed of the 10th hussars, under Colonel Quentin; the 18th hussars, under Colonel the Hon. H. Murray, and of the 1st hussars of the German Legion, under Colonel De Wissel. A piquet of the 10th, under Captain Taylor[8], was thrown into Smohain in the valley; their videttes were posted on the rising ground beyond.

Before the battle began, a Prussian patrol arrived at this piquet, and informed Captain Taylor, that part of Bülow's (4th) corps was at St. Lambert; this intelligence was immediately sent to the Duke of Wellington.

On Vivian's right was the 4th cavalry brigade, under Major-General Sir J. Vandeleur, composed of the 11th light dragoons, under Colonel Sleigh, the 12th, under Colonel the Hon. F. Ponsonby, and the 16th, under Colonel J. Hay. In advance of the hedge, in front of the centre of the left wing, was Bylandt's brigade of the Netherlands, deployed in line, composed of the 27th Dutch light infantry, the 5th, 7th, and 8th Dutch militia, and the 7th of the Belgian line; the 5th Dutch was in reserve.

On the left of the Genappe road, in rear of Picton's division, was the 2nd cavalry brigade, under Major-General Sir W. Ponsonby, composed of the 1st Royal dragoons, under Colonel Clifton, the 2nd or Scots Greys, under Colonel Hamilton, and the 6th, Inniskilling, under Colonel Muter.

Near the farm of Mont St. Jean[9], was the 10th brigade of the 6th division, which was to have been under Lieutenant-General the Hon. Sir L. Cole, but he had not joined; the brigade was under Sir J. Lambert, composed of the 4th, under Colonel Brook, the 27th, Inniskilling, under Major Hare, and

---

8. Now Major-General Taylor and deputy governor of Sandhurst College.
9. Every house in the neighbourhood was used for the wounded; the farm of Mont St. Jean was the chief hospital, or the headquarters for the medical staff.

the 40th, under Major Heyland; they had just landed from America, and had made forced marches from Assche. These were what the Duke termed Spanish or old tried infantry, most of whom being on their way from America did not arrive until the battle was fought Sir Harry Smith, the hero of Aliwal, was on Sir J. Lambert's staff.

In the hollow, on the right of the highroad in rear of Ompteda, was the 1st or household brigade, under Major-General Lord E. Somerset, *viz.* the 1st Lifeguards, Colonel Ferrior; the 2nd ditto, Colonel the Hon. E. Lygon; the Royal horse-guards (Blues), Colonel R. Hill; 1st dragoon guards, Colonel Fuller.

In rear of Alten's centre were the 3rd hussars of the King's German Legion, under Colonel Sir F. Arentschild. Behind the centre was the cavalry division of the Netherlands, under Lieutenant-General baron Collaert: the 1st brigade, under Major-General Trip, the 1st and 3rd Dutch, and 2nd Belgian carabineers. The second brigade, under Major-General De Ghigny, consisted of the 4th Dutch light dragoons and the 8th Belgian hussars. The 3rd brigade, under Major-General Merle, was composed of the 6th Belgian light dragoons and the 6th Dutch hussars.

On the right of the 3rd German hussars were the Cumberland Hanoverian hussars, under Colonel Hake.

In rear of Halkett's right was the 3rd cavalry brigade, under Major-General Sir W. Dornberg, consisting of the 23rd light dragoons, under Major Cutcliffe, and of the 1st and 2nd light dragoons of the King's German Legion.

In rear of Byng was the 6th cavalry brigade, under Major-General Sir C. Grant, composed of the 7th hussars, under Colonel Kerrison, of the 15th hussars, under Colonel L. Dalrymple, and of the 13th light dragoons, under Lieutenant-Colonel Boyse. The 13th did not properly belong to this brigade.

The 3rd division of the Netherlands, under Lieutenant-General Chassé, (who so gallantly defended the citadel of Antwerp in 1832,) was under Lord Hill: its 1st brigade, under Colonel Ditmers, was composed of the 33rd battalion of Belgian light infantry, and the 2nd of the line, with the 4th, 6th, 17th, and 19th battalions of Dutch militia, and it occupied the town of Braine-Lalleud; the 17th was posted a little nearer to the 2nd British division, to keep up the communication.

The 2nd brigade, under Major-General D'Aubremé, composed of the 36th Belgian light infantry, the 3rd, the 12th, and the 13th line, and the 10th militia, was at the farm of Vieux-Forêt, beyond Braine-Lalleud, for the security of our right flank, and to keep open the communication with our detached forces at Hal, etc., for the protection of our extreme right. The 6th British brigade thus detached was composed of the 35th, 64th, 69th, and 91st regiments, under Major-General Johnstone, with the 6th Hanoverian brigade, under Major-General Sir James Lyon, and two regiments of Hanoverian cavalry, under Colonel Estorff, and a division of Netherlanders, under Prince Frederick of Holland. These troops were thus posted for the protection of Brussels against a *coup de main* (surprise) by any detached force of the enemy.

The reader will observe that the principal advantages of the allied position were:

1: The junction of the two highroads immediately in rear of our centre, from which the paved broad road to Brussels, our main line of operation, branched off. This added to the facility of communication, enabled us to move ammunition, guns, troops, the wounded, etc., to or from any part of our main front line, as circumstances demanded.

2: The advanced posts of Hougoumont, La Haye Sainte, Papelotte, and La Haye farms, near which no enemy could pass without being assailed in flank by musketry.

3: The continuous ridge from flank to flank towards which, undiscovered, no hostile force could advance within range of our artillery upon the crest, behind which our troops could manoeuvre, or lie concealed from the enemy's view, while they were in great measure protected from the fire of the hostile batteries.

4: Our extreme left was strong by nature, and the buildings, hollow-ways, enclosures, trees and brushwood, along the valley from Papelotte to Ohain, thickly peopled with light infantry, would long have kept a strong force at bay. Our batteries on the left on the knoll commanded the valley and the slopes, while the ground from those batteries to Ohain, occupied till near eight o'clock p. m. by Vandeleur's and Vivian's brigades, was admirably adapted for cavalry.

5: Our extreme right was secured by numerous patches of brushwood, trees and ravines, and further protected by hamlets, and by Lord Hill's troops *en potence,* part of which occupied the town of Braine-Lalleud and the farm of Vieux-Forêt, on the height above it.

Between nine and ten o'clock, the French began to take up their position in our front, on a corresponding ridge and nearly parallel to ours; their centre being near La Belle-Alliance, about fourteen hundred yards from ours; their right running east along the ridge towards Frischermont. At two hundred yards behind La Belle-Alliance is a crossroad that leads from Planehenois to the Nivelles road, intersecting the latter about midway between Hougoumont and Mont-Plaisir, at which point there are now two small houses, built near where the French left terminated, which are visible from the allied right wing.

The French right wing was the 1st corps, under Lieutenant-General Count D'Erlon, the same, (with the exception of Durutte's infantry and Jacquinot's cavalry divisions, which were at Ligny,) that had been marching and countermarching between Gosselies, Ligny and Frasnes on the 16th, and which, up to this time, had not fired a shot during the campaign. It was composed of four divisions of infantry, and one of light cavalry. The 2nd or left division, under General Donzelot, had its left upon La Belle-Alliance. It consisted of the 13th light, and 17th, 19th, 51st of the line, and was drawn up, like the whole of their front, in two lines about sixty yards apart. On their right was the 1st division, under General Alix: the 28th, 54th, 55th, and 105th of the line. On their right was the 3rd division, under Lieutenant-General Marcognet: the 21st, 25th, 45th, and 46th of the line. On their right was the 4th division, under General Durutte: the 8th, 29th, 85th, 95th of the line. The 1st division of cavalry, under General Jacquinot, was on the right of this corps: it consisted of the 3rd and 7th light dragoons, and the 3rd and 4th lancers, with seven batteries to the corps.

The left wing was the 2nd corps, under Lieutenant-General Count Reille, composed of three divisions of infantry and one of cavalry. The right division, the 5th, under Lieutenant-General Bachelu, rested its right upon La Belle-Alliance, and its left in the valley that runs round the south enclosures of Hougoumont: it comprised the 12th, 61st, 72nd, and 108th line. Girard's division was at Ligny during the 16th and 17th, where it was left on the 18th, it is said, by mistake.

Upon their left, and facing the wood of Hougoumont, was the 9th division, under Lieutenant-General Foy; *viz.* the 4th light, the 92nd, 93rd, and 100th line. On the left of the 9th division, upon the ridge facing the buildings of Hougoumont, was the 6th division, under General Prince Jérôme Napoleon, comprising the 1st and 2nd light, and 1st, 2nd, and 3rd line; the last three regiments were composed of three battalions each. On the left of the corps was the 2nd cavalry division, under Lieutenant-General Piré, being the 1st and 6th light dragoons, and the 5th and 6th lancers; they crossed the Nivelles road in lines, and threw forward piquets towards Braine-Lalleud and Uphain; thus keeping a look-out upon the extreme left of their army. Their artillery, composed of five batteries, was ranged along the front of the divisions.

Behind their centre, close along their left of the Genappe road, was the 6th corps, under Lieutenant-General Count Lobau. The 19th and 20th divisions only were present: they were formed in close columns of battalions, by divisions. The 19th division was about two hundred yards behind the right of the 2nd corps; the 20th about two hundred yards in rear of the 19th division. The former was under Lieutenant-General Simmer, being the 5th, 11th, 27th, and 84th of the line. The 20th division, under Lieutenant-General Jeannin, was formed of the 5th light, and 10th, 47th, and 107th line. There were five batteries to this corps. The 21st, or Teste's division, was with Grouchy.

Upon the right of the 6th corps, separated only by the road, was the 3rd cavalry division, under Lieutenant-General Domont, being the 4th, 9th, and 12th light dragoons: and the 5th cavalry division, under Lieutenant-General Subervie, being the 1st and 2nd lancers, and the 11th light dragoons. They were in close columns. Their two troops of artillery were on their right.

Behind the centre of the right wing was the 4th cavalry corps, under Lieutenant-General Count Milhaud.

The 13th cavalry division, under Lieutenant-General Wattier, comprised the 5th, 6th, 9th, and 10th cuirassiers; and the 14th division, under Lieutenant-General Delort, consisted of the 1st, 4th, 7th, and 12th cuirassiers.

Their two troops of artillery were in the centre.

In rear of those divisions, in reserve, was the light cavalry of the Imperial Guard, composed of light dragoons and lancers, under Generals Lefebvre—Desnouettes and Colbert, like the rest, drawn up in two lines; their artillery in the centre.

In rear of the centre of the left wing was the 3rd cavalry corps, under Lieutenant-General Kellermann. It comprised the 11th cavalry division, the 2nd and 7th dragoons, and 8th and 11th cuirassiers, under Lieutenant-General L'Héritier; and the 12th division, *viz.* the 1st and 2nd carabineers (brass-clad cuirassiers), and 2nd and 3rd cuirassiers, under Lieutenant-General Roussel.

Their two troops of artillery were upon their flanks.

In rear of those two divisions were the horse-grenadiers and dragoons of the Imperial Guards, under the Generals Guyot and Hoffmeyer, in reserve; their artillery was in their centre. In rear of the 6th corps and the 3rd and 5th cavalry divisions, near the farm of Rossomme, was the infantry of the Imperial Guard in reserve, under Lieutenant-General Drouot: it consisted of four regiments of grenadiers, four regiments of chasseurs, two regiments of tirailleurs and two of voltigeurs, of two battalions each. The 1st and 2nd regiments of grenadiers and chasseurs formed the old guard, under Lieutenant-General Friant, and the 3rd and 4th regiments of grenadiers and chasseurs formed the middle guard, under Lieutenant-General Count Morand. The four regiments, of voltigeurs and tirailleurs formed the young guard, under Lieutenant-General Duhesme, drawn up in six lines of four battalions each; the Genappe highroad divided them into two equal parts; their artillery (six batteries) was on their flank. The reserve artillery of the guard (twenty-four guns) was in their rear.

Such was Napoleon's disposition of his eager and gallant followers. Siborne says:

This admirable order of battle, at once grand, simple and imposing, and presenting to its skilful designer the most ample means of sustaining, by an immediate and efficient support, any attack from whatever point he might wish to direct it, and of possessing everywhere a respectable force at hand to oppose any attack made upon himself, from whatever quarter it might be made, was no less remarkable for the regularity and precision with which the several masses, constituting thirteen distinct columns, advanced to their destined stations, than for the unusual degree of warlike pomp and high martial bearing with which the lines drew up in this mighty battle array.

Both positions, whatever some prejudiced French writers may assert, offered everywhere fair fighting ground, on which all arms could act without any disadvantage.

The Eve of Waterloo

Kneel, warrior, kneel: tomorrow's sun
May see thy course of glory run;
And batter'd helm and shiver'd glave
May lie neglected near thy grave.
Kneel, for thy prayer in battlefield
May sanctify thy sword and shield,
And help to guard, unstain'd and free,
Our altars, home and liberty.

Arm, warrior, arm: the hostile bands
Now grasp in haste their whetted brands,
And seek the vantage of the height,
Ere the first blush of morning light;
And hark! the trumpet's stormy bray!
God speed thee, warrior, on thy way!
The stirring word of onset be,
Our altars, home and liberty!

Shout, warrior, shout: the field's thine own,
The Emperor's ranks are all o'erthrown;
His columns dense and squadrons vast
Were but as dust before the blast.
Shout, till the mountain voice replies
In thunder, as Napoleon flies;
Add leaves again, unstain'd and free,
Our altars, home and liberty.

Sunday the 18th June, 1815, which cast such a brilliant lustre on the military annals of Britain, broke but slowly through the heavy clouds. The rain descended in torrents, succeeded, as the morning advanced, by a drizzling shower which gradually ceased. Soon after break of day, all who were able were on the move. Many, from cold and fatigue, could not stir for some time; fortunately, on most of us the excitement was too powerful to allow this physical inconvenience to be much felt; although many, in after years, suffered most severely from it.

Some were cleaning arms, others fetching wood, water, straw, etc., from Mont St. Jean, (my present place of abode;) some trying, from the embers of our bivouac, to light up fires, many of which had been entirely put out by the heavy rain. At this time there was a continual irregular popping along the line, not unlike a skirmish, occasioned by those who were cleaning their firearms, discharging them, when practicable; which was more expeditious and satisfactory than drawing the charges.

Our bivouac had a most unsightly appearance: both officers and men looked blue with cold; and our long beards, with our wet and dirty clothing drying upon us, was anything but comfortable. As morning advanced and all were in motion, one might imagine the whole plain itself to be undergoing a movement. Imagine seventy thousand men huddled together. The buzzing resembled the distant roar of the sea against a rocky coast.

Between nine and ten o'clock, the Duke of Wellington, with his usual firm countenance, passed along the line and was loudly cheered. His Grace was dressed in his field costume, white buckskin pantaloons, Hessian boots and tassels, blue frock coat with a short cloak of the same colour, white cravat, sword, a plain low cocked hat without plume or ornament, on which was attached the large black cockade of Britain, and three smaller ones of Spain, Portugal and the Netherlands. In his right hand he carried a long field telescope, drawn out ready for use. His Grace was mounted on his favourite chestnut charger, Copenhagen. He was followed by a numerous staff, several foreign officers, and the Russian, Austrian, Prussian and Spanish ministers, Count Pozzo di Borgo, barons Vincent and Müffling, and General Alava. I observed several in his train dressed in plain clothes. Their number was much diminished ere the day was over.

The Duke generally rode alone, or rather without having any one by his side, and rarely spoke, unless to send a message or to give orders; sometimes he would suddenly turn round and glide past his followers; halting occasionally, and apparently paying no attention to his own troops, His Grace would observe and peer at those of the enemy through his telescope, which the docile Copenhagen appeared perfectly to understand, from his showing no impatience nor getting restive.

The troops had been previously placed in their respective positions, and afterwards the cavalry dismounted.

About this time, the French bands struck up, so that we could distinctly hear them. I have no doubt, this was the moment when Napoleon assembled all his Generals, and forming a circle, placed himself in the centre, and gave his orders. This was in the hamlet of Maison-du-Roi, about a mile in the rear of his centre.

Not long after, the enemy's skirmishers, backed by their supports, were thrown out; extending as they advanced, they spread over the whole space before them. Now and then, they saluted our ears with well-known music, the whistling of musket-balls.

Their columns, preceded by mounted officers to take up the alignments, soon began to appear with the flashing of bayonets over dark masses at different points, accompanied by the rattling of drums and the clang of trumpets.

Could anyone behold so imposing a spectacle without awe, or without extreme excitement? Could anyone witness the commencement of the battle with indifference? Can anyone forget the impressions that are made upon the mind at such a moment? What a magnificent sight! Napoleon the Great, marshalling the chosen troops of France, against those of Britain and her allies under the renowned Wellington! Here, on one side, were the troops that had held nearly all Europe in bonds, and by whom kings and Princes had been humbled and deposed; and although it was not the first time that many of us had faced them, yet, on the present occasion, they were under the immediate command of their idolized Napoleon. It was impossible to contemplate so formidable a power in battle array, without a feeling of admiration towards such noble antagonists.

It presented altogether a sight that must be seen and felt to be duly appreciated, a sight that "survivors recollect in after years."

Such a scene fires the blood of the brave, and excites them to feelings and hopes, compared with which all other emotions are cold and powerless:

To him who's born for battle's strife,
Or bard of martial lay,
'Twas worth ten years of peaceful life,
One glance at this array.

Picture their infantry in front, in two lines sixty yards apart, flanked by lancers with their fluttering flags. In rear of the centre of the infantry wings were the cuirassiers, also in two lines. In rear of the cuirassiers, on the right, the lancers and chasseurs of the Imperial Guard, in their splendid but gaudy uniforms: the former clad in scarlet; the latter like hussars, in rifle-green fur-trimmed pelisse, gold lace, bearskin cap. In rear of the cuirassiers on the left, the horse-grenadiers and dragoons of the Imperial Guard, with their dazzling arms.

Immediately in rear of the centre was the reserve, composed of the 6th corps, in columns; on the left, and on the right of the Genappe road, were two divisions of light cavalry.

In rear of the whole, was the infantry of the Imperial Guard in columns, a dense, dark mass, which, with the 6th corps and cavalry, were flanked by their numerous artillery. Nearly seventy-two thousand men, and two hundred and forty-six guns, ranged with matches lighted, gave an awful presage of the approaching conflict.

The enemy were quite in hand, all within call, there was

nothing to prevent a movement being made. Why tarries Napoleon? so often termed, "the thunderbolt of war." Every minute's delay is loss to him and gain to Wellington, whose game it was to stand fast until the Prussians arrived. Was the Emperor tampering with a portion of the allies who had formerly fought in his ranks, and who might again rally round his eagles, (as he had been led to believe,) should a favourable opportunity present itself? French writers reply, and with some justice, that Napoleon waited for the partial drying of the ground, which the night's rain had rendered very unfavourable for cavalry and artillery. The grand martial display was calculated to heighten the enthusiasm of his legions, at the same time that it gratified the Emperor's unbounded ambition.

The allied army, a motley group, of nearly sixty-eight thousand men and a hundred and fifty-six guns, though almost as numerous as that of the enemy, did not present so imposing a spectacle, being for the most part drawn up in chequered columns of battalions at deploying intervals, the cavalry being on the flanks and in the rear. According to the nature of the ground, the guns were skilfully ranged at points whence the melancholy work of destruction could be best effected, yet, from its undulating form, it concealed a great portion of our force from the enemy's view.

"Never," said Napoleon, "had my troops been animated with such spirit, or taken up their ground with such precision. The earth seemed proud of being trodden by such combatants. . . . Never yet, I believe, has there been such devotion shown by soldiers, as mine have manifested for me; never has man been served more faithfully by his troops."

The two armies were now fairly in presence of each other.

The French lines being completed, the Emperor passed along them, attended by a brilliant and numerous staff: a forest of plumes waved around him. The troops hailed him with repeated shouts of *Vive l'Empereur!* the infantry raising their caps upon their bayonets, and the cavalry their *casques* or helmets upon their swords and lances. The parade over, the whole instantly formed columns.

With an army thus animated by one sentiment, and doubtless calculating on being joined during the fray by more than a few of the motley group who stood in his front, it may readily be conceived that Napoleon fully participated in the General confidence of a signal victory.

"The force of the two armies," said the Emperor just before the battle began, "could not be estimated by a mere comparison of numbers; because the allied army was composed of troops more or less efficient: so that *one Englishman might be counted for one Frenchman;* but two Netherlanders, Prussians, Germans, or soldiers of the Confederation, were required to make up one Frenchman."

CHAPTER 3

The Battle Commences

Just before the commencement of the battle, and after taking a minute survey of his troops on the position, the Duke rode down to Hougoumont, and following the footpath that traversed the wood, halted at the eastern boundary, from whence he surveyed the enemy's masses in that vicinity. He afterwards returned to the buildings, and casting a hasty glance around, made a few observations to Colonel Macdonnell, ordered a slight change to be made in the troops holding the wood and out-grounds, and then he rode away.

At about half-past eleven o'clock, His Grace was near the bit of hedgerow on the roadside, about midway between where\the Lion now standsand Hougoumont, in conversation with one of his staff, when a strong force of light troops of Prince Jerome's division commenced an attack in the wood of Hougoumont upon our light troops, who being under cover of the hedge and trees kept them at bay for some time: the French however pressed on briskly into the wood, and drove our troops back towards the buildings. The rattle of the musketry was kept up in the wood for some time; and thus opened the memorable day of Waterloo.

Upon Jerome's supporting columns being put in motion, (about ten minutes to twelve, according to Lord E. Somerset

61

and General Shaw Kennedy's watches,[1]) Captain Cleeve's German battery first opened upon them, and produced a most terrific effect, making a complete road through the mass:[2] the leading column was broken, and fell back behind the ridge; upon which our artillery more to the right opened upon the French rear columns which had slightly changed their position. Reille's guns now opened, and a heavy cannonade was carried on. Napoleon ordered Kellermann to push forward his horse batteries: thus the fire augmented like thickening peels of thunder, and the whole kept up a continual roar.

And from their deep throats
The shot and shells did pour.

Our Nassau and Hanoverian light troops were forced out of the wood by the enemy, when the light companies of the British guards advanced on the right of the buildings, and also from the orchard into the fields, driving the enemy before them.

During the time the enemy occupied the wood, the Duke, after explaining the danger attending the howitzers' range, as, from the proximity of the hostile forces, friends might be destroyed as well as foes, ordered Bull's howitzer battery to throw shells into it A shower of shells was soon sent flying into the wood, which forced Jerome's light troops and their supports to retire. Up to this time, except a little skirmishing, the battle was confined to Hougoumont. The roar of artillery was increasing. At this period a body of the enemy's cavalry approached our left at a good pace; upon which, Best's Hanoverians formed square; but the French cavalry went about. It was a reconnoitring party, to see whether we had thrown up any field-works, as our position, when seen from the French right, had all the appearance of being entrenched. Fresh columns of Jerome's division, supported by Foy's, were sent upon

---

1. Both those officers told me this on the field in 1842.
2. I have been told by an officer who accompanied this column, that seventeen men were killed by the first shot.

our post at Hougoumont; they united, extended their front, and pressed through the wood and open fields.

The horse battery upon the French left opened upon our right, and a sharp cannonade was kept up between the batteries. Our light troops in the wood and orchard made a desperate resistance, but were ultimately obliged to fall back upon the flanks of the buildings. As the French approached the hedge that masked the loop-holed wall, they pressed up to it, thinking our troops were behind it, but they were suddenly brought to a stand, by the fire through the loop-holes and from the scaffold over the top of the wall. Most of their advance were brought down, and those who followed were staggered, not being able to make out whence the fire came that made such havoc in their ranks; little thinking that a masked battery of muskets was within forty yards of them. They at length perceived that a well-directed fire through and over the masked wall had greatly increased their loss. Still they returned with redoubled fury to the attack, in hopes of carrying this important post. Not thinking it prudent to attempt an escalade, they covered themselves, as best they could, by the banked-up hedge and trees, and continued a dropping fire upon the wall, which was so peppered as to lead one to suppose they had an idea of battering it down with musketry, or mistook the red bricks for our red coats. At length some of the more daring, and there were many in their ranks, rushed over the hedge up to the wall, and seized the muskets which protruded through the loop-holes.

The enemy were making their way out of the wood, through a gap, into the large orchard, when Lord Saltoun charged them with his light troops and drove them back. Our howitzers upon the right of the main ridge began again plying with shells the enemy in the wood: they falling back, and our men moving on slowly, the shells were thrown in another direction, upon some supports. The enemy were again reinforced, and pressed on in a most daring manner.

Our guards on the right, under Colonel Macdonnell, fell back upon the haystack (afterwards burnt) that stood between the buildings and the wood, and upon the hedges and the right enclosures; while those on the left or orchard side, under Colonel Lord Saltoun, fell back to the south banked-up hedge of the orchard. Those on the right were assisted by their comrades from the windows of the house, as well as from the loopholes of the south stables. They managed upon that point to keep the enemy at bay for some time; but perceiving some of Jerome's troops out-flanking them on the allied right of the buildings, thus exposing our men to the danger of being turned on their right and cut off from retreat, they hastily fell back and entered the buildings by the north gate, which they attempted to block up: but the French were too close upon them, and forced an entrance. Our men quickly taking the best cover they could find, opened a rattling fire upon the intruders, then darted forward, and a struggle ensued, distinguished by the most undaunted courage on both sides. At length Colonel Macdonnell and his small force, amongst whom was Sergeant Graham, succeeded in overpowering the enemy and closing the gate. All of the enemy who had entered were either killed or severely wounded. Shortly after a French soldier climbed to the top of the gateway, and Sergeant Graham immediately shot him, by order of Captain Windham, who at the time was holding Graham's musket, whilst the latter was further securing the gate.

At this moment the position was nearer falling into the hands of the enemy, than at any other period during the day. A party of French drove back our light companies and passed the avenue hedge, turning the post on the allied right being favoured by the brushwood and high crops, they got close up under the ridge on the right of our line, and destroyed some of our artillerymen, causing Webber Smith's battery to be drawn back into the hollow road, where his guns were refitted. Colonel Woodford, with the rest of the Coldstreams, went down and drove the French before him; but, before his arrival, such a numerous body of the enemy had congregated at the north-gate and wall of Hougoumont, that our artillery opened fire upon them. Colonel Woodford's advance caused it to cease, from the fear of destroying our own men. Woodford cleared all before him, and leaving a detachment to guard the avenue, he entered the building from the lane by a small door of the barn (now bricked up).

Sergeant Graham, some time after this, asked permission to fall out for a few minutes: a request which surprised Colonel Macdonnell, and induced him to inquire the motive. Graham replied, that his brother was lying in the buildings wounded, and, as the flames were then fast extending, he wished to remove him to a place of safety. The request was granted, and Graham, having rescued his brother from the fate which menaced him, speedily returned to his post. Graham died an inmate of the Royal hospital, Kilmainham, Dublin, in 1846.

The French on our left of Hougoumont pressed on, and turned Lord Saltoun's troops on their left, driving them across the orchard to the friendly hollow-way; but upon the enemy following through the south hedge, all within musket range received, from the Coldstreams stationed inside the east garden wall, such a severe fire upon their left flank, as staggered and brought them up. Upon which Lord Saltoun, who had been reinforced upon his left by some of the 3rd guards from the main line, advanced, drove the enemy before him, and again occupied the front hedge; than which there was not a more secure position on the field, as long as the enemy did not outflank it: but this the French frequently attempted to do by attacking, from the open field beyond the east hedge of the enclosure, Saltoun's left, posted at the south-east angle of the orchard.

The enemy now occupied the wood and open fields on

both flanks. Outside the left enclosures there was cavalry-skirmishing. About this time small bodies of cavalry, supposed to be Prussians, were observed on the heights on our left, near St. Lambert.

In consequence of the determined resistance the enemy met with at our advanced post of Hougoumont, which proved a regular stumbling-block to Napoleon, he resolved upon attacking the left of our main line.[3] Marshal Ney had been making preparations for doing so, by pushing forward part of his artillery to the intermediate ridge of their right wing, placing his guns so that their range was not beyond half a mile; they were to cover, as is usual, the advance of their columns of attack, formed of the whole of D'Erlon's corps, supported by part of Reille's corps.

Napoleon's aim was to turn our left, force the left centre, and get possession of the farms of La Haye Sainte and Mont St. Jean, in order to cut off our communication with Brussels, and to prevent our cooperation with the Prussians. The French columns had been moved to the hollow, between the main and inner ridges. All was ready for the grand attack, of which Ney apprized Napoleon;[4] who, before he gave the order to begin, took a General survey upon his right, when, perceiving in the direction of St. Lambert, what he thought to be troops, he asked his Adjutant-General (Soult,) what the cloud of troops were that he saw in the distance? Soult replied, "I think I see five or six thousand men: possibly part of Grouchy's corps."

The telescopes were all put in requisition; but the day being hazy, the opinions were various and conflicting. Upon this General Domont was sent for, and ordered to proceed with two light cavalry divisions in the direction of St. Lam-

---

3. Why this attack was not made simultaneously with that upon Hougoumont, and at the same time a demonstration upon the allied centre, to prevent troops being drawn from it to support the points assailed, I am at a loss to say.
4. Soult, Ney, Napoleon and Wellington were all born in 1769.

bert, and ascertain what the supposed troops were. Domont and Subervie immediately moved to the right, and drew up *en potence* on the right of the French army, and facing the wood of Paris. This must have occurred about one o'clock. Soon after, an officer of the light cavalry brought in a Prussian hussar who had been taken prisoner, and who had been charged with a letter for orders from Bülow to Wellington. The Prussian was very communicative, and answered all questions in a loud tone; he said that his corps had been that morning at Wavre, near which the other three Prussian corps had encamped; that his regiment had sent out patrols for six miles in all directions, but had not fallen in with any part of the French army, consequently they had concluded that Grouchy had joined the Emperor at Planchenois; and that the column seen near St-Lambert was the advance-guard of Büllow's (4th) corps, about 30,000 strong, that had not been present at the battle of Ligny.

This intelligence obliged Napoleon to hold a considerable force in hand, in order to defend his right flank. It is therefore evident, that more caution and vigilance should have been used by him in that direction.

Soult, who was at this time writing a despatch to Grouchy, informed him that the Emperor wished him to manoeuvre in the direction of the main army; to find out the point where it was, to keep up a close communication, and to be at hand to fall upon and destroy any enemy that might attempt to disturb their right flank.

At this moment we are engaged in battle on the line of Waterloo. The centre of the English army is at Mont St. Jean; so manoeuvre to join our right without loss of time.
Duke of Dalmatia
One o'clock, 18th June

It was sent off with the intercepted letter, but did not reach Grouchy till after seven p. m. Domont soon after made the communication, that he had fallen in with the enemy in the direction of St. Lambert, and the Emperor might be assured that the troops he had seen were enemies, and that he had sent out patrols to find out Grouchy and to open a communication with him.

Napoleon remarked to Soult, "This morning we had ninety chances for us; the arrival of Bülow loses us thirty, but we have still sixty against forty; and if Grouchy repairs the horrible fault which he committed yesterday in amusing himself at Gembloux, and sends his detachment with rapidity, the victory will be more decisive, because Bülow's corps will be quite destroyed."

The Emperor still felt sanguine as to the successful result of the battle, notwithstanding up to this time he had received no intelligence from Grouchy, nor any respecting the Prussians that could be considered satisfactory. It was only by a gross oversight on the part of Napoleon, that Bülow was allowed to approach his right. Had he detached six or eight thousand men of all arms on the 17th, or at an early hour on the 18th, to command the entrance to the defiles of St-Lambert, through which Bülow had to pass, and not above ten minutes' gallop from the French right, (consequently the force could have been recalled at any moment,) Napoleon could have kept Büllow's corps out of action until the arrival of Zieten's (1st) corps, which was not until near eight o'clock, and before that hour he might with his whole force have assailed Wellington's position.

The appearance of the Prussians at St. Lambert was ominous for Napoleon: it compelled him to alter his plan of battle, and tended to paralyze part of his reserves. The Prussians were between Grouchy's corps and the French right. Grouchy might indeed fall upon the Prussian rear; but he might also be retarded at the passage of the Dyle, or by some other difficulty or misfortune. However it might be, the prospect was sufficiently gloomy to make Napoleon detach some cavalry for the purpose of observing Bülow's corps, and also to keep a strong force in hand ready to check the Prussians, should they attempt to disturb his right.

The Emperor now sent word to Ney to commence the attack. D'Erlon's four massive columns advanced, accompanied by Ney, who halted on the highroad where it cuts through the bank, before reaching La Haye Sainte. As soon as the columns reached the inner ridge, and were passing between their batteries, our guns opened upon them; they were scarcely down the slope so as to be under cover from their own guns, when their batteries of between seventy and eighty pieces, posted on their main and inner ridges, opened with a tremendous roar upon our lines, causing dreadful havoc in Picton's division and Bylandt's brigade. The balls that went over tell with terrific effect amongst our cavalry in the rear. The flank columns which were detached to attack La Haye Sainte and Papelotte, Smohain and La Haye on our left, soon became engaged. Papelotte and the orchard of La Haye Sainte were carried. The German rifles from the orchard of La Haye Sainte opened first; then the Nassau on the left, and soon the skirmish became General along the whole front of attack.

As the columns approached the rise of our position, they appeared *en échelons* from their left. Bylandt's brigade of the Netherlands was overpowered and gave way before the overwhelming force which advanced against it, but was rallied again in rear of the ridge, where it remained for the rest of the day.

Some of this brigade, particularly the 6th militia, had behaved with great gallantry on the 16th, at Quatre-Bras. The flanking fires from La Haye Sainte and the enclosures of Smohain induced the enemy's flank columns to swerve away towards the centre, before they dropped off their supports: so much so, that their central columns had not sufficient space to deploy. The left column got a strong fire from the walls of La Haye Sainte, which it had scarcely cleared, when our sandhole rifles began; this at first staggered the column, but still it pressed on with deafening shouts of *Vive l'Empereur!* and turned our sand-larks, who fell back behind the knoll.

The enemy had dislodged the green Germans from the orchard of La Haye Sainte, and were desperately disputing for the buildings, which were a most serious impediment to the French, whose attacking columns were advancing towards the hedge. The French artillery now suspended their fire, for fear of destroying friends as well as foes: whilst our few but well-served batteries were carrying destruction through the enemy's columns, who gallantly pressed on, regardless of the iron, hail, until within forty yards of the hedge, when the undaunted Picton ordered Kempt's brigade to deploy into line. Moving up to the hedge, this brigade fired a volley into the enemy while deploying, and then with a loud Hurrah! rushed through it, receiving a murderous volley in return. This caused some disorder and delay, particularly to the 79th regiment: but the delay was momentary; they rallied, and levelling their bayonets, presented a line of British infantry at the charge. Picton's gallant example at Quatre-Bras had so inspired his troops, that nothing could now resist the impetuosity of their attack.

By the terrific fire of our infantry, the assailing columns were soon turned into a shapeless mass of men, destitute of order, although still endeavouring to hold their ground; pouring out a straggling fire, yet unable to withstand the storm about to burst upon their devoted heads. During this time a portion of the first light battalion of the German Legion crossed the highroad to support our advancing brigade. The French left attacking column became panic-stricken, and, in utter confusion, fled precipitately down the slope. As the British pressed forward, their front was crossed by a body of cuirassiers hotly pursued by the 2nd British Lifeguards. The cuirassiers dashed in amongst their own broken infantry, who flung themselves on the ground to allow both cavalries to ride over them, they then rose up and fired after the Lifeguards. The cuirassiers coming nearer to their own position pulled up their steeds, and boldly faced their pursuers, but in vain; after many an isolated and individual combat, they were obliged again to turn and fly. It was here that Shaw, the famous Lifeguardsman, fell in the *mêlée*, mortally wounded by a carbine-ball, after having, it is said, killed nine of his steel-clad opponents.

During this same attack, a French officer, whose horse had been shot under him, seized the regimental colour of the 32nd, which was carried at the moment by Lieutenant Belcher: a struggle ensued: the Frenchman was in the act of drawing his sword, when he received a thrust in the breast from a Sergeant's halbert, and instantly after, notwithstanding the Major (Toole) called out, (alas! too late,) "Save the brave fellow!" He was shot by a man named Lacey, and fell dead at Lieutenant Belcher's feet. This officer and Lieutenant-Colonel Brown, both actors in this scene, revisited the spot in 1845. They related all that took place on this part of our line during the day, and further told me, that in collecting their wounded on the morning after the battle, they found, near where the Hanoverian monument now stands, a most beautiful young lady who had been shot dead in the costume of an officer of the French hussars.[5]

It was during this gallant and eminently successful repulse of the enemy, that the brave Picton fell:[6] he was struck by a musket-ball in the right temple, and died immediately. His last words were, "Charge! Charge! Hurrah!" His life had been spent in fighting the battles of his country: his end was suited to his stormy career; and although he had attained the meridian of military glory, no one of the many that fell that day was so lamented, as no one had

---

5. Many females were found amongst the slain, although not of the same class as the heroine alluded to. As is common in the camp, the female followers wore male attire, with nearly as martial a bearing as the soldiers, and some even were mounted and rode astride.

6. Picton appears to have had a presentiment that this campaign would close his glorious career. What a pity he did not survive to see the effect of his charge!

been so admired and loved by the British army. His renown had attracted the notice of Napoleon, who on the morning of the battle inquired, "Where is Picton's division?"

His desire to know this might be attributed to his thinking, that, as they had been so roughly handled and lost so many men at Quatre-Bras, their morale was shaken and they might be easily overpowered.

It appears that Picton had been wounded on the 16th, at Quatre-Bras; but it was not discovered till his body was laid out on the 19th, at Brussels.

He was succeeded in the command of the division by Sir James Kempt; Colonel Belson, of the 28th, taking command of the brigade.

The 95th rifles were soon in the midst of the broken French infantry, over which the two cavalries had ridden; they took a vast number of prisoners and sent them to the rear. The rifles then reoccupied the knoll and sandpit, and Baring's gallant Germans the little garden and orchard of La Haye Sainte, from whence the enemy had been driven.

Ponsonby's brigade had advanced close up to the ridge, and was waiting the proper moment to charge; for the French columns on Kempt's left, having had nothing in their front to check them after Bylandt retreated, were making through the hedges that lined the road. Part of the Royal Dragoons dashed into the head of the enemy's column in their front, and at the same moment a portion of the 28th regiment brought their right shoulders forward and fired a volley into its left flank. At this time, part of Pack's brigade, formed of the redoubtable remains of the 92nd Highlanders, was in rear of the ridge, their left brought forward, resting in front of the brushwood upon the knoll on our left.

Part of another French column had passed the straggling hedge, and was pressing on towards the position of this brigade, bearing directly on its left. This handful of tried soldiers, partially aided by the Royal Scots and 42nd Highlanders, immediately advanced in order to come to close quarters with the enemy, whose fire they received without returning, until within thirty yards; they then threw in a concentrated and destructive volley, which completely staggered the French, who however soon sufficiently recovered themselves to return the fire.

At this moment, the Scots Greys came up, and the Highlanders opened out to let them pass. The wild shrill squeaking bagpipes, mixed with the shouting of "Scotland forever!" heightened the national enthusiasm, and many of them, breaking from their ranks, caught hold of the Greys' stirrups to be able to keep up with them, and to take their part in completing the destruction of the enemy.

Where streamed fair Scotia's banners high,
Or nodded where her bonnets blue,
Where pealed the bagpipe's deafening cry,
Or where the varied tartans flew:
There did the rush of battle first
Announce the deadly fight begun;
There did the shouts of triumph first
Proclaim the Gallic host o'ercome.

While in this fact we see ample proof of the ardour which fired the breasts of our brave Scottish troops, yet we must allow that this mingling of broken infantry with cavalry advancing to an attack, must have materially impeded the impetus and efficiency of both. The cavalry having the advantage of the descent, bore down all before them. Unfortunately this splendid result was not enough for the gallant spirits who achieved it. Wild with their success and carried away by the ardour of the fight, they hurried in utter confusion up the opposite slopes, sabring every living thing that came in their way. This was not the only instance of our cavalry getting disordered and out of hand by their own headlong rashness, and in consequence causing most serious loss of life.

The eagle and colour of the 46th regiment in the French

column, attracted the particular attention of Sergeant Ewart of the Greys; he gallantly rushed forward to secure the trophy. The following is his account of the affair:

> It was in the charge I took the eagle from the enemy: he and I had a hard contest for it; he made a thrust at my groin, I parried it off and cut him down through the head. After this a lancer came at me; I threw the lance off by my right side and cut him through the chin and upwards through the teeth. Next, a foot-soldier fired at me, and then charged me with his bayonet, which I also had the good luck to parry, and then I cut him down through the head; thus ended the contest As I was about to follow my regiment, the General said, "My brave fellow, take that to the rear; you have done enough till you get quit of it." I took the eagle to the ridge, and afterwards to Brussels.[7]

The Greys, with the Highlanders, took and destroyed nearly the whole of the front attacking column. Upon the right of the Greys were the Inniskilling Dragoons, who dashed through the straggling hedge[8] down upon the supporting columns, and made fearful havoc amongst them; and although they had not the good fortune to capture an eagle, their attack was as brilliant as that of the other regiments of the brigade. On the right of the brigade were the Royal Dragoons, as before mentioned, who, like the Greys,[9] met the head of the

7. Ewart got a commission the following year. Like Shaw, the Lifeguardsman, he was a man of Herculean strength, and of more than ordinary stature, being six feet four inches, and of consummate skill as a swordsman. He died in 1845, having attained the age of seventy-seven.

8. It was here, and at this period, that a gentleman in plain clothes called out to the dragoons, "Go along, my boys! now's your time!" It was the late Duke of Richmond, come out merely as an amateur, and to see how his ball-guests, and his sons, three of whom were on the field, were faring. He was not attached to the staff of this army: otherwise he would have been second in command, as, besides being Colonel of the 35th, he was full General.

9. The Greys and Royal Dragoons having each captured an eagle at Waterloo, they were both ordered to wear an eagle on their colours, accoutrements and buttons.

enemy's column on our side of the Wavre road and hedge; the column threw out a straggling fire, and attempted to re-pass the hedge; but the Royals were soon among them, cutting and slashing away, and causing a panic, which, from the enemy's situation, was not to be wondered at.

In the centre of this column was the eagle of the 105th regiment; this caught the eye of Captain Clarke of the Royal Dragoons. The following extract is from the records of the regiment:

I was in command of the centre squadron of the Royal Dragoons in this charge; while following up the attack, I perceived a little to my left, in the midst of a body of infantry, an eagle and colour, which the bearer was making off with towards the rear. I immediately gave the order, "Right shoulders! Forward!" to my squadron, at the same time leading direct upon the eagle and calling out to the men with me to secure the colour; the instant I got within reach of the officer who carried the eagle, I ran my sword into his right side, and he staggered and fell, but did not reach the ground on account of the pressure of his companions: as the officer was in the act of falling, I called out a second time to some men close behind me, "Secure the colour, it belongs to me." The standard coverer, corporal Styles,[10] and several other men rushed up, and the eagle fell across my horse's head against that of corporal Styles's, who came up on my left: as it was falling, I caught the fringe of the flag with my left hand, but could not at first pull up the eagle: at the second attempt however I succeeded. Being in the midst of French troops, I attempted to separate the eagle from the staff, to put it into the breast of my coatee, but it was too firmly fixed. Corporal Styles said, "Sir, don't break it;" to which I replied, "Very well;

10. Styles received a commission; and Captain Clarke, now Colonel Kennedy, the order of the Bath and the Hanoverian Guelphic order.

carry it off to the rear as fast as you can;" he did so. Though wounded, I preferred remaining on the field in command of my squadron, which I did till near seven o'clock in the evening, when I was obliged to withdraw; having had two horses killed under me, and having received two wounds, which confined me to my quarters at Brussels for nearly two months.

During this conflict, the valley and slopes of both positions presented a sight indeed! they were covered with broken troops of both armies: ours, both infantry and cavalry, bringing up prisoners singly and in groups. Some few of our fellows were helping themselves to any little valuable article they could lay hand on, until driven back by their officers.

Many French officers were brought up prisoners; they delivered up their swords to our officers. The enemy upon the opposite heights were similarly employed in taking prisoners, and destroying such of our cavalry as had ventured too far, particularly the Scots Greys, who, by their ill-timed impetuosity, lost many men and horses. In fact most of Ponsonby's brigade, with a portion of the household brigade, animated by their first success, pursued their advantage too far; they crossed the valley in disorder, and galloped up to the French position in two's and three's and groups, brandishing their swords in defiance, riding along the ridge, sabring the gunners and rendering about thirty guns useless: the bugles, or trumpets, sounding to rally, were unheeded.

General Ponsonby rode forward to stop their wild career, but he was intercepted in a ploughed field by the lancers, and killed. The command of the brigade devolved on Colonel Muter of the Inniskillings. The enemy's cuirassiers, lancers and chasseurs, perceiving the isolated and unsupported position of our broken dragoons, rushed forward and made serious havoc, pursuing them down the slope into the valley. Those of our men whose horses were blown, became an easy prey to the enemy; but at length the 12th and 16th light dragoons, part of Vandeleur's brigade, came forward. The 12th, under Colonel F. Ponsonby, charged some unsteady infantry in the valley, and then attacked the lancers, whom they overpowered, thus relieving and rendering a great service to our broken cavalry. In advancing, the 12th suffered most severely from the fire of some of Durutte's division, who were concealed by a high bank in the valley, in front of our left.

The 16th light dragoons charged some of the enemy's cavalry; part of Merle's Dutch-Belgian cavalry came up as a support; a portion went down the slope. Vivian's brigade moved from our extreme left towards the scene of action, but like Merle's it was not required. Both sides were now employed in reforming upon their original positions, except our two light cavalry brigades, which took position somewhat more to their right. The skeleton remains of Ponsonby's brigade, at a later period of the day, crossed the Charleroy road, and joined Lord E. Somerset's. Meanwhile our rockets were playing with destructive effect upon the enemy, whilst rallying opposite to our left.

After this sanguinary conflict, Napoleon rode along his right wing, and as usual he was loudly cheered. Sir Hussey Vivian, who at the time was in front of the knoll on our left, told me that he distinctly saw the Emperor: he was galloping towards some of his lancers that were reforming; upon the near approach of Napoleon they waved their lance flags and shouted, *Vive l'Empereur!* Shortly before this, Vivian ordered two of Major Gardner's guns which were attached to his brigade, to open fire. Upon this the French artillery opened, and a shot striking one of our ammunition tumbrels, it blew up, which called forth a shout from the French gunners.

We may remark upon this attack,[11] which the Duke pronounced the most serious that occurred during the day, that

---

11. I am quite at a loss to explain the most unaccountable remissness of the enemy's cavalry in not supporting this attack; or why our light cavalry on the left, did not more promptly carry out the orders given by Lord Uxbridge before the battle began, to vigorously support offensive operations in their front.

it was entirely defeated; that it gave us a great many prisoners, led to our disabling many of their guns, and that its failure frustrated Napoleon's entire plan. Nor can any doubt be entertained, that, if Wellington's forces on this eventful day had been wholly composed of his Peninsular soldiers, of whom he had said, "I always thought, I could go anywhere and could do anything with that army!", we should not have looked so anxiously for the arrival of the Prussians, nor would they have been up in time to have taken any share in the victory.

Meanwhile the enemy's attack upon La Haye Sainte had been continued; they had again dislodged the German riflemen from the orchard, although a most determined resistance had been made by Major Baring. During the advance of D'Erlon's columns, the Duke, observing the dreadful havoc made in his front troops by the enemy's batteries, ordered them to retire behind the crest of the ridge for shelter, which movement was mistaken for one of retreat by Napoleon, who immediately launched forward Kellermann's cuirassiers and carabineers to pick up our guns. Shortly before this, His Grace ordered Lambert's brigade forward into front line, and advanced a reinforcement to La Haye Sainte, having observed that the enemy was about to make another attack.

Upon the arrival of the reinforcement, Baring tried to recover the orchard, as well as the little garden on our side of the farm, which had fallen into the hands of the French. The Germans were advancing, when they observed some cuirassiers moving forward. Lord E. Somerset, whose brigade was now in line immediately in rear of this part of the position, had placed two officers on the ridge, to give a signal of the enemy's advance, in order to time his charge. Upon the cuirassiers approaching the line of skirmishers in front of our light of the farm, the latter ran in upon Baring's troops, who were near the orchard, and threw them into confusion. They took to flight, but were overtaken, ridden down and sabred.

While the cuirassiers were ascending the ridge, our artillery opened with grape and case-shot, which laid many low, and disordered their ranks: they however pressed forward most gallantly. Somerset's line was now coming over the ridge, led by Uxbridge, and, at the moment our front squares fired into the cuirassiers, the two cavalries dashed into each other: the shock was terrific; the swords clashing upon the casques and cuirasses so that, as Lord E. Somerset humorously observed to me when he visited the field in June 1842, "You might have fancied that it was so many tinkers at work." But it was of short duration. The British household cavalry soon cleared the ridge of the cuirassiers, although they made a most gallant resistance: they fled down the slope on both sides of La Haye Sainte, closely followed by the brigade; those on the allied left of the farm, by the 2nd Lifeguards.

It was in following up this charge, that part of this brigade mixed with Ponsonby's broken dragoons on the French position, and fell upon and sabred some of the enemy's infantry who had been assaulting La Haye Sainte. Part of the 1st Lifeguards pursued some cuirassiers, till both became wedged in between the two high banks of the Genappe road, beyond the orchard of La Haye Sainte. Some of Reille's troops, who had advanced in support of D'Erlon's attack, fired down from these banks upon our Lifeguards, who had to get back to our line as well as they could. Most of the King's Dragoon Guards had dashed over the road and were falling back to reform; but they lost many men and some officers, by the enemy's fire from the little garden of La Haye Sainte.

In leading this charge, Lord E. Somerset lost his cocked hat, and went to the charge bare-headed. On his return, whilst looking for his hat, a cannon ball took off the flap of his coat and killed his horse. During the rest of the day he appeared in a Lifeguard's helmet.

Captain Siborne concludes his narrative of the attack and defeat of the enemy, upon our left and centre, between half-past one and three o'clock, in the following spirited manner:

Thus terminated one of the grandest scenes which distinguished the mighty drama, enacted on the ever-memorable plains of Waterloo: a scene presenting in bold relief genuine British valour, crowned with resplendent triumph; a scene which should be indelibly impressed upon the minds as well of living British warriors, as of their successors in ages yet unborn.

Britons, before other scenes are disclosed to your view, take one retrospective glance at this glorious, this instructive spectacle. Let your imagination carry you to the rear of that celebrated position, and a little to the left of the Charleroy road. Behold, in the foreground on the right, a British line of cavalry advancing to the charge, exulting in the consciousness of its innate courage, indomitable spirit and strength of arm. Whilst you are admiring the beautiful order and steadiness of their advance, your eyes are suddenly attracted by the glittering of a line of horsemen in burnished coats of mail, rising above the brow, and now crowning the summit of the ridge.

They are the far-famed cuirassiers of France, led on by a Kellermann: gallant spirits, that have hitherto overcome the finest troops that could be brought against them, and have grown grey in glory. Trumpets sound the charge; in the next instant your ears catch the low thundering noises of their horses' hoofs, and your breathless excitement is wound to the highest pitch as the adverse lines dash together with a shock, which at the moment you expect must end in their mutual annihilation. Observe the British, how they seem to doubt for a second in what manner to deal with their opponents.

Now they urge their powerful steeds into the intervals between the necks of those of the cuirassiers. Swords brandished high in air gleam fitfully in rapid succession throughout the lines, here clashing together, there clanging against helmet and cuirass, which ring under their redoubled strokes. See, the struggle is but a moment doubtful: the cuirassiers, seemingly encumbered by their coats of mail, are yielding to superior strength, dexterity and bravery combined; men and horses reel and stagger to the earth: gaps open out in their line; numbers are backing out, others are fairly turning round, their whole line now bends and breaks asunder into fragments: in the next moment they appear, as if by a miracle, to be swept from off the crest of the position, and being closely and hotly pursued by the victors, the whole rushing down the other side of the ridge, are snatched from your view. Your attention is now irresistibly drawn to that part of the foreground immediately facing you, where you have barely time to catch sight of a line of British infantry just as it forces its way through the hedge that runs along the crest of the ridge, to charge a column advancing up the other side.

At the moment the shouts that proclaim its triumph reach your ear, you are struck by the majestic advance, close to your left, of another line of British horsemen. These halt just under the brow of the ridge. In their left front your eye now also embraces a line of British infantry moving quickly up the steep; whilst at the same time you see the heads of two hostile columns issuing through the hedge, and crowning the ridge amidst shouts of *Vive l'Empereur!* The one nearest to you, finding no immediate opposition to its farther advance, is rapidly establishing itself on the height; the other is met by the advancing line of infantry. A struggle ensues; the farther column is concealed from your view by the smoke by which it is suddenly enshrouded: but, at the very moment when doubts arise in your mind as to the result, the cavalry rushes forward, and passing through intervals opened out for it by the infantry, charges both those heads of columns, cutting them up, as it were, root and branch; and then bounding through the hedge, the whole disappears as if by magic.

Now let your imagination, keeping pace with the intensity of feeling excited by such a scene, carry you up to the summit of the ridge. Behold, at once, the glorious spectacle spread out before you; the furious impetuosity of their onslaught overcomes all resistance: the terror-stricken masses, paralyzed by this sudden apparition of cavalry amongst them, have neither time nor resolution to form squares, and limit their defence to a feeble, hasty, straggling fire from their ill-cemented edges: a flight, commencing from the rearmost rank, is rapidly augmented by the outward scattering, occasioned by the continually increasing pressure upon the front; the entire slope is soon covered with the dispersed elements of the previously attacking force: parties of infantry are hurrying over the brow of the ridge to aid others of the cavalry in securing their prisoners; three thousand of these are swept to the rear, and two eagles are gloriously captured. From the momentary contemplation of these trophies, your eyes instinctively revert to the course of the victors, whom you now perceive in the middle distance of the view; a broken line of daring horsemen rushing up the opposite height.

Their intoxicating triumph admits of no restraint. They heed not the trumpet's call to halt and rally; but, plunging wildly amidst the formidable line of batteries ranged along the French position, they commence sabring the gunners, stabbing the horses, and seem to clear the ground of every living being. But physical efforts, however powerfully developed and sustained, have their limit; exhausted nature yields at length, and their fiery steeds, subdued not by force but by exhaustion, retire with lagging, faltering pace. You look in vain for a support; there is none: but your eye is suddenly caught by the fluttering of lance-flags of a column of the enemy's cavalry approaching from the left, and you become nervously alive to the danger that awaits the valiant band of heroes, who are only now made sensible of the necessity of retiring to collect and rally their scattered numbers. Seeing no support ready to receive them, and becoming aware of the near approach of hostile cavalry, they make a last and desperate effort Those who are best mounted, and whose horses are least blown, succeed in regaining the allied position unmolested; but a very considerable number are overtaken by the lancers, with whom they now contend under a fearful disadvantage in point of speed and order.

But mark! a rescue is at hand: a gallant line of friendly cavalry throws itself against the right flank of the lancers, the farther portion or left of that line first dashing through and scattering an unsteady mass of infantry, the sole remaining column out of the entire attacking force that has yet kept together; the tide of destruction now sets in strongly against the lancers. Their pursuit is checked. The heavy dragoons are relieved from the pressure. A *mêlée* ensues, but you are not kept long in suspense; for in another moment this newly arrived force, making good its way, succeeds in driving the lancers in confusion down to the foot of the valley. The arena in your front is speedily cleared of both friends and foes; the discharge of rockets which now attracts your attention appears like a display of fireworks in celebration of the glorious triumph. The affair has terminated.

But stay to witness the concluding part of the scene. Observe the splendidly attired group entering upon the right, just above La Haye Sainte.

It is headed by one whom you cannot for a moment mistake, the illustrious Wellington. Lord Uxbridge, returning from his brilliant charge, now joins the Duke, while the whole *Corps diplomatique et militaire* express in the strongest terms their admiration of the grand military spectacle of which they have been spectators. Among them are representatives of nearly all the continental nations; so that this glorious triumph of your valiant countrymen may be said to have been achieved in the face of congregated Europe. Honour, imperishable honour, to every British soldier engaged in that never-to-be-forgotten fight.

When Britain again puts forth her strength in battle, may her. sovereign's guards inherit the same heroic spirit which animated those of George, Prince Regent, and inspire them with the desire to maintain, in all their pristine purity and freshness, the laurels transmitted to them from the field of Waterloo; and when the soldiers of the three united kingdoms shall again be found fighting side by side against the common enemy, may they prove to the world that they have not degenerated from the men of the Union Brigade, who, by their heroic deeds on that great day, so faithfully represented the military virtues of the British empire.

Several instances of extraordinary heroism were displayed by Lord Uxbridge,[12] especially when he was leading on to the charge, between one and two o'clock, the admiring men of the two heavy cavalry brigades. It was perhaps not less prudent than gallant to kindle a daring spirit in our cavalry, and rouse them to the highest pitch of emulation by the dashing valour of their chief. There was not a man amongst us who did not feel certain that Uxbridge would have led the charge,

---

12. Personal intrepidity in a chief is no doubt important, and those under him acquire courage at times from the example of their leader. But be it said, without any disrespect to my high-spirited old commander, discretion may sometimes be outstripped, when personal intrepidity passes the bounds of prudence.

even if the whole French army had been moving in mass against him; yet it is well known that there was one looking on, who did not wear a black stock nor carry a musket,[13] that would have been better pleased if our chivalric leader had been a little more cautious to support, and more successful in, keeping the cavalry well in hand.

But on the British heart were lost
The terrors of the charging host;
For not an eye, the storm that view'd,
Changed its proud glance of fortitude.

---

13. His Grace has said, he would rather carry a musket than be attached to the emperor of Russia. (*Despatches,* vol. XII, page 268.)

CHAPTER 4

The Great Charges

Skirmishing continued along our whole front: the entire space between La Haye Sainte and Hougoumont was up to this time defended by Alten's skirmishers, commanded by Colonel Vigouroux, (30th regiment). The light companies of the guards were, as already stated, fully engaged at Hougoumont, to which post, about two o'clock, Sir J. Byng ordered Colonel Hepburn to advance, with the remaining companies of the 3rd guards. When they reached the first hedge of the orchard, the hollow-way, they met with Lord Saltoun, who, in consequence of the severe loss of his light troops, gave up the command to Colonel Hepburn, and returned to his own regiment, (the 1st guards,) posted on the main ridge.

General Cooke having lost an arm by a round-shot, the command of the division devolved on General Byng, and the latter's brigade on Colonel Hepburn, who soon after, crossed the orchard, driving the French before him, and occupied the south hedge; this he considered his position. The French went through a gap at the south-west corner of the orchard, into the wood, and, being huddled together, suffered severely from the concentrated fire of their pursuers, as well as from that of the Coldstream upon the scaffolds and through the loopholes of the wall. I have been told by a British staff-officer, who passed along the south hedges on the morning of the 19th, that, notwithstanding he had been at most of the battles in the Peninsula, he had never seen, except at a breach, dead and wounded men lie thicker than along those hedges.

About this time, the 7th hussars were in line, and near the right of the main ridge. Our officers and men were falling fast, from the fire of musketry; at length it was discovered that a dropping fire came from a spot covered with standing rye. Sergeant Montague and a few hussars galloped to the place, and surprised a group of the enemy's skirmishers, all of whom they cut down.

A strong line of the enemy's cavalry passed Hougoumont and ascended our position, apparently regardless of the fire of our artillery, although it somewhat disordered their ranks. The 7th, with a portion of the 15th hussars, was led against them. After a few cuts and points, the enemy went about, and rallied behind another well-formed body of their cavalry; we rallied in rear of our position. About the same time Colonel Hepburn's troops were warmly attacked, out-flanked, and again obliged to retire to their friendly hollow-way; but when the enemy passed the south hedge and entered the orchard, all within musket range got again such a severe fire from the Coldstream at the east wall that they were staggered; Hepburn again advanced, and recovered his position.

About the time the 2nd brigade of guards advanced to Hougoumont, the Brunswickers came into line on the right. A column of French infantry was now seen advancing towards Alten's and the left of Cooke's divisions. Our skirmishers were pushed forward to feel them; upon which they changed their direction towards Hougoumont through a winding valley, and got as it were under our position, so that they could not be seen. The officer of artillery, who fired the first shot, was posted near where the Lion now stands;

judging the course they were taking, he allowed them to proceed to a point where he could best exercise his engines of destruction, and opened upon the mass with fearful precision and awful effect. The whole column was thrown into confusion, and moved to some lower ground for protection; there it was reformed, and put in motion towards the enclosures of Hougoumont; the guns opened again upon them with similar results, which probably prevented a serious flank attack on this post.

Napoleon, finding his repeated attacks upon Hougoumont quite unavailing, ordered General Haxo to establish a battery of howitzers to set it on fire. The shells fell into the buildings, and flames shortly burst forth: at about three o'clock, the whole of the château and a portion of the out-offices were on fire. From the right of the allied position the appearance was awfully grand. It is surprising that the enemy, with so large a force of artillery, chiefly twelve-pounders, did not level Hougoumont with the ground. With his left batteries near the Nivelles road, from whence it was completely commanded, he might have soon beaten it about the ears of its defenders; he preferred however burning them out with shells.

The Duke considered it of great importance to withhold this position from the enemy, and directed that it should not be abandoned, whilst there was a man left to defend it, although it was in flames. He deemed the maintaining of the post essential to the success of the day's operations. Many of the wounded who were in the buildings perished in the flames; those in the chapel escaped, as the flames did not extend far beyond the entrance; and it is a remarkable fact, that they ceased at the feet of the wooden image of our Saviour.

Yes! Agincourt may be forgot,
And Cressy be an unknown spot,
And Blenheim's name be new;
But still in story and in song,
For many an age remember'd long,

Shall live the walls of Hougoumont,
And field of Waterloo.

The Duke's orders were carried down to Hougoumont by Major Hamilton, aide-de-camp to General Barnes, the adjutant-General, and given to Colonel Home, commanding some of the 3rd guards on the right of the building, near the wood. After delivering the order, Major Hamilton went away, but shortly returned and asked Colonel Home, if he perfectly understood His Grace's instructions: "I do," replied the Colonel, "and you can tell the Duke that, unless we are attacked more vigorously than we have hitherto been, we shall maintain the post without difficulty."

Shortly afterwards Colonel Home entered the buildings, which, together with some stacks, were in a blaze, and found in the walled garden the Colonels Macdonnell and Woodford, to whom he gave up the Duke's orders. Colonel Woodford, at this time, commanded in the interior of Hougoumont, and Colonel Hepburn in the orchard. To have allowed the enemy to establish himself in such a post, so near our front and flank, might certainly have been followed by the most serious consequences. But why our gallant assailants wasted so much ammunition against brick and stone walls, that might elsewhere have been used with effect against the enemy, is not easily answered. A post of the description of Hougoumont never before sustained such a succession of desperate attacks: the battle began with the struggle for its possession, which struggle only terminated on the utter defeat and rout of the enemy.

The attack upon La Haye Sainte[1] was repeated, notwith-

---

1. Our advanced posts of Hougoumont. La Haye Sainte, and Papelotte, were of the utmost importance to us, more particularly the former. An eminent military writer (Jomini) says, "Posts that can be readily defended, are of greater value in battle than insurmountable obstacles; since it is sufficient if such posts can be maintained for a few hours by means of mere detachments. Hougoumont with its enclosures, the farm of La Haye-Sainte and the rivulet of Papelotte, presented more serious impediments to Ney, than did the celebrated position of Elchingen."

standing the punishment the enemy had received at the hands of the German rifles. They again pressed on to closer combat with determined bravery. The principal attacks were directed to the barn and yard doors leading into the open fields towards the Lion.

About four o'clock, the 13th light dragoons and 15th Hussars (part of the brigade in which I served,) were sent off in haste, under General Grant,[2] towards Braine-Lalleud, to watch the movement of a portion of the enemy's lancers moving in that direction. The 2nd German dragoons also were ordered on the same service, to act as a support, if needful.

The fire of the enemy's artillery had been continued with great vigour; it was now increased upon that part of our position which was between the two highroads. Our squares, which were lying down behind the crest of the ridge and could not be seen by the enemy, were protected in a great degree from the round and grape-shot, but not from the shells, which were bestowed upon them most liberally. They sometimes fell amongst us with great effect. Those missiles may be both seen and heard as they approach; so that by keeping a look-out many lives were saved; the ground too was so saturated with rain that the shells in some instances sunk beneath the surface, and bursting threw up mud and sand, which were comparatively harmless. The oldest soldier however had never witnessed so furious a cannonade. The Duke, writing to Lord Beresford, says, "I never saw such a pounding match."

The havoc was dreadful in the extreme, for some considerable time before the impetuous Ney came on with his grand cavalry attack, made by forty squadrons. On their right, close to La Haye Sainte, were the cuirassiers; then the lancers and chasseurs *à cheval* of the Imperial Guard. They advanced in lines, *en echelons,* their left reaching nearly to the east hedge of Hougoumont.

As those on the right neared the ridge, their artillery dis-

---

2. General Grant had three horses shot under him.

continued firing; and ours opened with grape, canister and Shrapnel shells, which rattled like hail on the steel-clad warriors; but they still pressed on, regardless of our fire, towards the guns, the horses of which had been sent to the rear. Every discharge (the load was usually double,) threw them into great disorder; but excited by the trumpets sounding the charge, they rode up to the cannons' mouths, shouting, *Vive l'Empereur!*

Our gunners fled to the squares, which were all ranged in chequer; the front ones had advanced again nearly close to the guns. The French, not perceiving the advantage which the squares afforded the gunners, and imagining that they had captured the guns, shouted out in triumph, and then crossed over the ridge; here they were assailed by a rolling fire from our squares, which were all prepared, the front ranks on the right knee, the next rank at the charge.

When the cuirassiers had passed over the ridge, they were out of sight of the lancers and chasseurs, who immediately pressed on to share in the contest. Our artillery received them in a similar manner; some of the men rushing back to their guns, and after discharging them at the foe, taking shelter again within the squares, or under the guns. The firing produced a much greater effect upon such of the enemy's cavalry as were not protected by the cuirass and casque; consequently their ranks were much more disordered than were the cuirassiers'; still they pursued their onward course, passed the guns, raised a shout and swept round the squares. Some halted and fired their pistols at the officers in the squares; others would ride close up, and either cut at the bayonet or try to lance the outside files. No sooner had the broken squadrons passed the guns, than the gunners were again at their post, and the grape rattled upon the retiring hosts; but frequently, before a succeeding round could be discharged, the hostile cavalry were again upon them, and compelled them to seek shelter.

During the cavalry attacks, those of the enemy were at one

time on the allied position, riding about amongst our squares for three quarters of an hour; all cannonading having ceased between the two highroads.

When the enemy's squadrons became broken and disordered, our cavalry, who were kept in hand till the favourable moment, again attacked them and drove them down the slope, often following too far, by which they burned their fingers, and likewise prevented our gunners from keeping up a constant fire.

Our position was scarcely free from the enemy's cavalry, before their numerous artillery began to ply us again with shells and round-shot. After the first cavalry charges, our infantry squares, finding the odds in their favour, gained confidence, and it was soon evident they considered the enemy's cavalry attacks as a relief, and far more agreeable than their furious cannonade, which was invariably suspended on their attacking force crowning our ridge.

I am confident, from what I saw and heard, as well during as after the battle, that most of our British infantry would rather, when in squares, have the enemy's cavalry amongst them than remain exposed to the fire of artillery. The 1st foot-guards had the enemy's cavalry on every side of their squares several times, and beat them off. Our squares often wheeled up into line, to make their fire more destructive: on this, the cuirassiers would suddenly wheel round to charge; but our infantry were instantly in square, and literally indulged in laughter at the disappointment and discomfiture of their gallant opponents.

Throughout the day our squares presented a serried line of bristling bayonets, through which our enemy's cavalry could not break. Had the enemy made their attacks throughout with infantry and cavalry combined, the result must have been much more destructive; for, although squares are the best possible formation against cavalry, there can be nothing worse to oppose infantry. I am not aware of any parallel to the extraordinary scene of warfare now going forward: most of our infantry were in squares, and the enemy's cavalry of every description riding about amongst them as if they had been our own, for which, but for their armour and uniforms, they might have been mistaken.

An ammunition wagon in a blaze passed about this time in full gallop close to our rear, and one of our men, I think Fowler, afterwards the Sergeant saddler, drew his pistol and fired at the horses, but without taking effect: the wagon shortly after blew up.

The skirmishing at the farms of La Haye and Papelotte, which were retaken, and in the hamlet of Smohain, went on with unabated fury: the attacks upon La Haye Sainte and Hougoumont were continued. The artillery on both sides was now pealing forth its thunders. The earth trembled with the repeated concussions. Ney and his Imperial master, no doubt, expected to bear down all before them by the aid of the thirty-seven additional squadrons they were about to bring forward; whilst we could only command in addition two regiments, the 13th light dragoons and the 15th Hussars, under Grant, who, on discovering that the *ruse* of the enemy was to draw off a part of our cavalry from the right of our main front line, had now returned and driven some of the enemy's cavalry down the slope, but were obliged to retire immediately, as their cavalry was collected in great force in the valley, as also in the hollows near La Haye Sainte.

Being there exposed to the fire of our batteries, the French horsemen would at times call out aloud, *"En avant, en avant!* (Forward, forward!) here we are knocked to pieces;" upon which their chiefs would again advance and assail our position. About this period our attention was drawn to the firing of a battery in our rear; we all, to a man, looked round, as if by word of command: but found it to be our own guns, which were firing from the second ridge across the Nivelles road upon some lancers that were attacking our Brunswick squares, upon the rear face of our right wing, and were twice driven off by Bolton's battery.

The allied position was again cleared of the enemy, and skirmishers were thrown forward along the valley; and some were sent to cover the front from the Hougoumont orchard as far as La Haye Sainte. At this point the attack had been carried on with great vigour: Colonel Baring had made another application for rifle ammunition, which, from some cause or other, was not supplied.

In consequence of the enemy's not closely pursuing the Prussians from Ligny upon Wavre, between the evenings of the 16th and 17th, they had, during their retreat, scoured with strong patrols the whole country between their own left and the right of Napoleon's army, which was then advancing, by the Charleroy road, towards Waterloo. Thus the movements of both Grouchy and his Emperor were closely observed, and correct information forwarded from time to time to the Prussian headquarters.

The great caution they exercised, not only retarded the communication between the Emperor and his detached Marshal, by forcing the bearers of their despatches to take a circuitous route, and at times to turn and dodge, like hares, to avoid the vigilant Prussians, but enabled them to perform the contemplated and most important flank movement, without molestation, in order to join us on the field of Waterloo. Some of the Prussians had shown, during the battle of Ligny, a bad spirit, and many even had abandoned their colours and gone over to the enemy, while eight thousand of those belonging to the newly incorporated provinces with Prussia had returned home; still the *morale* of the great mass of the army remained arm and unshaken.

The example of their venerable and heroic commander, "Marshal *Vorwärts*" as he was termed by his soldiers, no doubt stimulated their courage. The Prince, notwithstanding his advanced age, and his toil-worn frame being severely shaken and bruised from his fall on the 16th, was mounted and amongst those he termed his children, early on the morning of the

18th. By an order of the day his troops were thus addressed, "I shall immediately lead you once more against the enemy; we shall beat him, because it is our duty to do so."

The difficulties encountered by the Prussians on their march from Wavre by St. Lambert to the field of Waterloo, would have tried and put to the test the endurance of any troops. The roads, from the heavy rains, were ankle deep, and the defiles of St. Lambert turned into a regular swamp, almost impassable for men and horses, and still worse for the guns and tumbrels of ammunition, that were very numerous and far from being well horsed, and which, at intervals, sunk up to the axle-trees; horses floundering and causing a stoppage, the most robust soldiers, in endeavouring to extricate the guns and ammunition wagons, would drop down, overcome by the fatigue of their exertions, and declare "they could not get on."

"But we must get on," said their veteran commander, who seemed to multiply himself, and might be seen at different points along the line of march, exciting his men to exertion by words of encouragement: "I have promised Wellington to be up," said Blücher, "and up we must get. Surely you will not make me forfeit my word: exert yourselves a little more, and victory is certain."

The Duke of Wellington was in constant communication throughout the day with the Prussians, by means of General Müffling, who was attached to our headquarters' staff, as also by Colonel Freemantle, aide-de-camp, Colonel Stavely, and Captain (now Lieutenant-Colonel) Basil Jackson of the Royal Staff Corps, and on the Duke's staff.

The four corps of Blücher's army had been concentrated at and near Wavre on the evening of the 17th, and the guns of the three corps which had fought at Ligny refitted, and with the troops supplied with fresh ammunition, as well as put into an efficient state for another battle.

The 4th (Bülow's) corps, which, up to this time, had not fired a shot in the campaign, was put in motion at sunrise on the 18th towards the French right flank, by way of St. Lambert; they were preceded by strong patrols to ascertain whether Napoleon had yet taken precautionary measures to obstruct their junction with us, or protect his own right. It was soon discovered that this precaution, so essential to the protection of his right, had been overlooked by Napoleon: the Prussians immediately availed themselves of the advantage which his neglect thus afforded, by throwing a force into the wood of Paris, which commanded the defiles of the Lasne and St. Lambert. Zieten's, or the first corps, was to march, by Fromont and Ohain, direct upon our left: Pirch's, or the second corps, was to follow Bülow's; they were delayed by a part of Wavre being on fire, and by the great difficulty of making progress through the defiles of St. Lambert. They were expected, nevertheless, to be up by or before two o'clock. It was near five o'clock when the first two brigades of Bülow's corps debouched from their covered position in the wood of Paris.

The 15th brigade, under General Losthin, and the 16th, under Colonel Hiller, with some cavalry, (altogether about 16,000 men and forty-four guns,) drew up perpendicularly to the French right flank; upon which Durutte's division, which formed the right of the French main front line, was thrown back *en potence.* The Prussian commanders detached some battalions to Frischermont and Smohain to secure their right flank; they also sent a few battalions to the Lasne, the woods of Virère and Hubremont, to support their left flank. So stealthily and cautiously did the Prussians approach Smohain, that both the enemy and allies seemed astounded upon their debouching from the enclosures.

General Domont's cavalry were still *en potence,* but at a considerable distance from the Prussians, whose advanced batteries opened upon the French cavalry, although at a long range; but this was merely to acquaint Wellington and Napoleon of their arrival, which doubtless alarmed the latter, whilst, by the former, it was listened to with joy.

Domont sent on part of his force to attack the Prussians, and moved forward his line. Some Prussian cavalry passed through the infantry to meet them, and drove back the French advance: the Prussian cavalry were soon obliged to fall back; but, as the infantry were advancing, and their artillery kept up a sharp fire, Domont did not attack. The Prussian battalions, detached to Smohain, cleared the enclosures, and drew up near the French right flank: they were attacked and driven back by a part of Durutte's division; but upon the Prussians reaching the enclosures and hollow ways, they maintained their ground and kept up a rattling fire. This was after six o'clock. Napoleon had ordered the 6th corps, under Count Lobau, to move to the right, and take up a position, where with six to eight thousand men of all arms, and favoured by the strong ground in front of Planchenois, he could keep in check thirty thousand of the enemy: at the same time the old and middle guard were advanced into the plain, and occupied the ground vacated by the 6th corps.

Durutte's light troops had been previously reinforced, and made a desperate effort to force back the Nassau-men at Papelotte and Smohain, for the purpose of preventing the junction of Bülow's corps with the allied left, when, after a sharp and close skirmish, the enemy's intention was frustrated. Blücher, observing Lobau's advance, extended his line; his right rested upon Frischermont, and his left upon the wood of Virère. Part of Prince William's cavalry was in reserve. Lobau's corps moved forward; Domont's and Subervie's cavalry remained as a second line. Lobau's guns soon opened a brisk cannonade upon Bülow's corps, and were answered with spirit. Some time after, the remaining two brigades of Bülow's corps debouched, and forming into columns sent their batteries to the front, which made the Prussian artillery more formidable than that of the French. Blücher's left was making toward Planchenois, in the right rear of the enemy. At this time, seven o'clock, the Prussian force in the field amounted to nearly

29,000 men and sixty-four guns. Their guns commanded the whole of the French right *en potence;* which, like the Prussian line, was parallel to the Genappe road, and nearly at right angles to their former front. The undulating ground over which the Prussians were advancing, rose like an amphitheatre, and their guns, in consequence, could open from the summit of numerous little heights; whilst at the intervals between the batteries, their troops advanced into the plain. Nothing could be more favourable for a force attacking an enemy's flank.

A Prussian battery dislodged a French one on the heights near Chantilly, and at once established at the point their own battery, whose fire was directed upon the enemy posted between Planchenois and La Belle-Alliance.

An incident occurred, as related by Siborne, worthy of notice:

> It was about six o'clock, that Napoleon replied to Ney's demand for fresh infantry, "*Où voulez-vous que fen a prenne? Voulez-vous que fen fasse?* (Where can I get them? Can I make them?)"

An expression, the force of which is rendered sufficiently obvious by the critical circumstances of his position, and clearly proves that his operations had taken an unfavourable turn; this was further manifest by the great anxiety and impatience he exhibited for the result of the battle.

CHAPTER 5

The Prussians Arrive

The Prussian left was now close approaching the village of Planchenois, which, up to the present period, had not been occupied. The French force, being less numerous than the Prussian, Lobau fell back towards the Genappe road, where the Prussian round-shot was now thickly falling upon both sides of La Belle-Alliance, near which was Napoleon during the greater part of the day.

The only reserve he now had was the infantry of the Imperial Guard, and the pressure upon his right flank was so great, that he was obliged to send the eight battalions of the young guard, with their divisional and two twelve-pounder reserve batteries, under General Duhesme, to the village of Planchenois, as the only means of preventing the Prussians from getting in the French rear.

At this time Blücher received intelligence that his 3rd corps, which had been left at Wavre as a rear-guard to check the enemy's corps under Grouchy, had been attacked by a superior force and obliged to retire.[1] But the veteran saw clearly that the field upon which he was now engaged was the spot where the fate of the campaign would be decided. He therefore sent orders to Thielmann, to hold out as well as

1. See chapter X, Grouchy's Report, and the English, Prussian, and French official accounts.

99

he could; and ordered his left wing to move upon Planche-nois, and to get possession of it, if possible.

Duhesme, with the young guard, had arrived at the village and made his dispositions. As the Prussians neared Planche-nois, they were received with a stinging fire of musketry from the French skirmishers, and some French guns opened upon the advancing columns, but did not arrest their progress; they gallantly pressed on, took three guns, and got possession of the churchyard, a strong position, which shortly after they were compelled to abandon, though not without making a most resolute defence. They rallied near, the village, and, be-ing reinforced, advanced to make another assault: this being observed by Napoleon, he sent General Morand with two battalions of the old guard and two twelve-pounder batter-ies, and shortly after General Pelet, with another battalion of the guard and a reserve battery; this force, in conjunction with Lobau's line on their left, attacked and routed the whole Prussian force, pushing them back upon their first position on the opposite heights.

This convinced Napoleon that Blücher was not up in sufficient force to make an effective effort against his right flank, and he could, therefore, hold the Prussians in check without making any change in his line of battle opposed to Wellington.

Whilst those operations were in progress, the skirmish-ing had continued at Hougoumont, as well as along our left wing and at La Haye Sainte. Ney's cavalry attacks had been renewed, his force being nearly doubled by the addition of a part of General Guyot's heavy cavalry of the guard, and Kel-lermann's cuirassiers.

Ney, with this additional force, had a stupendous body of cavalry in comparison with ours. The attack, like the previous ones, was covered by a tremendous fire of artil-lery, which played on every part of our right wing, the round-shot ploughing up the ground, or tearing open the files of the close and serried ranks, with shells exploding in all directions, and at every moment the flashes of the guns, amidst expanding volumes of dense smoke, challenging the attention of every man to the sources of destruction, the well-worked batteries on both sides. Nothing could be more imposing than the advance of Ney's cavalry, (flanked by infantry to assail our advanced posts,) as they swept up the slope of the allied position under a murderous fire of our double-shotted guns, of which they again succeeded in getting temporary possession. Our devoted squares at times seemed lost amidst the hostile squadrons, who, in vain, made repeated endeavours to penetrate these impregnable barriers; as before, their squadrons got mixed, broken, and their ardour sobered down, when a retrograde movement was commenced, which soon became General.

The allied cavalry, who had been kept in hand to act at the favourable moment, now darted forward and completed the disorganization of the French cavalry. Our undaunted artillery-men, ever on the alert, were to be found, as usual, at their guns, plying the retiring hostile cavalry with grape, canister, or case-shot.

But the enemy's cavalry, which frequently reformed in the valley just under our position, where their lances and the tops of their caps might be seen, were soon again on the position and amongst the squares. Some of the most daring would ride up to the squares and cut aside the bayonets. Such parties seldom escaped unhurt; the man or horse was almost sure to be brought down, but not near so many saddles were emptied as might have been expected.

During the attacks made by the French cavalry, not a single individual set an example of soldier-like devotedness by rushing upon the bristling bayonets; certainly no agreeable task, nor to be attempted without imminent danger, but one, when required and gallantly done, that raises men to military rank and renown, and that may hasten the crisis and lead to victory. Of the fifteen thousand French horsemen, it is doubtful whether any perished on a British bayonet, or that any of our infantry in square fell from the French cavalry's sabres; few, comparatively, of the enemy's cavalry were destroyed, even by our musketry.[2]

Many pretend that good infantry in square can resist the onset of cavalry, however skilful, bold and determined: my opinion is the reverse; much depends on circumstances.

The menacing approach of the French cavalry, who rode amongst and round our squares, was not quietly witnessed by our own horsemen: we made many spirited charges between and on every side of the allied squares. All the British and German, and Trip's Dutch-Belgian cavalry, that were between the two highroads, were more or less engaged during these attacks.

It was quite amusing, at times, to see some of the foreign troops cut away from the angles of their squares, and our staff officers galloping after them to intercept their flight. It was surprising to see how readily they returned to their squares.

The fire of volleys from our squares did no great damage; the independent file firing was the most destructive to the enemy's cavalry, to such particularly as were not clad in steel or brass. The killed and wounded men and horses, the broken guns, etc., afforded excellent cover to the skirmishers, whilst they impeded the movements of the horsemen, and augmented their disorder and confusion.

It is not difficult to conceive from the foregoing circumstances, what was the rage, the ungovernable fury that animated those attacks; and how, after unceasing combats for above two hours, in a limited space, no result was obtained

---

2. This might be attributed to many of our infantry, when hard pressed, adopting the French skirmishers' method of loading, *viz.* after priming, shaking the rest of the powder into the barrel, dropping the ball after it, and then giving the butt a rap or two on the ground, which, from the rain, was quite soft. The ball, in consequence, not being rammed down to confine the powder, came out at times nearly harmless.

by the French but a most horrible and bloody carnage. It was one of the greatest of their errors, on that eventful day, to get their cavalry into such a labyrinth, from which there was no extricating it before the pride of their fifteen thousand horsemen had been completely broken. It was now evident, from the enemy's attacks becoming less animated and frequent, that they began to see the utter folly of their attempts against our invincible infantry. It is, in my opinion, very doubtful, whether the enemy's cavalry ever came into actual collision with our squares.[3]

It has been said by Napoleon, and it is also the remark of most of the French writers, that Guyot went into action without orders. Napoleon despatched General Bertrand to stop the heavy cavalry of the guard; but they were so engaged that a retrograde movement would have then been dangerous. This, Napoleon observed, had deprived him "of a cavalry reserve at about five o'clock, because they went two hours sooner than they should have gone into action, and that the same troops well employed had many times gained him a victory."

I cannot reconcile to myself the idea that a division of cavalry would go into action without orders; it is much more probable that there was some mistake in the transmission of them; but why was not the advance countermanded? Most of their cavalry movements were so slow towards the end of the day, in consequence of the jaded condition of their horses, and the saturated and encumbered state of the ground, that an order sent on foot might have soon brought them back.

At one time during that memorable afternoon, the ridge and rear slope of our position were literally covered with every description of horsemen, lancers, cuirassiers, carabineers,

---

3. That His Grace ever threw himself into a square, is untrue; but, from the commencement of the battle till the close, he was more exposed than many of his troops: whenever there was a chance of rendering service, let the danger be what it would, the Duke was there, and, as on all occasions, showed the most perfect coolness and self-possession.

horse-grenadiers, light and heavy dragoons and hussars; during which our guns stood in position, abandoned by the artillerymen, who took refuge in and around the squares: when at length the enemy's gallant but fruitless efforts became exhausted, our cavalry appeared and cleared the allied position.

On one occasion a body of cuirassiers passed along the Nivelles road, closely followed by a party of my regiment under Captain Verner. Upon the high bank on the right of the Nivelles road, a party of the 51st regiment was firing upon the enemy, and our advanced files narrowly escaped being shot. As the cuirassiers neared the avenue between the Nivelles road and Hougoumont, they came upon an *abattis,* or barricade, near which was a party of the 51st, under Captain Ross, who fired upon them; about a hundred and fifty were killed, wounded or taken prisoners.

Ney's grand cavalry attack has called forth the following lively description from the pen of Captain Siborne:

> When the tremendous cavalry force, which Ney had now assembled, moved forward to the attack, the whole space between La Haye Sainte and Hougoumont appeared one moving, glittering mass; and as it approached the Anglo-allied position, undulating with the conformation of the ground, it resembled a sea in agitation. Upon reaching the crest of the ridge, and regaining temporary possession of the batteries, its very shouts sounded on the distant ear, like the ominous roar of breakers thundering on the shore. Like waves following in quick succession, the whole mass now appeared to roll over the ridge; and as the light curling smoke arose from the fire which was opened by the squares, and by which the latter sought to stem the current of the advancing host, it resembled the foam and spray thrown up by the mighty waters, as they dash on isolated rocks and beetling crags: and as the mass separated and rushed in every direction, completely covering the interior slope, it bore the appearance of in-

numerable eddies and counter-currents, threatening to overwhelm and engulf the obstructions by which its onward course had been opposed. The storm continued to rage with the greatest violence, and the devoted squares seemed lost in the midst of the tumultuous onset. In vain did the maddening mass chafe and fret away its strength against these impregnable barriers, which, based upon the sacred principles of honour, discipline and duty, and cemented by the ties of patriotism, and the impulse of national glory, stood proudly unmoved and inaccessible. Disorder and confusion, produced by the co-mingling of corps and by the scattering fire from the faces of the chequered squares, gradually led to the retreat of parties of horsemen across the ridge: these were followed by broken squadrons, and at length the retrograde movement became General.

Then the allied dragoons, who had been judiciously kept in readiness to act at the favourable moment, darted forward to complete the disorganization of the now receding waves of the French cavalry.

About this time, Chassé's Dutch-Belgian division was moved from Braine-Lalleud, and drawn up on the allied right of and parallel to the Nivelles road.

La Haye Sainte[4] was again to be attacked, and the west gates soon became the scene of a most dreadful struggle and carnage. Colonel Baring had again applied for a reinforcement and ammunition: the former was sent; but the latter, of which he stood so much in need, was not supplied. The gallant defenders were now cautioned to be sparing of the few

---

4. The very dilapidated state of the buildings after the battle, is proof, were any wanted, of the furious efforts made by the enemy to obtain the post, and the determined desperate courage of the little garrison which defended it. The entire edifice was a scene of ravage and devastation. One half of the little door of the barn, taken away and preserved by the proprietor, was perforated by upwards of eighty musket-balls.

cartridges left, and to take deliberate aim at the assailants, who seemed to press on with renewed vigour.

On this occasion, the enemy set fire to the barn, which caused considerable alarm to those on the defensive; but fortunately the reinforcement arrived. The Nassau-men, with their huge camp kettles, which supplied the place of buckets, arrived most opportunely, and Baring, with his officers and men, soon extinguished the flames, but not without the loss of many a brave fellow. At this time a portion of the enemy again succeeded in getting into the little garden, and made an effort to force an entrance by the back door. Swarms of their skirmishers passed the buildings and established themselves immediately under the crest of our position, where they not only found cover from the fire above, but, as before, cut off the communication between the farm and our main line. The 5th and 8th line battalions of the German Legion were led against the assailants; they pressed on at a good pace, the enemy giving ground: but a body of cuirassiers was at hand and fell upon the 5th Germans, who, being supported by a portion of the remnant of Lord E. Somerset's brigade, but little; the 8th however were dropped upon quite unawares, and nearly all destroyed. Colonel Schröder was wounded mortally; ensign Moreau, who carried the King's colour, was severely wounded, and the colour carried off by the enemy.

Every arm on the right of our front line was much annoyed by some of the French left batteries, which had been pushed forward. My horse was killed by a round-shot from that direction; I was however soon mounted again on a cuirassier's horse.

At length Lieutenant Louis was ordered to turn two guns upon those on the enemy's left; he soon silenced them, and thus rendered essential service, particularly to us, who being on the right, were completely enfiladed by them. A battery was run up to the bank on the side of the crossroad, about a hundred and fifty yards on the Lion side of where the crossroad leads down towards the north-east angle of the orchard of Hougoumont. The muzzles of the guns rested upon the bank, on a level with the ridge in their front, which screened the carriages and wheels from the enemy's observation and fire. Soon after, a strong body of the enemy's cavalry advanced upon the battery, which reserved its fire until they came within fifty yards, when, with terrific effect, it opened, doubly charged with grape. The space in front of the battery was quickly covered with killed and wounded. The fire of our artillery during the action surpassed everything of the kind ever before witnessed, frequently making wide roads through the enemy's masses. From our infantry being generally kept recumbent behind the crest of our position screened from the enemy's observation, our gunners suffered most dreadfully from the constant exposure to the direct fire of the French artillery, who at times saw nothing else to aim at.

From certain movements in the enemy's line, there was reason to expect an attack of infantry towards the right of Alten's division. Part of the King's Dragoon Guards and Blues were moved towards that point. The Cumberland Hanoverian Hussars, posted some distance from the front, were also moved close up to General Halkett's squares; but a few musket-balls whistling about them, and a shell railing into a Nassau square close by, so alarmed them, that they took themselves off.

Upon seeing this, Lord Uxbridge sent an aide-de-camp, Captain T. Wildman, to bring them back, but to no purpose, and Uxbridge, thinking him long gone, sent Captain H. Seymour, who, finding that the Colonel and his men were very anxious to quit the scene of action, took the former by the collar, and nearly shook him out of his saddle; he then inquired for the next in command, but it appeared there was no one; Seymour then laid hold of the bridle of Colonel Hake's horse, to lead him back to his post, hoping that the men would follow, but to no purpose: the Colonel and his regiment preferred going to Brussels in whole skins, to the chance of having them perforated in the field; of all the honours that a gallant bearing might win they had no perception, so strong was their dislike to the smell of gunpowder. The cowards proceeded forthwith to Brussels, spreading a false alarm throughout the journey. The regiment was soon after disbanded, and the Colonel cashiered.[5]

The expected attacking infantry were now seen in motion on the heights in front of La Belle-Alliance; a body of cuirassiers from the valley under our position near La Haye Sainte joined them, keeping a little on their right rear. As they neared the point about where the Lion now stands, Lord E. Somerset led part of his brigade down to meet them: he was received with a heavy fire; his men however galloped down upon the head of the column, but, being at this time very much reduced, they could not penetrate it; they nevertheless checked the enemy. Lord Uxbridge rode up to Trip's brigade, and after addressing a few words to them, turned round to lead them on: he had scarcely crossed the ridge and begun to descend the slope towards the enemy, when he found that he was alone, no one following him; upon which he returned to Trip, expressed himself in severe terms, and rode off in anger. After this, one of the German light cavalry regiments was led on, and it succeeded in stopping the enemy, but it was much cut up.

During this time, Wellington, observing that Napoleon's attention was directed towards the Prussians advancing upon his right, and His Grace seeing there was no danger of his own extreme right being disturbed, had ordered Lord Hill to move Chassé's Dutch-Belgian division from Bràine-Lalleud towards the scene of action. Some short time afterwards, the hero of Almaraz and Aroyo-de-Molinos[6] brought into front

---

5. In a work of the highest pretensions, I observe that these dastardly hussars are called Belgian: let the saddle be put upon the right horse: they were the Duke of Cumberland's Hanoverian Hussars.
6. Lord Hill rendered himself most conspicuous by the energy and zeal he displayed, and the efforts he used to support the gallant defenders of Hougoumont, as also to repel the repeated desperate assaults upon our right wing; thus vigorously assisting the chief, under whom he had immortalized himself during the Peninsular campaign.

line Duplat's German Legion brigade, followed by General Adam's light brigade, which latter took position on the rear slope of our right wing; those were followed shortly after by Colonel Hugh Halkett's Hanoverians. Altogether these reinforcements were a sight more reviving to our part of the line than a double share of grog, though even that would have been most welcome. Soon after the Germans bad passed us, the steel-jacket cavalry were at them while in motion; but the Germans, many of whom were riflemen, emptied many a saddle and made many a horse rear, plunge and fall, and ultimately they beat off the cuirassiers.

Our 23rd fusiliers, who came into front line after Byng's brigade was advanced to Hougoumont, and suffered severely from-the enemy's fire, received an unfriendly visit from some cavalry, whom they eventually disposed of in most gallant style.

At this time part of the Brunswick troops were with us on the right, and Duplat's Germans with part of Halkett's Hanoverians were between the right of the main line and Hougoumont orchard. These, with the troops at the loopholed wall and hedges on the right and along the avenue, were kept wide awake, particularly those under Hepburn in and about the orchard, which must have changed masters at least a dozen times during the day.

Adam was now in our left rear, and his men most anxious to have a shy at their old acquaintances. Their wishes were soon gratified, by orders from the Duke in person, to drive back some fellows, as His Grace always called them, who had crept close up to our ridge, near where the hedgerow is on the roadside between the Lion and Hougoumont; they were concealed by the smoke of the crashing fire which they threw into our gunners and front squares. The order was received with joy from the white cravat man whom they were wont to follow, and acknowledged by a hearty cheer from the Lights, who felt gratified that the old order of things was about being renewed, and that they at Waterloo, as well as through the Peninsula, should take an active part in the battle's front.

His Grace was here again exposed to a shower of leaden hailstones, one of which severely wounded in the shoulder our fire-eating Adjutant-General, Sir Edward Barnes, who sported a gold-embroidered scarlet coat; most of our staff officers wore blue frock coats in the field.

Adam's fine fellows were much excited, and forward they pressed up the slope, in line, four deep; for some reason, their old acquaintances, the French infantry, would not stay to receive them, but made a retrograde movement down the outer slopes, followed by the brigade, until its right, which was thrown rather forward, was near the corner of the orchard of Hougoumont, and its left at the point where the valley terminates, in right front of the Lion. The brigade was formed of the 71st and two companies of the 95th on the right; the 52nd in squares of wings in the centre, and the second battalion of the 95th on the left. Here, as if to fetch up for lost time, they were pounded by the artillery, and charged by cavalry continually.

Soon after five o'clock, La Haye Sainte was taken by the enemy, who, led by Ney, and perceiving that the fire of the defenders had greatly slackened, made a rush at the open barn-door, and broke open the west yard-door; some climbed upon the wall and fired down upon our poor fellows, who, for want of cartridges, could not return the fire. After a desperate struggle with the sword-bayonet, and butts of their rifles, at the western gates, they were obliged to retreat to the house, where the remains of the gallant little garrison, with their spirited commander, again made a most determined resistance, in the passage through the house to the garden. They were ultimately obliged to abandon the post altogether, and to fall back upon the main position.

This was what the French erroneously called carrying the village of Mont St. Jean, (full three quarters of a mile off.) We can afford however to be good-tempered at their mistake; for the taking of *the farmhouse,* La Haye Sainte, which was in our front, while Mont St. Jean was in our rear, was the only advantage they gained during the battle. It seems that the loss of this post displeased the Duke[7]. Yet the place was most gallantly defended as long as there was a round of ammunition to use.

While Adam's brigade was in its advanced position, it was frequently charged, and on one occasion, when in line; the 52nd, directed by the Duke in person, stood firm and received a charge from the enemy's cavalry, but without any effectual result Nor ought our foes to have expected anything else:[8] they had not succeeded against any of our skeletons of squares, when they themselves were at their full strength. There is not a doubt that our gallant enemy and admirer, General Foy, who commanded a division on that great day, and was stationed in the field beyond the orchard of Hougoumont, alludes to this brigade and Maitland's 1st guards, with Halkett's, when he says:

We saw these sons of Albion formed upon the plain, between the wood of Hougoumont and the village of Mont St. Jean. Death was before them and in their ranks, disgrace in their rear. In this terrible situation, neither the cannon balls[9] of the Imperial Guard, discharged almost at point-blank, nor the *victorious* cavalry of France, could make the least impression on the immovable British infantry: one might have been almost tempted to fancy that it had rooted itself in the ground, but for the majestic movement[10] which its battalions

---

7. See his letter of the 17th August 1816, in the Appendix, No. II.

8. The brigade was above two thousand strong.

9. Although according to appearances, those gentry are quite harmless, and might be stopped like a cricket-ball when bounding along, one of them would take off a leg or an arm, in much less time than the most skilful operator.

10. General Foy, no doubt, alluded to the right-shoulder-forward movement of Adam's brigade, together with the movements of Maitland's and Halkett's brigades, towards the close of the day. Foy had also, before the battle began, declared to his Emperor, that he had an infantry opposed to him, which he (Foy,) had never known to yield.

commenced some minutes after sunset, when the approach of the Prussian army announced to Wellington that he had just achieved the most decisive victory of the age.

We may imagine that those steel-clad gentlemen had some particular pique against the 1st foot-guards and Halkett's brigade, from the repeated visits they paid them. The lancers also frequently visited them. Whatever was the cause, not a brigade in the line was visited more than Sir Colin Halkett's by the enemy's cavalry;[11] and they were not forgotten by the Duke, who frequently passed the brigade, it being rather a central point. The Duke at one moment sent Colonel Gordon to Halkett, to inquire what square of his was so much in advance: it was a mass of killed and wounded of the 30th and 73rd, of his brigade!

---

11. Halkett's left, (30th and 73rd regiments,) in square, was attacked eleven times by the enemy's cavalry. The late Lord Harris, (then Colonel of the 73rd,) in a letter which is in my possession, alludes to the gallant conduct of these two regiments in the following manner, "My impression is that the gallant and enduring stand made by the 30th and 73rd regiments against *thirteen* charges of cuirassiers and an unceasing discharge of artillery for seven hours, besides the fact of successfully driving the French cavalry away by a charge in square, has not been done sufficient justice to by historians of the battle, with the exception of a French writer." Would that His Lordship had survived to have read my pages!

CHAPTER 6

The Struggle for the Centre

La Haye Sainte was no sooner in the power of the French, than they received orders to press as much as possible that part of our line, and clear the way for the guard.

In order to avail themselves of the advantages of so valuable a position, they loop-holed the gable-end of the house, erected a scaffold along the garden wall, cut holes through the garden hedge, resembling windows, and threw a force in advance of the garden, which was protected from the fire above by the natural slope, in addition to an artificial bank that abutted upon the natural one, extending along the roadside to where the monument to Colonel Gordon is erected.

This breastwork enabled the enemy to throw a front fire into the riflemen at the knoll and in the sand-hole, as well as an oblique fire into Lambert's and Kempt's brigades along the Wavre road. Those arrangements were scarcely completed, when a rattling fire was thrown among our sand-larks, who, being unable from their position to return it with any effect, took to flight towards their reserve, followed by all the riflemen from the knoll. The enemy immediately sent a force to the knoll and sand-hole, which annoyed our 27th; and the troops on that part of the front were kept under a very galling fire, at times muzzle to muzzle, until the advance of the whole line.

The French brought two guns round the garden hedge, and, placing them between the north-east angle of the garden wall and our position, threw grape-shot into the 1st, 4th, 27th, 28th, 40th, 79th, and 95th; but before they had time to fire a second round, a concentrated fire from the riflemen destroyed their gunners; they then pushed on a crowd of skirmishers, who crept along the banks close in upon Alten's, Lambert's and Kempt's troops, but protected from our fire. As we could not get at them with powder and ball, it was thought advisable to try the effect of steel: Colonel Ompteda led on the 5th German line; upon which they gave way, and took shelter, as well as they could, round the garden hedge, when a line of cavalry from the hollow rushed upon the Germans; and, as Captain Kincaid of the rifles observes, "Every man of them was put to death in a short time, except an officer on a little black horse, who went off to the rear like a shot out of a shovel."

Some of our light cavalry attempted to rescue the Germans; but our 95th, who had previously pointed their rifles at the cuirassiers, but had suspended their fire through fear of destroying our own infantry, now let fly and entirely cleared the whole front. Their skirmishers then moved to the left, towards Halkett's brigade and the 1st guards; but the eagle eye of the Duke saw it, and he ordered the guards to form line and drive the enemy off, which they did, when some, cuirassiers approached, but our lads were in square again. The cuirassiers moved off but received the fire from the squares of the guards, as well as from those of the 52nd and 95th.

Onset now followed onset in rapid succession, and before one assault was met and repulsed, another was prepared and pressing on.

His Grace, when he observed the diminished numbers of his brave troops, presenting still the same fearless attitude, felt there must be a limit to human endurance, and frequently turned his telescope in the direction where he expected the Prussians to arrive, and who were to cooperate more immediately with his left.

Hougoumont, as has been stated, had been repeatedly attacked: the large orchard and wood continued the scene of a dreadful carnage. The enemy generally outflanked our men upon their left; and at times stealing along under the east hedge from the south-east angle of the orchard, opened a flank fire upon them, when driven through the north hedge near our friendly hollow-way; but whenever our foes attempted to cross the orchard near the east garden wall, the Coldstream sent a galling flank fire into them. Hougoumont had been reinforced by the 2nd line and light companies of Duplat's brigade, as well as by the advance guard battalion of Brunswickers, who, together with the guards and the remainder of the Nassau-men and Hanoverian riflemen, drove the enemy out of the orchard into the wood.

During the time Duplat's brigade was in its advanced position, it suffered dreadfully from the French light troops: nearly all the officers were killed or wounded; Duplat was killed.

Skirmishing had gone on briskly at the farms of Papelotte, La Haye, the hamlet of Smohain, and along our left, where the want of ammunition was so great, that the enemy pressed close up to the hedge, driving in our skirmishers:[1] but they were soon driven back, when a fresh supply arrived.

From the time that La Haye Sainte had been taken by the enemy, the attacks upon our centre were carried on with the greatest desperation. The French crowded in swarms round

---

1. It is not easy to give a satisfactory reason why the enemy's infantry skirmishers were allowed to press so closely up to our position and inflict such severe losses upon our gunners and infantry, when our cavalry could have driven them off or destroyed them.

the knoll and sand-hole, and behind the artificial and roadside banks, which formed excellent breastworks for the advanced skirmishers to lay their muskets on the bank at the level of the plain, and to sweep it in all directions.

Our advance, at times, moved forward and dislodged them; but they returned on the falling back of our troops. This fire was replied to vigorously by Lambert's and Kempt's brigades, and Pack's Royals. Ompteda's brigade was reduced to a mere handful of men; Kielmansegge's was in a similar condition: in fact Alten's division had dwindled away to a weak brigade. The remains of Halkett's brigade were from the first formed into two weak squares. No portion of the line was more attacked both by infantry and cavalry, or more cannonaded than Alten's division. He himself was severely wounded. The 73rd, one of his regiments, was for a time commanded by a subaltern, (Lieutenant Stewart.) Pack's brigade was reduced to a skeleton, and had, by forming column, wheeling into line, and by edging and moving to its right, got close to the Genappe road, a little in rear of where stood the so called "Wellington tree". Adam's brigade had been subjected to so furious a cannonade and repeated cavalry attacks, that it was deemed necessary to draw it behind the position. On one occasion a French horse battery was pushed forward near the south-east angle of the orchard of Hougoumont, where it opened upon the brigade. Our batteries on the ridge concentrated their fire upon it, and drove it off. Our artillerymen cheered. I witnessed the great effect produced by some rockets which were thrown from the valley upon the French horse. Our batteries had been most successful on this part of the line in checking and destroying the enemy's cavalry.

It must have been evident to Napoleon, that, notwithstanding the battle had been raging for more than seven hours, the victory which he had calculated upon early in the morning was yet to be gained: although the day was far advanced, he showed no despair, but continued to feed the fight with fresh victims.

The result of the operations, up to this time, had been most destructive to both sides; more particularly so to our gallant foes, who, from acting on the offensive throughout, were much exposed to the close and direct fire of our batteries in advancing to the attack and retiring to reform, after each successive repulse. Our troops everywhere maintained a degree of cool forbearance and courage, which none but British could show under such trying circumstances.

About half-past seven p. m. the colours of the 30th and 73rd were sent to the rear, to the satisfaction of many; the Colonel of the latter regiment, the late Lord Harris, who was wounded soon after, taking the 73rd's colour from the officer, gave it in charge of a Sergeant, to carry to the rear.

The enemy's cavalry, who were now nearly sobered, would come up singly, and fire their carbines at the squares. Their horse artillery often galloped up, unlimbered, when *crash! crash!* came the grape into Halkett's squares, making gaps which it was admirable to see the fine fellows fill up, and that without orders.

Whenever the Duke came, which at this momentous period was often, there was a low whisper in the ranks, "Here's the Duke!" and all was steady as on parade. No matter what the havoc and destruction might be, the Duke was always the coolest man there: in the words of an eyewitness of this bloody scene, the Duke was coolness personified.[2] It really appeared that the more desperate the fight, the more determined were the few brave fellows that remained to hold their ground; yet often would a murmur escape them, such as, "This is thundering murderous work! Why don't we go into them?. . . . Let us give them the cold steel," etc., etc. But such murmurs were soon hushed, and again were displayed

---

2. All those who were near His Grace, and had full opportunity of observing him during the most critical and trying moments, agree in asserting, that it was impossible to learn from his countenance, voice or gesture, whether the affair in hand were trifling or important, quite safe, or extremely dangerous.

those traits of unyielding passive courage, the grandest, the most sublime characteristics of the British army.

The troops evinced in their resignation a discipline unparalleled in European armies. Though confident in their chiefs and themselves, their foes were not less so: a French cuirassier officer, a prisoner in Halkett's left square, replied, in a surly and snappish tone, to an officer of the 30th who asked him what force Bonaparte had, "You will see directly, Sir."

It was now past seven o'clock. The Prussians kept up a distant cannonade, and skirmished with the French right *en potence,* seeking a favourable opportunity to make a more powerful attack with the fresh troops that were then seen advancing. These war-breathing bands, fed by Blücher in person, full of determination, sure to strike home with the whole force of their arm, were seen streaming along in swarms, extending round Napoleon's right wing, and menacing his rear. The allied line stood firm and unbroken, the day was fast waning, and Napoleon must have imagined that a desperate effort to break our centre could alone prevent the defeat, which the arrival of the Prussians must render inevitable. Thus situated, he had no alternative but to rush into destruction, or success.

The political existence and future destiny of this renowned chief were fast drawing to a close; he could not reasonably anticipate assistance from Grouchy, therefore he at once resolved, as a *last resource,* his unsuccessful attempt to force the allied position with his devoted guards, that immovable phalanx which in the greatest emergencies had invariably stood as the rallying point and rampart of their army. Count Drouot was ordered to move forward into the valley (in front of and between La Belle-Alliance and Hougoumont enclosures,) the remaining twelve battalions of the old and middle guard, and form them into two columns of attack and a reserve. With these, Napoleon decided upon making a final struggle, directing their advance between La Haye Sainte and Hougoumont, upon the allied centre, undoubtedly impressed with the idea, that an overwhelming mass of fresh and chosen troops must succeed against an enemy shattered and reduced by furious attacks, and a ravaging cannonade.[3]

Four battalions of the middle guard, in mass of battalion columns, a favourite plan of the French, and formed left in front into one column of attack, were to advance towards a point, about where the Lion now stands, then occupied by Maitland's brigade, the 2nd and 3rd battalions of the 1st British foot-guards, (now Grenadiers,) and on their left by Halkett's British brigade, whose right was the 69th and 33rd, and his left the 30th and 73rd regiments. Four more battalions of the middle guard with two of the old guard, (chiefly chasseurs,) *en echelons* upon their left rear, formed a second column of attack, lower down the valley. The other two battalions of the old guard remained in reserve nearly opposite La Belle-Alliance, right and left; and in rear of them were drawn up in reserve the remains of the splendid cavalry force with which the Emperor had been making such desperate but fruitless attacks on our position. These constituted his last reserve. The attacking columns of the Imperial Guard were to be supported by the remains of D'Erlon's corps on their right, and Reille's corps on the left.

Towards the close of the action, many of our guns stood abandoned in position: some rendered useless by the enemy's fire, others had the muzzles bent down from the excessive heat, some were left for want of materials to load them, many touch-holes melted away, and numerous gunners were driven off by the enemy. Our confidence in the Duke was unbounded; notwithstanding, our army was much exhausted and reduced. Disorder and confusion continued in our rear, the roads were crowded with broken carriages, baggage, wounded officers, soldiers, dismounted dragoons, and trains of followers from the combined army; more particularly the

---

3. It appeared throughout the day, that Napoleon was determined to exhaust our troops, the expense of which was only, to him, a *secondary* consideration.

foreigners, many of whom gave as a reason for abandoning the field, that Napoleon and his legions were invincible, and would certainly be victorious, and to contend against them would be quite absurd.

In fact, what with the killed, wounded, and those in attendance, with others who had gone to the rear through fear, our fighting army became reduced, towards the close of the day, to a handful of men, a mere wreck of its former self. It is on record that upwards of twelve thousand had sought refuge in the wood of Soigne, whose desertion imposed great hardships on those who so gallantly remained to support their cause, the result of which seemed certain; and renewed ardour completed their exertions, by a compensation in the glorious victory they were about to achieve. All those who remained seemed resolved to conquer or perish on this sanguinary field, and by none was this feeling more powerfully exemplified, than by the few remaining in Sir Colin Halkett's brigade, who were often heard to exclaim, "This is thundering murderous work: we shall see which will stand killing longest."

Vivian, who had been all day on the left of our line, observing the advance, towards his position, of part of the Prussian cavalry of General Röder, attached to the 1st corps under General Zieten, and being aware that fresh cavalry was wanted on the right, put his brigade in motion, and was soon met by Lord Uxbridge, who felt pleased that the Duke's wishes had been anticipated. Vandeleur, who was also on the left, was ordered to follow Vivian. The right regiment, the 10th hussars, was posted by Lord Uxbridge about a hundred yards in rear of the junction of the crossroads, the 18th hussars on their left stretching towards the Genappe road, behind the remains of Alten's division, and the 1st German Hussars were in second line. After posting Vivian, Uxbridge joined Vandeleur, whom he posted parallel with the Nivelles road, the 11th on the right, the 16th next, and on the left the remains of the 12th light dragoons, in rear of Adam's, Maitland's and Halkett's brigades; he then returned to Vivian.

His Lordship dismounted, and, unattended, advanced down the slope to try and get a view of the enemy, and to draw his own conclusions; Vivian rode after him and. begged him not to place himself in such imminent danger; on which he returned, saying that he was of Vivian's opinion, that it would be best to wait an opportunity to attack.

The opportune arrival of the fresh cavalry upon this part of our line added confidence in no small degree to the shattered remains of brave fellows who were left to defend the front of the position. Uxbridge returned to the Duke, who was at a short distance to the right, watching the formation of heavy columns on our right of La Belle-Alliance; they were preparing the coming storm:

'Twas now the chieftain's soul was mighty proved,
That in the shock of charging hosts, unmoved,
Amidst confusion, horror, and despair,
Examined all the dreadful scenes of war;
In peaceful thought the field of death surveyed;
To fainting squadrons sent the timely aid;
Inspired repulsed battalions to engage,
And taught the doubtful battle where to rage.

His Grace now despatched Colonel Freemantle in search of the Prussians, who were expected to join the left of our line, and to request Zieten, their chief, to send on a part of his force to strengthen some weak parts of the front Zieten did not feel himself authorized to comply with the Duke's request, but said that his whole force would soon be up.

Numerous applications reached the Duke for support and reinforcements, or to be relieved by the second line, as divisions, brigades and regiments had dwindled away to skeletons and handfuls of men. The only reply was, "They must hold their ground to the last man." Sir Guy Campbell delivered that answer to the gallant remains of Pack's brigade, and the Duke told Sir Colin Halkett, that there must not be the least symptom of falling back, as everything depended on the steadiness of the front troops. Frequently, as the Duke passed the men, he heard murmurs, such as, "Are we to be massacred here? Let us go at them, let us give them *Brummegum!*" *i e.* the bayonet; and he would calmly reply, "Wait a little longer, my lads; you shall have at them presently."

The ammunition was nearly exhausted, when, fortunately, along galloped an artillery cart, and dropped some casks into the squares, which raised their spirits and made them feel more satisfied.

The Duke, finding he must depend entirely on his own resources to ward off the blow about to be struck by his antagonist, made such dispositions as his means would allow. It was indeed high time to strain every nerve, to strengthen and defend the point where the fiercest storm of battle was about to burst, and repel the last and most desperate struggle, now about to be made. Maitland's and Halkett's right was advanced; the Brunswick battalions on the right were to move into the space between Halkett's British and Kruse's Nassau brigades. Chassé's Dutch-Belgian division was to cross the Nivelles road, and form, D'Aubreme on the right, and Ditmers on the left, in rear of Adam's, Maitland's and Halkett's brigades.

The remains of the allied cavalry were in rear of the position on the right of the Genappe road, and most of our infantry were deployed into four deep lines, and lay recumbent on the ground for shelter. About this time a French officer[4] of carabineers rode into the right of the 52nd regiment as a deserter, and announced to Major Blair[5] and Colonel Sir A.

---

4. I met this French officer on the field in 1844: he was a Captain in the 2nd carabineers, or brass-clad cuirassiers; the reason he gave for not coming over to us till the eleventh hour, was, that he expected a number of his regiment to desert with him.
5. See the Major's letter, Appendix, No. VII.

Fraser, that Napoleon was about to attack us at the head of his Imperial Guard; this was made known to the Duke. Napoleon, it appeared, was Marshalling the Imperial Guard for the approaching attack: of this His Grace was well aware.

The skirmishers in advance of their columns about La Haye Sainte, the knoll and sandpit, and along the valley right and left, threw out a rattling fire for the purpose of harassing and weakening our line, in order to clear the way for the grand attack by the Imperial Guard; this fire was replied to vigorously by our troops, who were partially covered from the enemy's fire by the hedgerow and banks on this part of the front. Our gallant 27th, upon the bank at the junction of the roads, was much exposed. Our 95th rifles and the 4th foot were extended along the Wavre road. The 40th, 79th, 28th, and 1st Royals were in line behind the rear hedge. The fire increased, and it appeared as if all would be borne down before it The banks on the roadside, the garden wall, the knoll and sandpit swarmed with skirmishers, who seemed determined to keep down our fire in front; those behind the artificial bank seemed more intent upon destroying the 27th, who at this time, it may literally be said, were lying dead in square; their loss after La Haye Sainte had fallen was awful, without the satisfaction of having scarcely fired a shot, and many of our troops in rear of the ridge were similarly situated. A British officer, who was an eyewitness of the gallant conduct of the 27th, says, "If ever the sovereign give them another motto, it should be, *Muzzle to muzzle;* for so they fought at Waterloo."

Efficient artillery upon this part of the line we had none; thus the enemy again brought up some guns near the corner of La Haye Sainte garden hedge, and placed them so that their muzzles were on a level with our ridge, from whence they rapidly dealt out grape upon Kielmansegge's two squares, completely smashing them, until they, like the rest, were reduced to a mere clump of men. The artillery and musketry fire was increasing. The skirmishers pressing on, and their drums beating, foretold the advance of columns to the charge. Upon this, the Prince of Orange ordered two battalions of the Nassau brigade, under General Kruse, to advance, and gallantly placed himself at their head: the Prince was struck by a musket-ball in the left shoulder, and the command of this part of our line devolved on Count Kielmansegge.

The Nassau-men were giving way, when the five battalions of Brunswick infantry moved into the interval between Halkett and Kruse; but were received by such a stinging fire from the French skirmishers, with a crashing fire of grape from their artillery, before they were in position, and became so enveloped in smoke, that they could not get into order until they were in close contact with the enemy, whose vigorous attack caused the part of Alten's division on Halkett's left, with the Nassau and Brunswickers, to give way, and fall back under the crest of the ridge. Now came really the tug of war, the poise or balance of the battle.

At this critical moment Wellington galloped to the spot, and addressing himself to the Brunswickers, succeeded, by the electrifying influence of his voice and presence, in rallying the discomfited columns. Lieutenant-Colonel Sir Alexander Gordon was mortally wounded on this occasion. By the example and encouragement on the part of the commanding officers, the other brigades were also rallied and formed up. The Duke went off hastily to the right again.

The battle had been now raging for nearly eight hours, and not a square had been broken, or the enemy gained more than one advantage, via. the capture of La Haye Sainte, through one of those mischances in war which often mar the best planned arrangements. But those continued furious attacks had not been met and repulsed without a most severe loss to the troops who had stood the brunt of the battle, and been so long exposed to the murderous cannonade. The exceeding small force on our side which really defended the crest of the position on this terrible day, is almost incredible, and their conduct beyond all praise. It was not only to stand the brunt of the strife, but upon their steadiness and determination depended entirely the holding of the position.

CHAPTER 7

The Imperial Guard Attacks

Vivian came to this part of the line about a quarter before eight p. m. The enemy's skirmishers had again pressed on in crowds up to the front, which, from its reduced state, was once more giving way. A battalion of the Brunswickers was retiring, having expended all its ammunition.

The Nassau-men were falling back in mass upon the horses' heads of the 10th hussars, and, as Sir Hussey Vivian said, if the 10th had not been there, they would have retreated. Captain Shakspeare of the 10th was with Sir Hussey, and they both did their utmost to encourage them. Vivian says that he must, in justice to many of their officers, state, that they endeavoured to stop the men, and one in particular, whom he saw take a drummer by the collar, and make him beat the rally.

The left of the division now pressed on, led by Kielmansegge. Those on the right took it up, as well as the Brunswick and Nassau-men, their drums beating, Vivian and his aide-de-camp and many of his officers cheering them on, whilst the hussars followed in support; the French and their artillery falling back before them.

One crowded hour of glorious strife
Is worth an age of peaceful life;

'Tis thus the soldier hurries on,
And faces death amidst the throng.

It was during this desperate effort of the enemy that the two attacking columns of the Imperial Guards,[1] amongst whom the most unbounded enthusiasm reigned, proudly led the van, and advanced *en echelons* right in front from the valley, between La Belle-Alliance and the enclosures of Hougoumont; the first or leading column, directed by Napoleon in person, until they came abreast of where the highroad is cut through the bank beyond the orchard of La Haye Sainte, a prominent point about two hundred yards to their left of the Genappe road, which they left obliquely on their right. Here the Emperor gave them in charge of Ney; when the guards passed before him, he addressed them with a few words of encouragement for the last time, but, from the noise, the words could not be heard, and Napoleon, in a significant manner, pointed to our position, when the shouts of *"Vive l'Empereur! Vive Napoléon! En avant!"* rent the air; those war-cries excited a frenzy of ardour as his devoted followers pressed on to death and destruction.

At this moment Blücher's artillery was blazing away upon the French right *en potence,* who returned the compliment, but not in full value. The firing was distinctly heard by Napoleon and his troops; and being apprehensive that it might damp their courage, he sent General Labédoyère through the line, with the false report,[2] that it was Grouchy's guns that had fallen upon

---

1. This force was never employed but in cases of great emergency. Had it been brought forward earlier and before the Prussians arrived, deployed into line out of range of our musketry, and supported by cavalry before that arm was so much cut up, certainly Napoleon would have stood a better chance. No doubt the attack ought to have been made earlier, or not at all. The Duke says, "Had they forced our position, instead of taking advantage of it and pressing on they must have turned round to face the Prussians, who were at that time in great force pressing the enemy's right and rear." Looking at the relative situations of Planchenois, Mont St. Jean, and the French army, reckless as Napoleon had doubtless then become, it is still surprising he made the attack.
2. See Ney's letter, Appendix, No. V.

the Prussian rear, and it now only required but a little firmness to complete the victory to which they were advancing.

The sanguinary drama was now, with the long and trying day, fast drawing to a close. The Imperial Guards, their country's pride, they who had never turned their backs on foe or fled the battlefield, were now, for the first time, about to attack men who, like themselves, acknowledged no victor; the unconquered were to measure their prowess with men who had never been vanquished, the world waiting with anxious expectation the result of this memorable day.

The French guards, led by the undaunted Ney, *"le brave des braves,"* advanced towards a point occupied by the first brigade of British foot-guards, and the 5th or Halkett's British brigade. The guards were lying down, for cover from the shower of round and grape-shot and shells thrown amongst them by the French batteries. The enemy's advance was, as usual, preceded by skirmishers and covered by a tremendous fire of artillery, although, at this time, considerably diminished, owing to a great many of the guns being rendered useless. The Imperial Guards were well supported on their right by D'Erlon's infantry columns, especially by those of Donzelot's division, who prolonged this attack to the Genappe road against the Brunswickers, Nassau troops, and the rest of Alten's division.

About this time, Vandersmissen's Dutch-Belgian brigade of guns most opportunely came in between the intervals of Halkett's brigade. Reille's columns on the left pressed on towards Hougoumont, which again became the scene of a severe struggle; Bachelu's division advanced on the right of its enclosures, and D'Erlon's columns *en echelons* pushed forward on the right of La Haye Sainte.

As the leading column of the Imperial guards began to ascend the tongue of ground leading to the spot where the Lion now stands, they suffered most severely from the destructive fire of our right batteries, which, from being ranged *en echelons,* every efficient gun played into the exposed long flank of the Imperial columns with double charges of round, canister, case, or grape-shot; they appeared to wave like high standing corn blown by sudden gusts of wind, from the terrific effect of each discharge. Caps and muskets might, at times, be seen flying in the air, after this dreadful fire. Ney had his horse killed under him, and gallantly led along on foot; at his side General Friant was killed, and General Michel mortally wounded.

To men quite enthusiastic, who felt certain they were advancing to a glorious victory, this was no check, and the Imperial Guards pursued their onward course with a firm step. The veterans of Jena, Wagram and Austerlitz could only be arrested in their progress by death or severe wounds: they had, by their invincible prowess, decided many a battle.

When the head of the column neared the line of the allies, it escaped the terrific fire of our right batteries, while at the same moment their own batteries ceased firing; a crowd of skirmishers rushed on and opened a stinging fire upon our artillery-men, who soon drove them back upon the columns by a discharge of grape, canister and case-shot; double charges were poured into the head of the enemy's columns from Bolton's guns, (now commanded by Napier,) and Vandersmissen's batteries: the front of the enemy appeared to stand still, from the men being mowed down as they laboured up the slopes, while their rear seemed pressing on. The Imperial Guards at length succeeded in crowning the ridge, upon which they saw nothing but the batteries; they descried through the smoke some cocked hats, and little imagined that one of them covered the head of the illustrious Duke, who was shortly to acquire a last and crowning laurel, or that the sun of Napoleon was to set with the one just retiring from their view on the field of Waterloo.

The enemy pressed on until within about fifty yards of the British foot-guards (who were lying down,) and Halkett's brigade, which quietly awaited the band of veteran heroes.

Wellington then gave the words, "Up, guards, make ready!"[3] and ordered General Maitland to attack. They rose in line four deep, and appeared to the French as if they had sprung out of the earth; whilst the French grenadiers, with their high bearskin caps and red plumes, looked like giants bearing down upon them.

Our guards and Halkett's right, the 69th and 33rd, the gallant Halkett waving the latter regiment's colour in their front, advanced a few paces and threw in a tremendous volley, that was followed up by independent file-firing, rapidly and steadily delivered. A stream of musketry and grape-shot was maintained with such coolness and precision, that the whole front of the enemy's columns was shaken: it was impossible to be otherwise; from four to five hundred of them were killed or wounded. This, however, did not check the mass that pressed on our troops. The French officers, waving their swords, and with shouts and words of encouragement, attempted to deploy and extend their front. But for this it was too late, the continued crossfire which assailed them drove the foremost of the enemy back on their mass. Many in the midst of the columns fired over the heads of their comrades, and the confusion in their ranks became greater every moment.[4]

---

3. "Up, guards, and at them!" or "Up, guards, make ready!"—what an idea of mutual confidence between the General and his men, does that simple order convey! No haranguing, which, if it excites the soldiers, also expresses a doubt of their exertions; nothing of that kind was considered necessary, but a command, which, from its very simplicity, shows the entire conviction, in the mind of him who gave it, that it would be most effectually obeyed.
4. A column or columns advancing to an attack, although steady as on parade, on nearing the line of a cool determined enemy, must be quickly shattered by the converging fire, which would drop their leading and flank flies, the only men that can really use their muskets; confused by different words of command from various officers, often enveloped in smoke and crowded together, the pressure is such, that every movement augments disorder and confusion. The imposing advance of large masses has often intimidated an enemy, notwithstanding they are only really formidable in the imagination, until deployed into line, during which evolution, a good volley, resolutely followed up by the application of the cold steel, would overthrow the best troops that ever pulled a trigger. The Duke says, "Napoleon did not manoeuvre at all; he

Their desperate situation being instantly perceived by the Duke, His Grace ordered the charge: Lord Saltoun, who had joined from Hougoumont, called out, "Now's the time, my boys!" Our guards and Halkett's left advanced with a loud cheer to the charge, the latter against a column which, on nearing our position, had inclined to its right from the rear of the leading column, and moved *en echelons* upon its right rear, steady as on parade, through the hollow on their right of the tongue of ground, where they were protected from the direct fire of our right batteries.

They gallantly advanced with a noble and admirable bearing; their officers in front, arms sloped, drums beating the *pas de charge,* with their brass guns severally loaded with grape, between them and on their flanks. When within ninety yards of Halkett's left, they halted, carried arms as if to salute, and round wheeled their guns, down went their port-fires, and crash came the grape, accompanied by a volley, into the 30th and 73rd regiments, that instantly returned the fire and came to the charge; and before the sharp report had died away, Vandersmissen's brigade of guns, double-charged with grape, went *bang! bang! bang!* every instant, right through the Imperial columns, that appeared to be rent asunder, and began to give way and disperse.[5]

Our guards were pursuing the discomfited enemy into

(continued from page 51) moved forward in the old style, in columns, and was driven off in the old style." (Despatches, vol. XII, page 589.) I will not go so far as to say that moving forward in any other formation would have gained them the battle, but I do think the old style of advancing in columns did not give them a chance.
5. From the circumstance of the columns of the Imperial Guards making their attack at the point of our line which ran curving forward, they must have become, on crowning the allied position, exposed to a crossfire of all arms, which may be thus described: Halkett's left and Vandersmissen's batteries formed the left of the curve, whilst the immediate right of it consisted of Halkett's right, our guards and Napier's battery, whose right was brought rather forward; thus the fires were diagonal, that is, the two fires evidently crossed. It is therefore not astonishing that the veterans of a hundred fights gave way under this, to use their own words, effroyable (dreadful) crossfire upon both front and flank.

the valley, when the left or second column of the Imperial Guards was observed "closely pressing on, undismayed by the defeat of their first column. To avoid being taken in flank, orders were given to the British guards to go about and resume their original position, but the word was misunderstood, and they fell into confusion; on recrossing the ridge however, and getting the command, "Halt, front, form!" notwithstanding the two battalions were mixed pell-mell together, they instantly fronted and formed four deep, and told off in companies of forties.

Halkett's left, which had charged, on getting clear of the smoke, saw the enemy broken and going off in confusion; and loud and deep were the execrations bestowed upon them for not waiting to meet the retaliating vengeance, now ready to be inflicted, for our slaughtered comrades. After the charge, the whole brigade got mixed together, and was for a few minutes in great confusion, occasioned by a terrific fire of musketry and grape-shot, the murderous effects of which so disordered Halkett's right that they gave way, and thus clashed with their left who were retiring; this caused the confusion that, fortunately however, was speedily restored, for a cry was heard, "Form square to resist cavalry!"[6] and a cheer burst forth from the 73rd; when Major Kelly, an officer of that regiment, but on the staff, seeing the confusion and consequent danger, resolved to remain with his men, they having no officer of rank left to command them.

---

6. Had the enemy's cavalry really been at hand, the remaining few fine fellows under Halkett must have been annihilated. This confusion and giving way, together with that on the immediate left of the brigade, as well as the disorder on its immediate right, at about the same time, and at so critical a juncture, might have caused the most serious consequences; but, thanks to the zeal and energy of the superior officers, as well as to the coolness, alacrity and discipline of our troops, they soon reformed with much steadiness and regularity, and aided by Vandersmissen's and Bolton's iron hail from their double-charged guns, the withering fire of Adam's light-bobs upon the enemy's left flank, together with that of our guards upon their front, our struggle terminated most satisfactorily.

During this most desperate assault, D'Aubremé's Netherlanders, formed in three large squares, in the immediate rear, fell into the greatest disorder; Vandeleur, whose brigade was in their rear, galloped forward, and with some of his own officers, and those of the Dutch-Belgians, did all in his power to restore order and encourage the men to hold their position. Colonel Monee, 69th regiment, was killed, and Sir Colin Halkett wounded, when the command of his brigade devolved on Colonel Elphinstone, who, when it had reformed, posted the left of the brigade at the hedgerow, where the road curves forward, (near where the Lion now stands;) the right was advanced anew[7] to protect the left flank of our guards against an attack of Donzelot's troops, who were again pushing on.

The left of our guards was brought slightly forward, to be parallel with the left or second attacking columns of the Imperial Guards,[8] who, passing the eastern boundary of Hougoumont obliquely on their left, were saluted, *en passant*, by Hepburn's skirmishers. Notwithstanding this, they pursued their onward course with the greatest sang-froid through the valley, towards where their first column was so severely engaged; our artillery on the ridge, from the Nivelles road to the curve in our line, was in full play upon them; the fire of our guns fell with ruinous precision upon the dense mass, and made them suffer dreadfully: but the men who had often, in a doubtful field, wrested victory from the obstinate foe, advanced firmly, their front and flank, as usual, covered by a numerous body of daring skirmishers, whose smoke from their rattling fire at times concealed the advance of the columns.

The fire of our guns was so severe that some cuirassiers

---

7. Their advance proves that this momentary confusion but little affected them.
8. A portion of this force might have been advantageously employed against us with their cavalry. Husbanding them so long, was, I suspect, an error of no small magnitude.

were sent to charge the batteries: this they did, and succeeded in driving the gunners away. They also drove in the skirmishers of Adam's brigade: upon which, a squadron of the 23rd light dragoons was sent down into the hollow near the orchard of Hougoumont. The cuirassiers advancing again, the 23rd, under Lieutenant Banner, charged them in flank, and drove them back upon their infantry columns, whose fire turned our dragoons about. They galloped back towards our lines, followed by some cuirassiers, most of whom, as well as their other cavalry, were, upon the advance of the Imperial Guards, drawn off and rallied on their own position between La Belle-Alliance and Hougoumont. Our officers on this part of the line were intently observing the movements of the enemy's columns; and our few fine fellows at the guns, disregarding the fire from the enemy, played incessantly with deadly aim into the close deep masses of infantry: changing, as the distance diminished, from round to grape and canister, and to double charges.

As the columns neared the ridge, they became impatient under this destructive cannonade; and their skirmishers rushed forward, prolonging the attack to Donzelot's division on their right, which, in a line of battalion columns, with their guns between them and on their flanks, and preceded by a crowd of daring skirmishers, were again assaulting the remains of Alten's division, as above related. Our gunners, under this close and severely-telling fire, could not long stand to their guns, but either lay down beneath them, or dropped behind the ridge; an expedient to which our artillerymen had frequent recourse during the day. Some brave fellows now and then would hastily load and fire, and again seek shelter. D'Aubremé's and Vandeleur's brigades sustained some casualties by this column's fire.

General Adam, and Colonel Colborne of the 52nd, (of the unmatched Peninsular school,) had been watching the enemy's columns, and the latter, (a real fire-eater,) upon his own responsibility, brought forward the right shoulder of his regiment, placing it across the oft-mentioned bit of hedgerow, and nearly parallel to the left flank of the attacking columns.

Thus was executed, with judgment, promptitude and spirit, worthy of the high character of the corps and its commander, a movement, which eventually enveloped the enemy's columns in an angle, at the apex of which was a battery, whose double-charged guns soon carried death and destruction through the mass, whilst a rapid and continued rolling fire of musketry assailed its front and flanks.

The Duke having seen the guards placed in their position, rode a little to the right, and observing the 52nd in a favourable situation, sent to Sir Henry Clinton to move forward the rest of Adam's brigade to charge the Imperial Guards who, with drums beating and deafening shouts of *"Vive l'Empereur!"* now crowned the summit of the position. The fire of Napier's and Vandersmissen's batteries, and of the British guards, opened on them, but still they gallantly pressed forward, as did also the columns of Donzelot, upon Alten's division; and the rest of D'Erlon's columns *en échelons, on* their right of La Haye Sainte, moved forward towards Lambert's, Kempt's and Best's brigades.

The fate of the battle seemed to quiver on the beam, when the 52nd in its complete four-deep line, previously screened from the enemy's view by the crest of our ridge, moved down upon the left flank of the Imperial columns in the most compact order. The columns halted, formed front to their left, and opened a fire upon the 52nd from their long flank. The latter also halted, and poured a most deadly fire into the mass: thus the finest infantry the world produced confronted each other.

At this moment (about eight o'clock,) the 2nd battalion of the 95th rifles came up on the left, and fired into the head of the column. The 71st and the 3rd battalion of the 95th were also rapidly advancing. This terrific fire told with most awful effect on the flank of the mass, already torn by the close discharges of case and grape-shot from our guns. From whose rapid fire, together with the musketry, a dense cloud of thick smoke hung on the ridge, and completely enveloped the contending parties. A still more rapid roll of musketry marked the highest efforts of the conflict, when on a sudden it began to slacken. Sir John Colborne gave the word to charge, which was answered by three hearty cheers that were heard above the shouts of "*Vive l'Empereur*".[9]

The French column now seemed to reel to and fro under the heavy fire upon both front and flank, and in truth it was unable to advance and unwilling to retire, and found itself in a position too trying even for its experienced veterans, notwithstanding they were animated by the best spirit. But the most daring in its ranks, and there were many such, made a determined resistance, and seemed to linger on the spot; one of these, no doubt, was Ney, who, upon the rout of the first columns, joined the second and led them also.[10]

The confusion and disorder which had been increasing now became uncontrollable. With the exception of the two rear battalions of the old guard, under General Cambronne,

---

9. Some French writers state that this hitherto victorious column was seized with a panic. If so, it was not to be wondered at: a crowd of men, heaped helplessly together, exposed to an incessant crossfire of musketry, round and grape-shot poured in like hail upon both front and flank, and our lines converging to enclose and bayonet them, was enough to occasion a panic. We may here observe, that the attack of the Imperial column is almost incredible, unaccompanied as it was and entirely unsupported by cavalry, with the flanks perpetually exposed, and never attempting to deploy into line, till fired into; halting to engage with musketry against troops in line. They sealed their own doom; for while utterly incapable of deploying or returning their enemy's fire with any effect, they were attacked by our infantry and turned by our cavalry. I must leave to the talented military historians to prove that this attack displayed Napoleon's former genius. The cause of the interval of some minutes between the two attacking columns, or why the attacks were not simultaneous, I am at a loss to explain; but it certainly was the cause of their being beaten in detail.
10. It is to be regretted that this gallant but inconstant soldier did not here meet a death far preferable to the one he afterwards found under the walls of the Luxemburg.

which at first, to appearance, formed a separate column of attack, and which alone retained the least semblance of order, the second attacking columns of the Imperial Guards shared the fate of the first, breaking into confusion, and in their flight carrying with them most of Donzelot's columns, who had prolonged the attack to the Genappe road against Alten's division, as previously mentioned, and were now falling back into the valley, from whence they had just emerged to make the attack. The 52nd and the second battalion of the 95th were pressing forward in pursuit, over ground literally covered with dead and dying, when a body of broken horsemen dashed through the smoke upon their front; and their whole fire was for a moment concentrated upon it, until it was discovered to be a part of the 23rd light dragoons pursued by some cuirassiers, one of whom broke through the 52nd and was killed in the rear by the Sergeant-Major, and another was cut down by an officer.

The front was scarcely cleared of the cavalry, when three of the enemy's guns opened a fire of grape, at about four hundred yards in prolongation of its right flank: Colonel Colborne galloped to the right of his regiment, and exclaimed, "Those guns will destroy us!" when instantly the right section, under Lieutenant Gawler, wheeled up and drove them off. The rest of the regiment continued the pursuit of the broken columns.

Colonel Hugh Halkett, on perceiving the forward movement of Adam's brigade, moved upon its right rear with the Osnabruck militia. Vivian's hussar brigade and the 2nd German light dragoons were immediately advanced to attack the French reserves,[11] drawn up between La Belle-Alliance and Hougoumont.

The feelings of our great antagonist on witnessing the to-

---

11. The French reserves were, for the most part, drawn up in chequer, presenting an irregular front, from La Belle-Alliance to the nearest enclosures of Hougoumont.

tal overthrow of his devoted guards, his last hope, and the deathblow to his political existence, may be imagined, but not described.

At this time, (eight o'clock,) says Captain Siborne, the General disposition of the Prussian forces, relative to that of Wellington's army, was, that the advance-guard of Zieten's (first) corps had joined our left; part of Pirch's (second) corps, with his reserve cavalry, had joined Bülow, who was on the advance, his right to attack Lobau, and his left to make a third attack upon Planchenois. The French opposed to them appeared determined to make a stand at all points.

CHAPTER 8

The Advance

The enemy's troops engaged in the last attack retired in the greatest confusion, which caused a panic throughout the remainder of the French army.

By this, the Prussians were relieved from the determined pressure made on them by the French right *en potence;* and it soon became evident that they were gaining ground. Zieten's (first) corps had just joined the left of our line by Ohain; Adam's brigade was most vigorously pursuing the fugitives, and Vivian's hussars were rapidly advancing on the enemy's reserve: all these things combined, convinced the Duke that the favourable moment for making a General attack, was arrived. Closing his telescope with an air of triumph, he ordered the advance of the whole line.

This order was received by the eager remains of the army with loud and tremendous cheers.

Then, Wellington, thy piercing eye
The crisis caught of destiny.
The British host had stood
That morn, 'gainst charge of host and lance,

As their own ocean rocks hold stanch;
But when thy voice had said, Advance!
They were their ocean's flood.

The Duke stood on the rise (immediately in front of the Lion,) with his hat raised in the air, as a signal to advance. The last parting rays of the beautiful setting sun at this moment (a quarter after eight,) shone most resplendently forth, as if to enliven the scene presented to our view, on emerging from the smoke, (that had long rendered invisible every object but the flashes of the enemy's batteries,) offering to the eyes of all who witnessed it, a spectacle which can never be forgotten by them. Were I to live to the age of Methuselah, never shall I forget that evening.

In front might be seen the retiring columns of the enemy, broken and mingled with crowds of fugitives of all arms, mounted and dismounted, mixed pell-mell together. In the right front was a dense smoke, curling upwards, from the Smouldering ruins of Hougoumont Far in the distance to the left front might also be dimly seen the dark columns of the Prussians, many of whom had arrived just in time to witness the overthrow of the French.

During this time Vivian's hussars had moved to the right, cleared the front and advanced on the right of Maitland's guards, who with Vandeleur's brigade cheered them on. On crossing the ridge the smoke was thick, but in the valley it became clear; and several columns of the enemy's infantry and cavalry, with guns on their flanks and between them, were visible in front. The Duke sent a message to Vivian by Colonel Campbell, not to attack till the infantry arrived, unless he thought he could break the French squares.

At this moment several men and horses of the 10th were killed by grape from the enemy's guns. Vivian observed to Sir Colin Campbell that, as our infantry advancing might not be in good order, it would be dangerous, if the French cavalry should fall upon them, and that he thought it would be better

140

for him to attack at once and drive the cavalry off,[1] leaving the enemy's squares to be attacked by our infantry. To this Sir Colin agreed, and returned to the Duke. Vivian now formed the 10th and 18th hussars into one line, and the 1st German hussars in second line. While forming, a broken body of the 23rd light dragoons, after being fired into by the 52nd, galloped along his front; his right was attacked by cuirassiers, and he lost many men, but beat off the enemy. Whilst the French were firing grape at the hussars, our own guns were also plying them with shot and spherical case, our gunners taking them for foes. Vivian sent an officer to correct the error.

The 10th hussars, on getting into line, charged and defeated the cavalry in their front. The 2nd Germans charged upon the right of the 10th. Vivian now rode to the 18th, who were near the two squares of the old guard which had been left in reserve; they had on each flank and between them, cavalry and guns.

The 18th was in line, and as steady as if exercising on Hounslow heath. On reaching its front, Vivian said, "Eighteenth, you will follow me;" on which the Sergeant-Major (Jeffs), afterwards adjutant of the 7th hussars, and many of the men, coarsely but fiercely exclaimed with an oath, "Ay, General, anywhere you choose to lead us."

The charge was ordered, and in an instant an attack was made on the cavalry and guns. Colonel Murray, commanding the 18th, in making this charge, leaped his horse over the traces between the wheelers and leaders of a French gun

---

1. My gallant friend and companion in arms the General, (See General Vivian's letter, Appendix, No. VII.) who, on all occasions, from my attending him as orderly, at the close of the day of Waterloo, until his death, so kindly took me by the hand, thought that what had occurred at Marengo, (when Kellermann's cavalry charged the advancing columns of Austrian grenadiers, and Desaix with a small force attacked their front and snatched a victory which the Austrians considered they had previously gained,) might probably take place at Waterloo, and was therefore most anxious to drive the enemy's cavalry off and prevent a like occurrence

which was dashing across his front in order to escape; but the hussars were upon the artillery, slaughtering the drivers and gunners and securing the guns: these destructive engines being now silenced, and the sting taken out of their cavalry, gave our infantry full scope to act.

In returning from this charge, Vivian found Major Howard, with a small body of the 10th, near a French square, from whose fire he was rapidly losing his men. At this moment a fine and gallant soldier, Lieutenant Gunning, fell. Vivian observed to Howard, "We have one of two things to do, either to retire a little out of the fire, or to attack;" and seeing some red-coated infantry approaching, who threw out a scattering fire upon the enemy's square, almost as destructive to friends as to foes, Vivian ordered the charge and accompanied it. The men galloped up to the bayonets of the Imperial Guards, and a fierce and bloody conflict ensued. Major Howard was shot by a musket-ball, and fell upon the enemy's bayonets—

And he was of the bravest, and when shower'd
The death-bolts deadliest the thinn'd files along,
E'en where the thickest of war's tempest lower'd,
They reach'd no nobler breast than thine, young gallant Howard!

The red-coated infantry were Colonel Halkett's Osnabruckers, who shortly before had captured General Cambronne of the Imperial Guards,[2] and a battery. Adam's brigade

---

2. It was Halkett himself who marked out Cambronne, and having ridden forward at full gallop, was on the point of cutting down the French General, when the latter cried out for quarter and received it. This fact does not well agree with the words popularly ascribed to Cambronne, *"La garde meurt, et ne se rend pas."* After having surrendered, Cambronne tried to escape from Halkett, whose horse fell wounded to the ground. But in a few seconds Halkett overtook his prisoner, and seizing him by the *aiguillette*, hurried him to the Osnabruckers, and sent him in charge of a Sergeant to the Duke of Wellington. Cambronne was subsequently sent to Ostend, with Count Lobau and other prisoners. It was only the old guard that wore the *aiguillette*. The words ascribed to Cambronne, "The guard dies, it never surrenders," of which we see such numbers of engravings, and which illustrates so many

had followed the broken columns of the French guards and Donzelot's into the valley in advance of the orchard of La Haye Sainte; but now there was something of more importance on the right of the Genappe road that required their attention; this was three squares of the enemy flanked on their right by cuirassiers: they were the remains of the first attacking column of the Imperial Guards, who had been rallied by Napoleon, and posted here to cover the retreat. The Duke galloped into the valley to Adam's brigade, and ordered Sir John Colborne to attack the rallied force of the Imperial Guards, saying, "They won't stand. Go on, Colborne, go on." Sir Colin Campbell rejoined the Duke, and explained the causes for which Vivian had decided on attacking the French reserves.

Lord Uxbridge, after having displayed the most brilliant acts of heroism during this sanguinary and arduous day, was about to join Vivian's hussars, when a grape-shot wounded his right leg, which rendered amputation necessary: the command of the allied cavalry consequently devolved on General Vandeleur, and that of his brigade on Colonel Sleigh, (11th Light Dragoons.)

Adam's brigade pressed gallantly up the slope towards the three squares and the cuirassiers; the former opened a heavy fire from both front and flanks. The Duke was still in rear of the 52nd. Sir Colin Campbell, finding the shot fly thick about the Duke, said, "Your Grace, this is no place for you; I wish you would move a little;" to which the Duke replied, "So I will, when these fellows are driven off."

As our line approached, the French squares went about by command; the Duke then galloped forward on the right of Ad-

---

(continued from page 63) so many pocket handkerchiefs, and ornaments so much of their crockery, etc., have, notwithstanding they were never uttered, made a fortune: all French historians repeat them. I am in possession of a letter, written to me by a friend of Cambronne's, and who asked the General, whether it was true that he had uttered the words in question; the reply was, I quote Mr. E. S. Dickson's own words, *"Monsieur, on m'a débité cette réponse."* ("The answer has been placed to my account.")

am's brigade, which was now about to cross the Genappe road. The cuirassiers accompanying the squares came down the road in a menacing attitude, as if to charge; but as no time was to be lost, the brigade lowered their bayonets, and in their four-deep line pressed on; but the cuirassiers declined the combat.

An incident occurred just at this time, relative to the Duke, which deserves to be noticed, as showing the great watchfulness which he at all times exercised.

Adam, who was now in the valley between the two ridges of the French position, and on the allied left of the Genappe road near La Belle-Alliance, not being able to see at any distance to his right, nor aware of Vivian's advance, was apprehensive that an attack might possibly be made upon his right flank, which by his movement had become exposed: he therefore desired his Brigade-Major to proceed and ascertain, whether there were any danger. In performing this duty, the Major fell in with the Duke, who was riding at a smart pace, followed by only one individual, whom Major Blair addressed; but he was immediately interrupted by the remark, *"Monsieur, je ne parle pas un seul mot d'anglais."* ("Sir, I cannot speak a word of English.") The Major then stated to him in French the object he was pursuing; and was answered, *"Le Duc lui-même a été voir, il n'y a rien à craindre."* ("The Duke has, himself, been to see, there is nothing to fear.") Upon this the Major hastened back with the satisfactory communication.

About a hundred yards on the allied left of La Belle-Alliance, the road running towards Planchenois becomes a complete hollow-way, out of which a broken column of French infantry was in the act of debouching with some guns, and making a hasty retreat, when the 52nd regiment in its advance came right upon them. The infantry tried to escape, and at the same time to defend themselves as best they could.

The artillery turned to their left and attempted to get up the bank, but their horses were immediately shot down by the 52nd. A young officer of the battery surrendered; but the commander, a veteran who wore upon his breast the decoration of the Legion of Honour, stood, sword in hand, in the midst of his guns, and in an attitude of bold defiance. A soldier started from the ranks and made a thrust at him, which the officer parried; a scuffle ensued, the man closed with him, threw him on the ground, and keeping him down with his foot, reversed his musket to bayonet him. The repugnance to the shedding of human blood unnecessarily,[3] (a feeling which we may proudly claim as belonging to British soldiers,) burst forth in a groan of displeasure from his comrades. It came too late; the fatal thrust had passed, and the life of the deserving member of the honoured Legion was extinct.

The battery and many prisoners were captured. The brigade, pressing on in pursuit of the squares, got upon the highest point of ground of the French position, and in the line of fire from the Prussian batteries: the Duke sent to Bülow to stop the fire. The 71st, on the right, captured a battery, and one of the guns, being loaded, was turned round and fired into the retreating foe by Captain Campbell of the 71st, aide-de-camp to General Adam. It is supposed that this was the last French gun, fired on that memorable day. Soon after, the squares followed by Adam, halted near the farm of Rossomme, threw away their knapsacks, and being thus lightened, disappeared in the twilight.

About the time that Howard was killed, Vandeleur's brigade was spanking along under the east hedge of Hougoumont; and overtaking some of the flying enemy between the Hougoumont enclosures and Rossomme, they made some charges and captured a great number of the enemy.

As soon as a part of Zieten's corps had joined our left,

---

3. It is notorious, that in the bosom of the truly brave, a spark of humanity is always smouldering, even when the ferocity of war rouses the savage passion to the greatest fury. The case above, that of Major Toole, 32nd regiment, with which our readers are already acquainted, that of General Pelet a few pages on, together with the anecdote of the French skirmisher with Lieutenant-Colonel F. Ponsonby, prove the difficulty of making brave men hate each other.

Blücher ordered the battery to open fire, the infantry to descend into the valley of Smohain, and in conjunction with the troops of Nassau to attack the French, who had been reinforced in order to prevent a junction between Bülow's corps and the allied left.

Zieten's advance infantry pushed down into the valley, where some shots were exchanged by mistake between them and the Nassau troops: the mistake was soon rectified, and both bodies united advanced, and dislodged the French from the houses in the valley of Smohain, and the farms of La Haye and Papelotte.

It was about eight o'clock, when Zieten's advance cavalry drew up on our left, and an infantry brigade and the reserve cavalry of General Pirch's (2nd) corps joined Bülow, and in conjunction made the following dispositions for the third attack upon Planchenois:

General Ryssel's and Colonel Hiller's infantry brigades of the 4th corps under General Count Bülow, and General Tippelskircher's brigade of General Pirch's (2nd) corps, formed in columns of battalions; on the left was a regiment of Prince William's reserve, and two battalions of infantry with their skirmishers in front; and three cavalry regiments, part of Prince William's, were in rear of the above brigades.

In rear of this cavalry was General Kraft's infantry brigade of the 2nd corps in reserve; and on the right of the infantry brigades were three lines of cavalry, under General Jurgass; and upon their right, and advancing simultaneously with the attack upon Planchenois, were Hack's and Losthin's infantry brigades of the 4th corps; in their rear were three battalions, part of Hack's brigade. On the right of those brigades was a small force of cavalry, part of Prince William's, and upon their right were four battalion columns, part of General Steinmetz's brigade of General Zieten's (1st) corps. Upon the ridge on the allied left, was part of General Roder's cavalry that had just reached the field, and whose battery opened fire in place of one belonging to the allies that had expended all its ammunition. A few battalions were detached to the left of Planchenois, to secure the flank, and, if possible, to turn the enemy's right. The whole Prussian force was preceded by skirmishers, and their batteries were most advantageously placed upon the heights.

A squadron of Prussian cavalry beat back a company of the Imperial Guards from the farm of Chantilly, above Planchenois. The latter retired upon the wood at the farm of Caillou, closely pursued by the hostile cavalry, which was beaten off by the Imperial baggage guard. The Prussian dragoons soon returned in such force, that the Emperor's suite, with bag and baggage, made a hasty flight towards Genappe.

Whilst Blüchers army stood as stated, Wellington had defeated both the attacking columns of the Imperial Guards; and Adam's brigade was driving them and Donzelot's division, that had broken and mixed with them, across the field, towards the Genappe highroad. Vivian's brigade and the 2nd German light dragoons were setting forward at a long trot towards the French reserves, drawn up between La Belle-Alliance and Hougoumont.

The whole allied line was now advancing, flanked on the left by Prussian cavalry. The enemy showed little resistance to any part of it. As Hepburn issued from the orchard of Hougoumont into the open fields, the enemy went off, scarcely firing a single shot. Those in the wood made a little resistance, until they saw that all their army was in full flight. The cavalry on the French left went off in order, skirmishers out covering their retreat. Bachelu's and Foy's divisions moved off, on witnessing the defeat of the second column of the Imperial Guards: on seeing this, the troops holding La Haye Sainte abandoned it. Alix's, occupying the sandpit and knoll, gave way on the advance of Lambert; and Marcognet yielded and broke before the advance of Pack and Kempt. Durutte's division broke before Zieten's and the Duke of

Saxe-Weimar's advance. De Lobau, on seeing the troops on his left giving way, together with the flight of the Imperial Guards, followed by British troops whom he perceived in his rear, as well as the now vigorous attack of Bülow, and the probability of his being cut off from all retreat with his whole corps, rushed into the stream of fugitives, that had set in towards Rossomme and Genappe.

During this time Planchenois had been the scene of a most dreadful struggle: the French in the churchyard held out, and the Prussians, finding it of no avail to continue the attack in front, turned the village on both flanks, driving the Imperial Guards before them; the latter, finding that they should be cut off from all retreat, fell into disorder, and mixed with the General mass of fugitives, who were flying in all directions towards Rossomme and La Maison-du-Roi, followed by the Prussians, who made a dash at the eagle of the Imperial Guards. General Pelet called out, *"A moi, chasseur! sauvons l'aigle, ou mourons autour d'elle!"* ("Rally round me, chasseurs! let us save the eagle, or die protecting it!") Upon this they formed square, and saved the eagle and the honour of the regiment.[4]

About nine o'clock, Napoleon threw himself, with a few of his staff, into a square of the 2nd chasseurs of the old guard, that had been under Cambronne; but upon the approach of our cavalry he galloped away. Wellington, with our advance brigades, reached the farm of Rossomme, between which and La Belle-Alliance some Prussian cavalry and our 18th exchanged blows, and some lives were lost. The 11th Light Dragoons and 1st German Hussars were also nearly coming in contact with each other, owing to the dimness of the twilight.

An arrangement by communication had previously been made by Wellington and Blücher, that the allied army should

---

4. Let it be recorded to General Pelet's credit, that he prevented the butchery of some Prussian prisoners, whom their captors, in their fruitless rage, were eager to sacrifice.

halt here, and that the Prussians should pursue and harass the routed enemy. The Duke was now, with all his advance, a little beyond Rossomme, upon a particular knoll with a gap through it, which can be distinctly seen from most parts of the right of the allied position.

As the Prussians passed us, (for I had the honour and good fortune to be an actor in this scene,) I heard their bands play, "God Save the King," which soul-stirring compliment we returned by hearty cheers.

In the pursuit of the enemy from Rossomme to Genappe, the Prussian lance and sabre were busy in the work of death. Many a brave soldier, that had escaped the bloody field, fell that night beneath the deadly steel. In vain did the French make a feeble effort at Genappe to check the Prussians, by barricading its long and narrow street with their few remaining guns and tumbrels. So entirely had their defeat destroyed their discipline, that the Prussians, by the first sound of the trumpet, beat of drum, or their wild hurrah, overcame every obstacle, and, pressing on, they captured sixty pieces of cannon.

The Duke, after clearing the highroad and its left of the allied troops, in order to give full scope to the advancing Prussians, to whom he now relinquished the pursuit of the flying enemy, remained for some time on the right of Rossomme with his advanced troops, in conversation with General Vivian, Colonel Colborne and others; after which His Grace, promising to send the provisions up, turned his horse round and rode away.

On returning leisurely towards Waterloo, about ten o'clock, at a short distance before reaching La Belle-Alliance, he, aided by a clouded moon, descried a group of mounted officers making towards the Genappe highroad from the direction of Frischermont; the Duke turned off to meet them: it proved to be Blücher and his staff; they most heartily congratulated each other on the glorious result of the contest in which they had been so intensely engaged. The conference lasted about ten minutes, when the veteran Blücher, promising to leave his inveterate foe no rallying time on this side of the frontier, shook hands with His Grace and proceeded to Genappe, sending forward to General Gneisenau, who led his advance-guard, orders to press and harass the enemy, and not suffer the grass to grow under their feet, or even allow them to take breath. Bülow's corps, which led the pursuit, was supported by Zieten's. Pirch's corps received orders to turn round and strike across the country, and, if possible, to cut off Marshal Grouchy's retreat.

Our gallant chief returned over the field to Waterloo, and before reaching La Haye Sainte was obliged to quit the highroad, on account of its being completely blocked up with guns, many of which were upset and lying topsy turvy; whilst the frequent snort and start of the horses told but too clearly that the ground they trod was studded and strewed with the slain. His Grace, on regaining the highroad, was so affected by the cries of the wounded and moans of the dying, as to shed tears, and on his way did not exchange a word with any of his suite, composed only of five persons, one of whom, the late Sir Colin Campbell, was armed with a cuirassier's sword.

The Duke was sombre and dejected, as well he might be: grim death had been busy, and had had a regular gala-day amongst His Grace's old and well-tried friends, who had followed him in distant climes, and through many an arduous and hard-fought field. The Duke, on this occasion, might have exclaimed with Pyrrhus, "Such another victory, and we are undone!" We may readily believe, that in writing the next day to the Duke of Beaufort and the Earl of Aberdeen, His Grace only yielded to the genuine dictates of his heart, when he expressed in these, as well as other letters, "The losses I have sustained have quite broken me down, and I have no feeling for the advantages we have acquired."[5]

---

5. See Appendix, No. II, or *Despatches,* vol. XII, page 488-9.

Napoleon, after quitting the square, which was about midway between La Belle-Alliance and the farm of Rossomme, rode on our right of the road for some distance, escorted by the gallant remains of the horse grenadiers of the guard, the only force in the whole French army that now retained the least semblance of order. But finding the ground very heavy, he crossed the road at the Maison-du-Roi, and rode along a crossroad which was also in a very bad state: he then made for the highroad again, passed Genappe, and arrived at Quatre-Bras about eleven o'clock; thence he proceeded to Charleroy.

The remains of the allied army bivouacked on what had been the French position. The 52nd, 71st, and 2nd and 3rd battalions of the 95th, halted on the ground that had been occupied by the Imperial Guards in reserve, near the farm of Rossomme. The remains of my regiment went to the vicinity of the farm of Hulencourt, with Vivian's brigade: I accompanied General Vivian and Colonel Sir E. Kerrison to the farm, acting as orderly, and still mounted on the cuirassier's horse.

Thus closed upon us the glorious 18th of June. Fatigue and extreme exhaustion, following such exertions and such excitement as had been our lot that day, left us little power to reflect either upon the completeness of our own triumph, or the extent of the disasters that overtook the remains of our vanquished foes. These fled in utter and hopeless disorder before the Prussians, who dashed into the pursuit, and continued the work of slaughter with a ferocious and avenging spirit, which the conduct of the French two days before had provoked.

Had however the enemy's cavalry been husbanded, the headlong rush of the victors might have been sufficiently checked, to have allowed the French army to retreat in something like order. But the wreck of that fine army fled, or rather was driven from the long-disputed field, in the wildest disorder and confusion.

More important or decisive events than those which so quickly succeeded each other between the 15th and 18th of June never before graced the pages of history. Never did the events of a few days produce such important consequences.

We, the conquerors of Waterloo, and many of us certainly never expected so glorious a termination to the battle, were glad to lie down among the dead and dying, and snatch a few hours of necessary repose:

Piled high as autumn shocks, there lay
The ghastly harvest of the fray,
The corpses of the slain.

The battle might be described to have consisted of a succession of assaults, sustained with unabated fury, and often with a boldness and effect that much perplexed our troops and put their firmness to the test. Every renewed attack diminished our numbers, and still the survivors yielded not an inch of ground, and, even without orders, made good the gaps. No other troops in the world would have endured, for so long a period, so terrible a struggle.

Our Imperial antagonist admitted that we went through and stood to our work, unlike any troops he had ever seen before, and the fact is well authenticated, that Napoleon repeatedly complimented us on our incomparable steadiness and forbearance. But this is not to be wondered at, when our chief, he who had so often directed our energy, affirmed that he had "never seen the British infantry behave so well." Our glorious contest had been maintained against the most renowned legions of Europe, that had never before shown such constant audacity and intrepidity.

They were led by Generals of undoubted skill and gallantry, who with their brave troops had won laurels in many an arduous, hard-fought battle, and who believed themselves to be, what their ambitious chief had so often declared, invincible, and as such they were still regarded by most of the continental nations.

At Waterloo we had to contend against soldiers of undaunted spirit, full of enthusiasm and careless of life. Never did these heroic men, grown grey in victories, better sustain their reputation than on this occasion. The French are a brave people, and no troops in the world surpass, if any equal them, for impetuosity of attack; but many men will stand fire and face distant danger, and yet shrink from the struggle when closing in desperate grasp with an enemy. It is not bravery alone which decides the battle, calmness is often absolutely necessary, and in this, the most valiant are at times found wanting. Never did a battle require more cool and determined courage than that of Waterloo. Nothing can be more trying to troops than passive endurance of offence; nothing so intolerable as to be incessantly assailed, and not permitted in turn to become assailants. A desperate struggle in a well-contested battlefield, differs greatly from acting on the defensive, from holding a position, or from being attacked and not allowed to return the aggression of an enemy. There is an excited feeling when assailing, which stimulates even the weak-hearted, and drowns the thought of danger. The tumultuous enthusiasm of the assault spreads from man to man, and timid spirits catch a gallant frenzy from the brave.

CHAPTER 9

The Pursuit to Paris

On our awaking next morning, each of us must have experienced something like astonishment, not unmingled, I hope, with feelings of gratitude, that amidst such carnage as he had witnessed, his life and strength were still spared, to fight again, if need should be, the battles of his country. We knew we had beaten the French, and that too, completely; for our last charge had succeeded at every point. But they were not defeated because they were deficient either in bravery or discipline. Their bearing throughout the day was that of gallant soldiers: their attacks were conducted with a chivalric impetuosity and admirably sustained vigour, which left no shadow of doubt upon our minds of their entire devotedness to the cause of Napoleon, of their expectation of victory, and the determination of many of them not to survive defeat.

The best and bravest of them fell; but not till they had inflicted almost equal loss upon their conquerors. To deny them the tribute of respect, admiration and pity, which their bravery and misfortunes claim, would tarnish the lustre of our martial glory. The British soldier is content with victory: he abhors insult and cruelty: he has a melancholy pleasure in being just and generous to a fallen foe. That the French in their flight from Waterloo were unnecessarily butchered during many hours by the exasperated Prussians, is a fact, which I can more easily explain than justify.

The field of battle, after the victory, presented a frightful and most distressing spectacle. It appeared as if the whole military world had been collected together, and that something beyond human strength and ingenuity had been employed to cause its destruction. Solicitude for the wounded prompted the Duke to ride back to Brussels immediately after the sanguinary contest.

The assistance of the town authorities was requested, in collecting and removing the wounded from the field, as well as to restore confidence amongst the population, and allay the extreme excitement which prevailed throughout Belgium. Right nobly did the inhabitants of Brussels respond to his appeal. The clergy, as might have been expected, were foremost in their exertions to relieve the dreadful agonies of so many gallant and innocent sufferers: the highest in rank rivalled the hardier classes in performing the most trying offices for the mangled heroes that filled the hospitals, and encumbered even many private dwellings. Ladies, of the honoured names of Merode and Bobiano, set an illustrious example, by their presence on the field the morning after the battle; the scene of carnage, so revolting to their delicate and tender nature, stimulating, instead of preventing, their humane exertions. Many other ladies, like ministering angels, shared in this work of mercy to the wounded, of whatever nation they might be, or in whatever cause they had fallen.

A number of poor fellows who were carried to the houses of the neighbouring villages, met with the most humane treatment: many there breathed their last, under circumstances somewhat less appalling than on the battlefield. There still lives in Waterloo a most respectable old lady, at whose house several of our officers were quartered before the battle. Madame Boucqueau (the lady in question) saw these gallant men go forth in the morning: they did not all return at the close of the day. She remembers well that an officer, who appeared to her to hold superior rank, came back to her house in the evening, and said to her exultingly, *"Me void encore, madame; es-tfini: ils sont à nous."* (" Here I am again; it is over: we have won the day.") The worthy dame has in her possession a silver cup, presented to her late husband by British gratitude. As it does honour to all parties concerned, and is a sample, no doubt, of many an interchange of kindly feelings amidst the horrors of war, I have great pleasure in recording here the inscription which is on this cup:

A small mark of grateful respect from
Colonel Sir W. Robe
of the British Royal Artillery
Knight Commander of the Bath
and Knight of the Tower and Sword
To Sieur Maximilian Boucqueau
of Waterloo
for kindness in the last moments
and attention to the remains of a beloved son
Lieutenant W. L. Robe
of the British horse artillery
who nobly fell at Waterloo

The allied army proceeded on the 19th to Nivelles, (a most wonderful military exploit after such a desperate battle,) where it was joined by the detached force under Prince Frederick and General Sir Charles Colville. His Grace overtook us on the 21st, on which day we entered France. On the day previous to the allied army entering the country, the Duke issued the following:

General Order
Nivelles, June 20th, 1815
1. As the army is about to enter the French territory, the troops of the nations which are at present under the

command of Field-Marshal the Duke of Wellington, are desired to recollect that their respective sovereigns are the allies of His Majesty the King of France, and that France ought, therefore, to be treated as a friendly country. It is therefore required that nothing should be taken either by officers or soldiers, for which payment be not made.

2. The Field-Marshal takes this opportunity of returning to the army his thanks for their conduct in the glorious action fought on the 18th inst., and he will not fail to report his sense of their conduct, in the terms which it deserves, to their several sovereigns.

Wellington

The Duke's headquarters on the 21st were at Malplaquet, the scene of one of the great Marlborough's victories, in 1709. He immediately issued a proclamation to the French people, which exemplifies the wisdom, firmness and moderation that ever marked the career of our illustrious commander. He worthily represented a brave, victorious, but humane people, the inhabitants of the British empire.

PROCLAMATION

Be it known to the French people, that I enter their country at the head of a victorious army, not as an enemy, (excepting to the usurper, the declared enemy of the human race, with whom we can have neither peace nor truce,) but to assist them to throw off the iron yoke by which they have been borne down.

For this purpose I have issued the accompanying orders to my army; let all who shall infringe those orders be reported to me.

The French people, however, must be aware that I have a right to require them so to conduct themselves, that I may be warranted in protecting them from all aggression.

They will therefore provide whatever shall be demanded of them by persons duly authorized, receiving in exchange receipts in proper form and order: they will remain peaceably in their dwellings, and will hold no correspondence nor communication with the usurper or his adherents.

All persons abandoning their homes after our entry into France, or absenting themselves in order to serve the usurper, shall be looked upon as his partisans and our enemies; and their property shall be confiscated and applied to the maintenance of the troops.[1]

Wellington

Given at headquarters, Malplaquet, June 22nd, 1815

Whilst the Duke was addressing this language to the French people, the fallen usurper, having awakened from his short dream of empire and spoliation, made a last but fruitless effort to continue to delude his discomfited partisans. On the very same day that Wellington's proclamation went forth from Malplaquet, Napoleon issued the following declaration:

Palace of the Elysée

June 22nd, 1815

French People!

In commencing hostilities to uphold your national independence, I relied upon the combined efforts and good-will of all classes, as well as the cooperation of all official persons in the country. Hence sprang my hopes of success, and willingness to set at defiance all the proclamations of the powers against me.

Circumstances appear to me to be altered. I tender myself in sacrifice to the hatred of the enemies of France. May they be sincere in their declarations! May their hostility really aim at nothing but me personally!

---

1. See the original in French, in Gurwood, vol. XII, page 484-5

My political life is at an end; and I proclaim my son, under the name of Napoleon the Second, Emperor of the French.

The present ministers will constitute provisionally the council of state.

My interest in my son's wellbeing leads me to invite the Chambers to proceed without delay to provide a regency by an enactment for this purpose.

Make united efforts to preserve the public peace and your national independence.

Napoleon

This production neither aroused the French to make fresh sacrifices for his sake, nor stayed the victorious march of the allies upon Paris.

On the 24th of June we took Cambray, which was given up on the following day to Louis the XVIII. This was the last occasion on which I saw a shot fired in a hostile manner.

Our first brigade of guards took Péronne on the 26th. The Duke on this occasion had a narrow escape. After directing his staff to get under shelter in the ditch of an outwork, he posted himself in a sally-port of the glacis. A staff officer, having a communication to make to His Grace, came suddenly upon him and drew the attention of the enemy, who treacherously discharged a howitzer loaded with grape at the point; it shattered the wall against which the Duke was standing, and made (to use the words of one who saw him immediately afterwards,) "his blue coat completely *red*."

Meanwhile Grouchy, who was at Wavre, having heard of the utter failure of his Imperial master at Waterloo, commenced a retreat on Paris, vigorously followed by the two Prussian corps under Thielmann and Pirch. During this retreat, Grouchy displayed more skill, energy and decision, than in his pursuit of the Prussians upon Wavre, on the 17th and 18th.

The Prussians, who were on our left, had several sharp engagements with the enemy during their advance upon Paris;

and both armies reached the environs of the capital on the 1st of July. Hostilities ceased, and a military convention was signed in the evening of the 3rd. On the morning of this day Zieten's corps had a sharp action, in which they were victors, at Issy, near Paris.

The campaign thus, by a singular coincidence, was brought to a close by the same troops that opened it. The allied and Prussian armies entered Paris on the 7th of July, and were followed next day by Louis XVIII. Before the end of the month, the armies of Europe congregated in and round Paris, amounted nearly to the most enormous number of a million of men in arms.

Napoleon, in the meantime, had left the capital. The Emperor surrendered at sea, on the 15th of July,[2] to Captain Maitland, of the *Bellerophon*. By a decree of the allied powers, he was sent to St. Helena, where he died May 5th, 1821.

Since these events, more than thirty years have passed over us; and peace between the two greatest nations of the globe, England and France, has been uninterruptedly maintained. Long may it continue, to the honour of those whose blood and valour purchased it, and to the lasting happiness of the civilized world! It was the prospect of securing this immense benefit to mankind that united all European nations against the ambition of Napoleon, and that afforded the best comfort under the distressing sacrifices made to ensure his overthrow. Perhaps no people benefited by his fall so much as the French themselves: his triumphs (often great in a military point of view,) left nothing in their hands, whilst they filled every family in France with mourning. The conscription was a more searching tyranny than civilized men had ever before endured; and all this blood flowed in vain. Our Gallic neighbours have sometimes mistaken the tone of triumph in which we speak of the downfall of Napoleon,

---

2. Those curious of historical coincidences will observe that Napoleon opened the campaign on the 16th of June.

and have regarded it as insulting to them: nothing is farther from the mind and heart of the British soldier who has ever stood in arms against them, and who is always ready to acknowledge their military excellence.

CHAPTER 10

Official Accounts

The despatch of the Duke of Wellington, written immediately after the battle, cannot fail to interest everyone. It is a document which has fixed the attention of statesmen and soldiers, not more on account of the importance of the event it describes, than for the noble simplicity, perfect calmness and exemplary modesty which characterise the great man who penned it: it stands in honourable contrast with the hurried, inflated, untrue accounts of military achievements not infrequently given by commanders of no small renown.

LONDON GAZETTE EXTRAORDINARY

Downing Street
June 23rd, 1815
Major the Hon. H. Percy arrived late last night with a despatch from Field-Marshal the Duke of Wellington, K. G., to Earl Bathurst, His Majesty's principal secretary of state for the war department, of which the following is a copy:

To Earl Bathurst
Waterloo
June 10th, 1815
My Lord,
Bonaparte, having collected the 1st, 2nd, 3rd, 4th and 6th corps of the French army, and the Imperial Guards, and nearly all the cavalry, on the Sambre, and between that river and the Meuse, between the 10th and 14th of the month, advanced on the 15th, and attacked the Prussian posts at Thuin and Lobbes, on the Sambre, at daylight in the morning.

I did not hear of these events till in the evening of the 15th; and I immediately ordered the troops to prepare to march, and afterwards to march to their left, as soon as I had intelligence from other quarters to prove that the enemy's movement upon Charleroy was the real attack.

The enemy drove the Prussian posts from the Sambre on that day; and General Zieten, who commanded the corps which had been at Charleroy, retired upon Fleurus; and Marshal Prince Blücher concentrated the Prussian army upon Sombreffe, holding the villages in front of his position of St. Amand and Ligny.

The enemy continued his march along the road from Charleroy towards Brussels; and, on the same evening, the 15th, attacked a brigade of the army of the Netherlands, under the Prince de Weimar, posted at Frasnes, and forced it back to the farmhouse, on the same road, called Les Quatre-Bras.

The Prince of Orange immediately reinforced this brigade with another of the same division, under General Perponcher, and, in the morning early, regained part of the ground which had been lost, so as to have the command of the communication leading from Nivelles and Brussels with Marshal Blücher's position.

In the meantime, I had directed the whole army to march upon Les Quatre-Bras; and the 5th division, under Lieutenant-General Sir Thomas Picton, arrived at about half-past two in the day, followed by the corps of troops under the Duke of Brunswick, and afterwards by the contingent of Nassau.

At this time, the enemy commenced an attack upon Prince Blücher with his whole force, excepting the 1st and 2nd corps, and a corps of cavalry under General Kellermann, with which he attacked our post at Les Quatre-Bras.

The Prussian army maintained their position with their usual gallantry and perseverance, against a great disparity of numbers, as the 4th corps of their army, under General Bülow, had not joined; and I was not able to assist them as I wished, as I was attacked myself, and the troops, the cavalry in particular, which had a long distance to march, had not arrived.

We maintained our position also, and completely defeated and repulsed all the enemy's attempts to get possession of it. The enemy repeatedly attacked us with a large body of infantry and cavalry, supported by a numerous and powerful artillery. He made several charges with the cavalry upon our infantry, but all were repulsed in the steadiest manner.

In this affair, His Royal Highness the Prince of Orange, the Duke of Brunswick, and Lieutenant-General Sir Thomas Picton, and Major-Generals Sir James Kempt and Sir Denis Pack, who were engaged from the commencement of the enemy's attack, highly distinguished themselves, as well as Lieutenant-General Charles Baron Alten, Major-General Sir Colin Halkett, Lieutenant-General Cooke, and

Major-Generals Maitland and Byng, as they successively arrived. The troops of the 5th division, and those of the Brunswick corps, were long and severely engaged, and conducted themselves with the utmost gallantry. I must particularly mention the 28th, 42nd, 70th, and 92nd regiments, and the battalion of Hanoverians.

Our loss was great, as Your Lordship will perceive by the enclosed return; and I have particularly to regret His Serene Highness the Duke of Brunswick, who fell fighting gallantly at the head of his troops.

Although Marshal Blücher had maintained his position at Sombreffe, he still found himself much weakened by the severity of the contest in which he had been engaged, and, as the 4th corps had not arrived, he determined to fall back and to concentrate his army upon Wavre; and he marched in the night, after the action was over.

This movement of the Marshal rendered necessary a corresponding one upon my part; and I retired from the farm of Quatre-Bras upon Genappe, and thence upon Waterloo, the next morning, the 17th, at ten o'clock.

The enemy made no effort to pursue Marshal Blücher. On the contrary, a patrol which I sent to Sombreffe in the morning found all quiet;[1] and the enemy's videttes fell back as the patrol advanced. Neither did he attempt to molest our march to the rear, although made in the middle of the day, excepting by following, with a large body of cavalry brought from his right, the cavalry under the Earl of Uxbridge.

---

1. Lieutenant-Colonel the Hon. Sir Alexander Gordon was sent, escorted by Captain John Gray's troop of the 10th hussars, to ascertain the real line of retreat of the Prussians, and to communicate with their headquarters, as to cooperation with the British army, ordered to retire to the position in front of Waterloo.

This gave Lord Uxbridge an opportunity of charging them with the 1st Lifeguards, upon their *débouché* from the village of Genappe; upon which occasion His Lordship has declared himself to be well satisfied with that regiment.

The position which I took up in front of Waterloo crossed the highroads from Charleroy and Nivelles, and had its right thrown back to a ravine near Merbe-Braine, which was occupied, and its left extended to a height above the hamlet Ter-la-Haye, which was likewise occupied. In front of the right centre, and near the Nivelles road, we occupied the house and gardens of Hougoumont, which covered the return of that flank; and in front of the left centre we occupied the farm of La Haye Sainte. By our left we communicated with Marshal Prince Blücher at Wavre, through Ohain; and the Marshal had promised me that, in case we should be attacked, he would support me with one or more corps, as might be necessary.

The enemy collected his army, with the exception of the 3rd corps, which had been sent to observe Marshal Blücher, on a range of heights in our front, in the course of the night of the 17th and yesterday morning; and at about ten o'clock he commenced a furious attack upon our post at Hougoumont. I had occupied that post with a detachment from General Byng's brigade of guards, which was in position in its rear; and it was for some time under the command of Lieutenant-Colonel Macdonnell, and afterwards of Colonel Home; and I am happy to add, that it was maintained throughout the day with the utmost gallantry by these brave troops, notwithstanding the repeated efforts of large bodies of the enemy to obtain possession of it.

This attack upon the right of our centre was accompanied by a very heavy cannonade upon our whole line, which was destined to support the repeated attacks of cavalry and infantry, occasionally mixed, but sometimes separate, which were made upon it. In one of these the enemy carried the farmhouse of La Haye Sainte, as the detachment of the light battalion of the German Legion, which occupied it, had expended all its ammunition; and the enemy occupied the only communication there was with them.

The enemy repeatedly charged our infantry with his cavalry, but these attacks were uniformly unsuccessful; and they afforded opportunities to our cavalry to charge, in one of which Lord Edward Somerset's brigade, consisting of the Lifeguards, the Royal horse-guards and 1st dragoon guards, highly distinguished themselves, as did that of Major-General Sir William Ponsonby, having taken many prisoners and an eagle.

These attacks were repeated till about seven in the evening, when the enemy made a desperate effort with cavalry and infantry, supported by the fire of artillery, to force our left centre, near the farm of La Haye Sainte, which, after a severe contest, was defeated; and, having observed that the troops retired from this attack in great confusion, and that the march of General Bülow's corps, by Frischermont, upon Planchenois and La Belle-Alliance, had begun to take effect, and as I could perceive the fire of his cannon, and as Marshal Prince Blücher had joined in person with a corps of his army to the left of our line by Ohain, I determined to attack the enemy, and immediately advanced the whole line of infantry, supported by the cavalry and artillery.

The attack succeeded in every point: the enemy was forced from his positions on the heights, and fled in the utmost confusion, leaving behind him, as far as I could judge, a hundred and fifty pieces of cannon, with their ammunition, which fell into our hands.

I continued the pursuit till long after dark, and then discontinued it only on account of the fatigue of our troops, who had been engaged during twelve hours, and because I found myself on the same road with Marshal Blücher, who assured me of his intention to follow the enemy throughout the night. He has sent me word this morning that he had taken sixty pieces of cannon belonging to the Imperial Guard, and several carriages, baggage, etc., belonging to Bonaparte, in Genappe.

I propose to move this morning upon Nivelles, and not to discontinue my operations.

Your Lordship will observe that such a desperate action could not be fought, and such advantages could not be gained, without great loss; and I am sorry to add that ours has been immense. In Lieutenant-General Sir Thomas Picton, His Majesty has sustained the loss of an officer who has frequently distinguished himself in his service; and he fell gloriously leading his division to a charge with bayonets, by which one of the most serious attacks made by the enemy on our position was repulsed. The Earl of Uxbridge, after having successfully got through this arduous day, received a wound by almost the last shot fired, which will, I am afraid, deprive His Majesty for some time of his services.

His Royal Highness the Prince of Orange distinguished himself by his gallantry and conduct, till he received a wound from a musket-ball through the shoulder, which obliged him to quit the field.

It gives me the greatest satisfaction to assure Your Lordship that the army never, upon any occasion, conducted itself better. The division of guards, under Lieutenant-General Cooke, who is severely wounded, Major-General Maitland, and Major-General Byng, set an example which was followed by all; and there is no officer nor description of troops that did not behave well.

I must, however, particularly mention, for his Royal Highness' approbation, Lieutenant-General Sir Henry Clinton, Major-General Adam, Lieutenant-General Charles Baron Alten (severely wounded), Major-General Sir Colin Halkett (severely wounded), Colonel Ompteda, Colonel Mitchell (commanding a brigade of the 4th division), Major-Generals Sir James Kempt and Sir Denis Pack, Major-General Lambert, Major-General Lord Edward Somerset, Major-General Sir William Ponsonby, Major-General Sir Colquhoun Grant, and Major-General Sir Hussey Vivian, Major-General Sir O. Vandeleur, and Major-General Count Dornberg.

I am also particularly indebted to General Lord Hill for his assistance and conduct upon this, as upon all former occasions.

The artillery and engineer departments were conducted much to my satisfaction, by Colonel Sir George Wood and Colonel Smyth; and I had every reason to be satisfied with the conduct of the Adjutant-General, Major-General Barnes, who was wounded, and of the Quarter-Master-General Colonel De Lancey, who was killed by a cannon shot in the middle of the action. This officer is a serious loss to His Majesty's service, and to me at this moment.

I was likewise much indebted to the assistance of Lieutenant-Colonel Lord Fitzroy Somerset, who was severely wounded, and of the officers composing my personal staff, who have suffered severely in this action. Lieutenant-Colonel the Hon. Sir Alexander Gordon, who has died of his wounds, was a most promising officer, and is a serious loss to His Majesty's service.

General Kruse, of the Nassau service, likewise conducted himself much to my satisfaction; as did General Tripp, commanding the heavy brigade of cavalry, and General Vanhope, commanding a brigade of infantry in the service of the King of the Netherlands.

General Pozzo di Borgo, General Baron Vincent, General Müffling and General Alava, were in the field during the action, and rendered me every assistance in their power. Baron Vincent is wounded, but I hope not severely; and General Pozzo di Borgo received a contusion.

I should not do justice to my own feelings, or to Marshal Blücher and the Prussian army, if I did not attribute the successful result of this arduous day to the cordial and timely assistance I received from them. The operation of General Bülow upon the enemy's flank was a most decisive one; and, even if I had not found myself in a situation to make the attack which produced the final result, it would have forced the enemy to retire if his attacks should have failed, and would have prevented him from taking advantage of them if they should unfortunately have succeeded.

Since writing the above, I have received a report that Major-General Sir William Ponsonby is killed; and, in announcing this intelligence to Your Lordship, I have to add the expression of my grief for the fate of an officer who had already rendered very brilliant and important services, and was an ornament to his profession.

I send with this despatch two eagles, taken by the troops in this action, which Major Percy will have the honour of laying at the feet of His Royal Highness. I beg leave to recommend him to Your Lordship's protection.

I have the honour to be, etc.

Wellington

TO EARL BATHURST

Brussels, June 19th, 1815

My Lord,

I have to inform Your Lordship, in addition to my despatch of this morning, that we have already got here five thousand prisoners, taken in the action of yesterday, and that there are above two thousand more coming in tomorrow. There will probably be many more.

Amongst the prisoners are the Comte de Lobau, who commanded the 6th corps, and General Cambronne, who commanded a division of the guards.

I propose to send the whole to England, by Ostend.

I have the honour to be, etc.

Wellington

MARSHAL BLUCHER'S OFFICIAL REPORT
OF THE OPERATIONS OF THE PRUSSIAN ARMY
OF THE LOWER RHINE

(The Marshal's account of the battle of Ligny is omitted, as, however interesting, it does not strictly belong to this work.)

On the 17th, in the evening, the Prussian army concentrated itself in the environs of Wavre. Napoleon put himself in motion against Lord Wellington upon the great road leading from Charleroy to Brussels. An English division maintained, on the same day, (16th) near Quatre-Bras, a very severe contest with the enemy. Lord Wellington had taken a position on the road to Brussels, having his right wing upon Braine-Lalleud, the centre near Mont St. Jean, and the left wing against La Haye Sainte. Lord Wellington wrote to the Field-Marshal, that he was resolved to accept the battle in this position, if the Field-Marshal would support him with two corps of his army. The Field-Marshal promised to come with his whole army; he even proposed, in case Napoleon should not attack, that the allies themselves, with their whole united force, should attack him the next day. This may serve to show how little the battle of the 16th had disorganized the Prussian army, or weakened its moral strength. Thus ended the day of the 17th.

Battle of the 18th

At break of day the Prussian army again began to move. The 4th and 2nd corps marched by St. Lambert, where they were to take a position, (covered by the forest, near Frischermont,) to take the enemy in the rear, when the moment should appear favourable. The first corps was to operate by Ohain, on the right flank of the enemy. The third corps was to follow slowly, in order to afford succour in case of need. The battle began about ten o'clock in the morning. The English army occupied the heights of Mont St. Jean; that of the French was on the heights before Planchenois: the former was about 80,000 strong; the enemy had above 130,000. In a short time, the battle became general along the whole line. It seems that Napoleon had the design to throw the left wing upon the centre, and thus to effect the separation of the English army from the Prussian, which he believed to be retreating upon Maestricht. For this purpose, he had placed the greatest part of his reserve in the centre, against his right wing, and upon this point he attacked with fury. The English army fought with a valour which it is impossible to surpass. The repeated charges of the old guard were baffled by the intrepidity of the Scottish regiments; and at every charge the French cavalry was overthrown by the English cavalry. But the superiority of the enemy in numbers was too great; Napoleon continually brought forward considerable masses; and, with whatever firmness the English troops maintained themselves in their position, it was not possible but that such heroic exertions must have a limit.

It was half-past four o'clock. The excessive difficulties of the passage by the defile of St. Lambert had considerably retarded the march of the Prussian columns, so that only two brigades of the 4th corps had arrived at the covered position which was assigned to them. The decisive moment was come; there was not an instant to be lost. The Generals did not suffer it to escape: they resolved immediately to begin the attack with the troops which they had at hand. General Büllow, therefore, with two brigades and a corps of cavalry, advanced rapidly upon the rear of the enemy's right wing. The enemy did not lose his presence of mind; he instantly turned his reserve against us, and a murderous conflict began on that side. The combat remained long uncertain, while the battle with the English army still continued with the same violence.

Towards six o'clock in the evening, we received the news that General Thielmann, with the 3rd corps, was attacked near Wavre by a very considerable corps of the enemy, and that they were already disputing the possession of the town. The Field-Marshal, however, did not suffer himself to be disturbed by this news; it was on the spot where he was, and nowhere else, that the affair was to be decided. A conflict continually supported by the same obstinacy, and kept up by fresh troops, could alone ensure the victory, and if it were obtained here, any reverse sustained near Wavre was of little consequence. The columns, therefore, continued their movements.

It was half an hour past seven, and the issue of the battle was still uncertain. The whole of the 4th corps, and a part of the 2nd, under General Pirch, had successively come up. The French troops fought with desperate fury: however, some uncertainty was perceived in their movements, and it was observed that some pieces of cannon were retreating. At this moment, the first columns of the corps of General Zieten arrived on the points of attack, near the village of Smohain, on the enemy's right flank, and instantly charged. This movement decided the defeat of the enemy. His right wing was broken in three places; he abandoned his positions. Our troops rushed forward at the *pas de charge,* and attacked him on all sides, while, at the same time, the whole English line advanced.

Circumstances were extremely favourable to the attack formed by the Prussian army; the ground rose in an amphitheatre, so that our artillery could freely open its fire from the summit of a great many heights which rose gradually above each other, and in the intervals of which the troops descended into the plain, formed into brigades, and in the greatest order; while fresh columns continually unfolded themselves, issuing from the forest on the height behind us. The enemy, however, still preserved means to retreat, till the village of Planchenoie, which he had on his rear, and which was defended by the guard, was, after several bloody attacks, carried by storm.

From that time the retreat became a rout, that soon spread throughout the whole French army, which, in its dreadful confusion, hurrying away everything that attempted to stop it, soon assumed the appearance of the flight of an army of barbarians. It was half-past nine. The Field-Marshal assembled all the superior officers, and gave orders to send the last horse and the last man in pursuit of the enemy.

The van of the army accelerated its march. The French, being pursued without intermission, were absolutely disorganized. The causeway presented the appearance of an immense shipwreck: it was covered with an innumerable quantity of cannon, caissons, carriages, baggage, arms, and wrecks of every kind. Those of the enemy who had attempted to repose for a time, and had not expected to be so quickly pursued, were driven from more than nine bivouacs. In some villages they attempted to maintain themselves; but as soon as they heard the beating of our drums, or the sound of the trumpet, they either fled, or threw themselves into the houses, where they were cut down, or made prisoners. It was moonlight, which greatly favoured the pursuit; for the whole march was but a continued chase, either in the cornfields, or the houses.

At Genappe, the enemy had entrenched himself with cannon and overturned carriages: at our approach, we suddenly heard in the town a great noise, and a motion of carriages; at the entrance we were exposed to a brisk fire of musketry: we replied by some cannon shot, followed by a *hurrah!* and an instant after, the town was ours. It was here that, among many other equipages, the carriage of Napoleon was taken: he had just left it to mount on horseback, and, in his hurry, had forgotten in it his sword and hat. Thus the affairs continued till break of day. About forty thousand men, in the most complete disorder, the remains of the whole army, have saved themselves, retreating through Charleroy, partly without arms, and carrying with them only twenty-seven pieces of their numerous artillery.

The enemy, in his flight, had passed all his fortresses, the only defence of his frontiers, which are now passed by our armies.

At three o'clock, Napoleon had despatched, from the field of battle, a courier to Paris, with the news that victory was no longer doubtful: a few hours after, he had no longer any army left. We have not yet an exact account of the enemy's loss; it is enough to know, that two thirds of the whole were killed, wounded, or prisoners: among the latter are Generals Mouton, Duhesme, and Compans. Up to this time, about three hundred cannon, and above five hundred caissons, are in our hands.

Few victories have been so complete; and there is certainly no example that an army two days after losing a battle, engaged in such an action, and so gloriously maintained it. Honour be to troops capable of so much firmness and valour!

In the middle of the position occupied by the French army, and exactly upon the height, is a farm called La Belle-Alliance. The march of all the Prussian columns was directed towards this farm, which was visible from every side. It was there that Napoleon was during the battle; it was thence that he gave his orders, that he flattered himself with the hopes of victory; and it was there that his ruin was decided. There, too, it was, that, by a happy chance, Field-Marshal Blücher and Lord Wellington met in the dark, and mutually saluted each other as victors. In commemoration of the alliance which now subsists between the English and Prussian nations, of the union of the two armies, and their reciprocal confidence, the Field-Marshal desired, that this battle should bear the name of La Belle-Alliance.

By order of Field-Marshal Blücher,

General Gneisenau

Paris
June 21st, 1815
Battle of Mont.-St. Jean
At nine in the morning, the rain having somewhat abated, the 1st corps put itself in motion, and placed itself with the left, on the road to Brussels, and opposite the village of Mont St. Jean, which appeared the centre of the enemy's position. The 2nd corps leaned its right upon the road to Brussels, and its left upon a small wood, within cannon-shot of the English army. The cuirassiers were in reserve behind, and the guards in reserve upon the heights. The 6th corps, with the cavalry of General Domont, under the order of Count de Lobau, was destined to proceed in rear of our right to oppose a Prussian corps, which appeared to have escaped Marshal Grouchy, and to intend to fall upon our right flank, an intention which had been made known to us by our reports, and by the letter of a Prussian General, enclosing an order of battle, and which was taken by our light troops.

The troops were full of ardour. We estimated the force of the English army at eighty thousand men. We supposed that the Prussian corps, which might be in line towards the right, might be fifteen thousand men. The enemy's force, then, was upwards of ninety thousand men; ours less numerous.

At noon, all the preparations being terminated, Prince Jérôme, commanding a division of the second corps, and destined to form the extreme left of it, advanced upon the wood of which the enemy occupied a part. The cannonade began. The enemy supported, with thirty pieces of cannon, the troops he had sent to keep the wood. We made also on our side dispositions of artillery. At one o'clock, Prince Jérôme was master of all the wood, and the whole English army fell back behind a curtain. Count D'Erlon then attacked the village of Mont St. Jean, and supported his attack with eighty pieces of cannon, which must have occasioned great loss to the English army. All the efforts were made towards the ridge. A brigade of the 1st division of Count D'Erlon took the village of Mont-St-Jean; a second brigade was charged by a corps of English cavalry, which occasioned it much loss. At the same moment, a division of English cavalry charged the battery of Count D'Erlon by its right, and disorganized several pieces; but the cuirassiers of General Milhaud charged that division, three regiments of which were broken and cut up.

It was three in the afternoon. The Emperor made the guard advance, to place it in the plain upon the ground which the first corps had occupied at the outset of the battle; this corps being already in advance. The Prussian division, whose movement had been foreseen, then engaged with the light troops of Count de Lobau, spreading its fire upon our whole right flank. It was expedient, before undertaking anything elsewhere, to wait for the event of this attack. Hence, all the means in reserve were ready to succour Count de Lobau, and overwhelm the Prussian corps when it should be advanced.

This done, the Emperor had the design of leading an attack upon the village of Mont St. Jean, from which we expected decisive success; but, by a movement of impatience so frequent in our military annals, and which has often been so fatal to us, the cavalry of reserve having perceived a retrograde movement made by the English to shelter themselves from our batteries, from which they suffered so much, crowned the heights of Mont St. Jean, and charged the infantry. This movement, which made in time, and supported by the reserves, must have decided the day, made in an isolated manner, and before affairs on the right were terminated, became fatal.

Having no means of countermanding it, the enemy showing many masses of cavalry and infantry, and our two divisions of cuirassiers being engaged, all our cavalry ran at the same moment to support their comrades. There, for three hours, numerous charges were made, which enabled us to penetrate several squares, and to take six standards of the light infantry, an advantage out of proportion with the loss which our cavalry experienced by the grape-shot and musket-firing. It was impossible to dispose of our reserves of infantry until we had repulsed the flank attack of the Prussian corps. This attack always prolonged itself perpendicularly upon our right flank. The Emperor sent thither General Duhesme with the young guard, and several batteries of reserve. The enemy was kept in check, repulsed, and fell back: he had exhausted his forces, and we had nothing more to fear. It was this moment that was indicated for an attack upon the centre of the enemy. As the cuirassiers suffered by the grape-shot, we sent four battalions of the middle guard to protect the cuirassiers, keep the position, and, if possible, disengage and draw back into the plain a part of our cavalry.

Two other battalions were sent to keep themselves *en potence* upon the extreme left of the division which had manoeuvred upon our flanks, in order not to have any uneasiness on that side; the rest was disposed in reserve, part to occupy the *potence* in rear of Mont St. Jean, part upon the ridge in rear of the field of battle, which formed our position of retreat.

In this state of affairs,, the battle was gained; we occupied all the positions which the enemy occupied at the outset of the battle: our cavalry having been too soon and ill employed, we could no longer hope for decisive success; but Marshal Grouchy, having learned the movement of the Prussian corps, marched upon the rear of that corps, which ensured us a signal success for next day. After eight hours' fire and charges of infantry and cavalry, all the army saw with joy the battle gained, and the field of battle in our power.

At half after eight o'clock, the four battalions of the middle guard, who had been sent to the ridge on the other side of Mont St. Jean, in order to support the cuirassiers, being greatly annoyed by the grape-shot, endeavoured to carry the batteries with the bayonet. At the end of the day, a charge directed against their flank, by several English squadrons, put them in disorder. The fugitives recrossed the ravine. Several regiments, near at hand, seeing some troops belonging to the guard in confusion, believed it was the old guard,, and in consequence were thrown into disorder. Cries of "All is lost, the guard is driven back!" were heard on every side. The soldiers pretend even that on many points ill-disposed persons cried out, *"Sauve qui peut."* However this may be, a complete panic at once spread itself throughout the whole field of battle, and they threw themselves in the greatest disorder on the line of communication: soldiers, cannoneers, caissons, all pressed to this point; the old guard, which was in reserve, was infected, and was itself hurried along.

In an instant, the whole army was nothing but a mass of confusion; all the soldiers, of all arms, were mixed pell-mell, and it was utterly impossible to rally a single corps. The enemy, who perceived this astonishing confusion, immediately attacked with their cavalry, and increased the disorder, and such was the confusion, owing to night coming on, that it was impossible to rally the troops, and point out to them their error. Thus a battle terminated, a day of false manoeuvres rectified, the greatest success ensured for the next day: all was lost by a moment of panic terror. Even the squadrons of *service,* drawn up by the side of the Emperor, were overthrown and disorganized by these tumultuous waves, and there was then nothing else to be done but to follow the torrent. The parks of reserve, the baggage which had not re-passed the Sambre, in short everything that was on the field of battle, remained in the power of the enemy. It was impossible to wait for the troops on our right; every one knows what the bravest army in the world is when thus mixed and thrown into confusion, and when its organization no longer exists.

The Emperor crossed the Sambre at Charleroy, at five o'clock in the morning of the 19th. Philippeville and Avesnes have been given as the points of reunion. Prince Jérôme, General Morand, and other Generals have there already rallied a part of the army. Marshal Grouchy, with the corps on the right, is moving on the lower Sambre.

The loss of the enemy must have been very great, if we may judge from the number of standards we have taken from them, and from the retrograde movements which he made; ours cannot be calculated till after the troops shall have been collected. Before the disorder broke out, we had already experienced a very considerable loss, particularly in our cavalry, so fatally, though so bravely engaged. Notwithstanding these losses, this brave cavalry constantly kept the position it had taken from the English, and only abandoned it when the tumult and disorder of the field of battle forced it. In the midst of the night, and the obstacles which encumbered their route, it could not preserve its own organization.

The artillery has, as usual, covered itself with glory. The carriages belonging to the headquarters remained in their ordinary position; no retrograde movement being judged necessary. In the course of the night they fell into the enemy's hands.

Such has been the issue of the battle of Mont St. Jean, glorious for the French armies, and yet so fatal.

Dinant

June 20th, 1815

It was not till after seven in the evening of the 18th of June, that I received the letter of the Duke of Dalmatia, (Soult,) which directed me to march on St. Lambert, and to attack General Bülow. I fell in with the enemy as I was marching on Wavre. He was immediately driven into Wavre, and General Vandamme's corps attacked that town, and was warmly engaged. The portion of Wavre, on the right of the Dyle, was carried: but much difficulty was experienced in debouching on the other side; General Gérard was wounded by a ball in the breast, whilst endeavouring to carry the mill of Bierge, in order to pass the river, but where he did not succeed; and Lieutenant-General Aix had been killed in the attack on the town. In this state of things, being impatient to cooperate with Your Majesty's army on that important day, I detached several corps to force the passage of the Dyle and march against Bülow. The corps of Vandamme, in the mean time, maintained the attack on Wavre, and on the mill, whence the enemy showed an intention to debouch, but which I did not conceive he was capable of effecting. I arrived at Limal, passed the river, and the heights were carried by the division of Vichery and the cavalry. Night did not permit us to advance farther, and I no longer heard the cannon on the side where Your Majesty was engaged.

I halted in this situation until daylight Wavre and Bierge were occupied by the Prussians, who, at three in the morning of the 19th, attacked in their turn, wishing to take advantage of the difficult position in which I was, and expecting to drive me into the defile, and take the artillery which had debouched, and make me re-pass the Dyle. Their efforts were fruitless. The Prussians were repulsed, and the village of Bierge taken. The brave General Penne was killed.

General Vandamme then passed one of his divisions by Bierge, and carried with ease the heights of Wavre, and along the whole of my line the success was complete. I was in front of Rosières, preparing to march on Brussels, when I received the sad intelligence of the loss of the battle of Waterloo. The officer who brought it informed me, that Your Majesty was retreating on the Sambre, without being able to indicate any particular point on which I should direct my march. I ceased to pursue, and began my retrograde movement. The retreating enemy did not think of following me.

Learning that the enemy had already passed the Sambre and was on my flank, and not being sufficiently strong to make a diversion in favour of Your Majesty, without compromising the troops under my command, I marched on Namur. At this moment, the rear of the columns were attacked. That of the left made a retrograde movement sooner than was expected, which endangered, for a moment, the retreat of the left; but good dispositions soon repaired everything, and two pieces which had been taken were recovered by the brave 20th dragoons, who, besides, took a howitzer from the enemy. We entered Namur without loss. The long defile which extends from this place to Dinant, in which only a single column can march, and the embarrassment arising from the numerous transports of wounded, rendered it necessary to hold for a considerable time the town, where I had not the means of blowing up the bridge. I entrusted the defence of Namur to General Vandamme, who, with his usual intrepidity, maintained himself there till eight in the evening; so that nothing was left behind, and I occupied Dinant.

The enemy has lost some thousands of men in the attack on Namur, where the contest was very obstinate; the troops have performed their duty in a manner worthy of praise.

De Grouchy

STRENGTH OF THE ALLIED ARMY AT WATERLOO AND ITS LOSSES						
Designation	Infantry	Cavalry	Artillery	Total	Guns	Killed, wounded missing
British	15,181	5,843	2,967	23,991	78	6,932
King's Ger. Legion	3,301	1,997	526	5,824	18	589
Hanoverians	10,258	497	465	11,220	12	1,602
Brunswickers	4,586	866	510	5,962	16	660
Nassauers	2,880			2,880		643
Dutch-Belgians	13,402	3,205	1,177	17,784	32	4,000
Total	49,608	12,408	15,645	67,661	156	14,426

British, killed and wounded, on the 16th, at Quatre-Bras: 2,504. On the 17th, in the retreat to the Waterloo position: 108. The greater number of the men (1,875) returned. as missing, had gone to the rear with wounded officers and soldiers, and joined afterwards. The officers are supposed kill. The names of British officers, killed and wounded, may be seen in the Appendix, No. IV.

PRUSSIAN FORCE AT WATERLOO, SOME OF WHICH BECAME ENGAGED TOWARDS THE CLOSE OF THE DAY				
			Artillery	
Arrived on the field	Infantry	Cavalry	Men	Guns
About half-past five o'clock p. m.	12,043	2,720	783	40
At three quarters after six	13,338		360	24
At a quarter before eight	15,902	6,138	660	40
Total	41,283	8,858	1,803	104
General total in the field	51,944 men			104
Loss at Waterloo, in killed, wounded and missing: 6,682 men				

			Artillery	
Designation	Infantry	Cavalry	Men	Guns
Imperial Guard	12,000	4,000	2,400	96
1st Corps	17,600	1,400	1,564	46
2nd Corps	15,760	1,865	1,861	38
6th Corps	6,600		1,007	30
3rd Cavalry Corps		3,300	300	12
4th Cavalry Corps		3,300	300	12
3rd Cavalry Division		1,400	150	6
5th Cavalry Division		1,250	150	6
Total	51,950	16,515	7,732	246
Deduct for previous losses	3,000	750	600	246
Under arms	48,050	15,765	732	
General total in the field	71,047 men			246

STRENGTH OF THE FRENCH ARMY IN THE FIELD AT WATERLOO

The French loss has been computed at nearly fifty thousand men during the campaign.

Of the French Generals, De Lobau (Mouton), Compans, Duhesme and Cambronne were made prisoners; and Girard, Devaux, Letort, Penne, Michel, Aix and Baudouin killed.

Perhaps we cannot arrive at a more accurate notion of the loss of the enemy than that conveyed by Ney, in his speech in the Chamber of Peers, four days after the battle, to which the reader's notice is drawn (chapter XI): "The guard was exterminated." And everybody knows that Napoleon always husbanded the guard, at the cost of all his other troops. The extermination of the guard implies then that the whole army was utterly routed.

The slaughter, in the absence of official reports, must be left to be computed by the sober judgment of the reader.

The French force detached under Grouchy to observe the Prussians amounted to thirty-two thousand men, and a hundred and four guns.

On the right, close to the Nivelles road, the Brunswick guns. Stretching towards the left, Major Bull's (howitzers), Captain N. Ramsey's, Major Webber Smith's, Captain Mercer's, Major Symper's (German), Captain Sandham's, Major Beane's batteries; and Captain Bolton's, at the angle between Adam's left and Mainland's right. Captain Sinclair's battery. Major Vandersmissen's batteries, at the interval between Halkett's brigade. Major Lloyd's, Major Sir H. Ross's batteries. Major Sir R. Gardner's battery, advancing. Major Whinyates' (rocket), Major Braun's (German), Major Rogers' batteries. A Dutch-Belgian battery. Major Rettberg's (German), just relieved by a Prussian battery. A Dutch-Belgian battery. Major Khulman's and Captain Cleeve's (German) batteries, advancing on the highroads, after refitting. Five Dutch-Belgian guns near Ditmers' brigade.

ARTILLERY TAKEN BY THE ALLIED ARMY AT WATERLOO	
12-pounder guns	35
6-pounder guns	57
6-inch howitzers	13
24-inch howitzers	17
Total guns	122
12-pounder spare gun-carriages	6
6-pounder spare gun-carriages	8
Howitzer spare gun-carriages	6
12-pounder wagons	74
6-pounder wagons	71
Howitzer wagons	50
Forge wagons	20
Imperial Guard wagons	52
General total	409
Exclusive of those taken by the Prussians, on the field and in the pursuit	

Our readers will give us credit for having observed a strict impartiality throughout our narrative of the battle; and in the same spirit would we desire to discuss those questions relating to it, which have given rise to so many false and exaggerated statements.

The first subject of controversy we shall notice, is the strange, but oft repeated charge, against Wellington's military judgment, in choosing his position in front of Mont St. Jean, with a forest in his rear, *in case of defeat*. I must be excused if I show some little indignation at the repetition of this charge; a British soldier must be allowed to be as jealous of the fame of his illustrious commander as our gallant opponents were of that of their idolized Napoleon. Well, what is the charge? That the Waterloo position was not well chosen for a retreat, having defiles and a wood in its rear.

We begin our examination of this point by remarking that Wellington chose the position, not in a hurry, nor because he was forced to do so, but most deliberately, and after having thoroughly reconnoitred it He chose it with the conviction that he could well maintain it, until the Prussians could form a junction with him; this accomplished, he knew that the French would not have a single chance left. He had but one apprehension; namely, that the enemy would push on by Hal, and turn the allied right. But Napoleon's holding us too cheap, his impetuosity, or his desperation, brought him headlong upon our chosen position: the very best for our purposes between Charleroy and Brussels. Let the event assist the impartial reader in deciding which commander showed the better judgment in selecting his ground for action. But as far as the Duke is concerned, it is quite unnecessary to say anything in his defence.

Nor should we have attempted to give a description of the Waterloo position, but for the judgment of Napoleon, at least as coming to us through the Generals De Montholon, Gourgaud, De Las-Cases, Mr. O'Meara, etc., being so directly at variance with that practically shown by the Duke of Wellington, who, we supposed, had previously both taken up and successfully defended too many positions, not to know the local requisites of a good one, and particularly as opposed to a French army. Waterloo was not fixed upon at the spur of the moment, as I have elsewhere shown; in addition to which, the Duke, his staff, and most of our Generals were so often over the ground before the battle, that the farmers complained of the damage done thereby to their crops.

It may be well to observe, for the information of those who are unacquainted with the position and localities, that the main-road from the field of Waterloo to Brussels is a very wide and well paved one. The road to the capital by Braine-Lalleud and Alsemberg is also paved. Several crossroads, in rear of our position, likewise traverse the forest of Soigne, and communicate with the highroad between this and Brussels. The trees of the forest, and the hedges, banks, and buildings on the sides of the roads, would have afforded excellent protection to light troops covering a retreat. Close in rear of the allied army and along the verge of the wood, was a most advantageous ridge, which might have offered an excellent second position, and from whence the guns could command everything within their range. The forest of Soigne itself, composed of lofty trees, afforded a shelter which resolute men could not be easily driven from: being nearly free from underwood, it was everywhere passable for broken infantry and cavalry, and from which no French force could have dislodged us, unless we willed it. When the Duke of Wellington, some years after the battle, was asked what he would have done, had he been driven from his position at Waterloo, His Grace replied, "I should have gone into the wood." The impartial opinion of the celebrated and able military writer Jomini may with propriety be here cited:

We have said that one of the essentials in a position is, that it should offer the means of retreat; which brings us to the consideration of a question created by the battle of Waterloo. Supposing an army to be posted in front of a forest, having a good road behind its centre and each of its wings; would it be compromised, as Napoleon asserts, in the event of its losing the battle? For my own part, I think, on the contrary, that such a position would be more favourable for retreating, than if the country were perfectly open; since a beaten army cannot traverse a plain without being exposed to the utmost danger. Doubtless, if the retreat should degenerate into a disorderly flight, a portion of the guns remaining in battery in front of the forest would probably be lost; but the infantry, the cavalry, and the rest of the artillery, would be able to retire with as much facility as across a plain. But if, on the contrary, the retreat takes place with order, nothing can possibly protect it better than a forest: provided always, there exist at least two good roads behind the lines; that the enemy be not allowed to press too close, before the requisite measures preparatory to retiring are thought of; and that no lateral movement shall enable the enemy to anticipate the army at the outlets from the forest, as happened at Hohenlinden. It would also greatly tend to secure the retreat, if, as was the case at Waterloo, the forest should form a concave line behind the centre; for such a bend would then become a regular *place d'armes*, in which to collect the troops and afford time to file them successively into the high road.[2]

General Jomini's doctrine, with the grounds on which it clearly rests, will have more weight with the honest reader, (be he a military man or a civilian, a Frenchman or an Englishman,) than the fond opinions of the admirers of Napoleon at St. Helena.

Let us now turn to the Duke of Wellington's plans and expectations, and we shall have ample evidence of his quick perception, consummate skill and unrivalled judgment.

---

2. Art of War, page 598.

The Duke was at Vienna at the moment the news reached him of Bonaparte's escape from Elba, and of his landing in France. The following letter records the first impressions made by this event in the Austrian capital, and the full conviction which Wellington immediately felt, that the enemy of Europe's peace would be speedily overthrown.

To Viscount Castlereagh, K. G.
Vienna
March 12th, 1815
My Lord,
I received here, on the 7th instant, a despatch from Lord Burghersh, of the 1st, giving an account that Bonaparte had quitted the island of Elba, with all his civil and military officers, and about twelve hundred troops, on the 26th of February. I immediately communicated this account to the Emperors of Austria and Russia, to the King of Prussia, and to the ministers of the different powers, and I found among all one prevailing sentiment, of a determination to unite their efforts to support the system established by the peace of Paris.

As it was uncertain to what quarter Bonaparte had gone, whether he would not return to Elba, or would even land on any part of the continent, it was agreed that it was best to postpone the adoption of any measure till his farther progress should be ascertained; and we have since received accounts from Genoa, stating that he had landed in France, near Cannes, on the 1st of March; had attempted to get possession of Antibes, and had been repulsed, and that he was on his march towards Grasse.

No accounts had been received at Paris as late as the middle of the day of the 6th, of his having quitted Elba, nor any accounts, from any quarter, of his farther progress.

In the mean time, the sovereigns, and all persons assembled here, are impressed with the importance of the crisis which this circumstance occasions in the affairs of the world. All are desirous of bringing to an early conclusion the business of the Congress, in order that the whole and undivided attention and exertion of all may be directed against the common enemy; and I do not entertain the smallest doubt that, even if Bonaparte should be able to form a party for himself in France, capable of making head against the legitimate government of that country, such a force will be assembled by the powers of Europe, directed by such a spirit in their councils, as must get the better of him.

The Emperors of Austria and Russia and the King of Prussia have despatched letters to the King of France, to place at His Majesty's disposal all their respective forces; and Austrian and Prussian officers are despatched with the letters, with powers to order the movement of the troops of their respective countries placed on the French frontiers, at the suggestion of the King of France.

The plenipotentiaries of the eight powers who signed the treaty of Paris, assembled this evening, and have resolved to publish a declaration, in which they will, in the name of their sovereigns, declare their firm resolution to maintain the peace and all its articles, with all their force, if necessary. I enclose the draught of what is proposed to be published, which, with the alteration of some expressions and the omission of one or two paragraphs, will, I believe, be adopted.

Upon the whole, I assure Your Lordship that I am perfectly satisfied with the spirit which prevails here upon this occasion; and I do not entertain the smallest doubt that, if unfortunately it should be possible for Bonaparte to hold at all against the King of France, he must fall under the cordially united efforts of the sovereigns of Europe.

I have the honour to be, etc.

Wellington

The Duke, though strongly urged by the allied sovereigns of Austria, Prussia and Russia to start for the Netherlands, remained in Vienna until he had completed his duties at the Congress, and received orders from England to take the command of the troops assembling in the Low Countries. He arrived at Brussels early in April. In less than twenty-four hours, he was master of the state of things, and immediately wrote the following despatch:

To General Kleist
Brussels
April 5th, 1815
General,
I arrived here during last night: I have spent the day in endeavouring to make myself master of the state of affairs.

The reports respecting the situation, number and the intentions of the enemy are always excessively vague: but it appears to me we ought to be prepared against a surprise *(coup de main)* which he might be tempted to try at any moment.

There can be no doubt that it would be an immense advantage to him to make us retrograde with the troops which we have in front of Brussels; to drive before him the King of France and the Royal family, and to compel the King of the Netherlands, with his establishments newly formed here, to make a retreat. This would be a terrible blow in public opinion, both here and in France: and, according to his usual management, *(allure,)* the news of his success would be known throughout France, whilst that of any reverse that might happen to him would be concealed from everybody.

After having placed 13,400 men as garrisons in Mons, Tournay, Ypres, Ostend, Nieuport and Antwerp, I can get together about 23,000 good troops, English and Hanoverian; amongst them about five thousand excellent cavalry. This number will be increased in a few days, especially in cavalry and artillery. I can also bring up 20,000 Dutch and Belgian troops, including two thousand cavalry; the whole having about sixty pieces of cannon.

My opinion is, that we ought to take measures to unite the whole Prussian army with this allied Anglo-Dutch army in front of Brussels; and that, with this view, the troops under Your Excellency's command should, without loss of time, march along the Maese, and take up cantonments between Charleroy, Namur and Huy.

By this disposition, we shall be sure to save this country, so interesting to the allied powers: we shall cover the concentration of their forces on the Rhine; and we shall escape the evils which would inevitably result from a sudden retreat in our actual circumstances. At the same time, Your Excellency would be just as able as you are in your present position, to march your troops to any point required by the service of the King; and we should have for our numerous cavalry a field of battle as favourable as any in the rear of Brussels.

I beg Your Excellency to take these reasons into consideration, and to let me know your determination; in order that I may decide what measures I ought to take in case I should be attacked, if Your Excellency should judge more fit to remain where you are.

I ought to apprize Your Excellency, that the King of the Netherlands has given orders for providing your troops with all they may want upon their advance into this country.

Wellington

My readers will remark in this letter the Duke's prompt decision on the importance of an immediate junction of a large Prussian force with the British allied army, and of protecting Brussels at all hazards. We shall see how much stress Napoleon laid upon keeping the British and the Prussians apart, and upon making a dash at Brussels. These two great commanders then took the same view: but the Duke's vigilance and energy baffled all Napoleon's exertions against the English allied army and the city of Brussels: the Prussians would have suffered less at Ligny, if the Duke's earnest entreaty for the earliest possible junction of the allies had been duly appreciated. Wellington also correctly anticipated, from the first moment, that Charleroy and its vicinity would probably be the point selected by Napoleon for his irruption into the Netherlands.

It seems from a letter dated 15th of April 1815, of the Duke to Gneisenau, that he had ascertained that two corps of the enemy, composed of 45,000 infantry and 7,200 cavalry, were in his front between the Sambre and the sea: he immediately set off to reconnoitre the whole frontier: this occupied him four days.

By reference to the "Secret Memorandum" in the Appendix to this work, it may be seen how prompt, energetic and comprehensive were the measures resolved upon by the Duke of Wellington. As early as the 30th of April, he wrote to Lord Uxbridge, "All the dispositions are so made that the whole army can be collected in one short movement, with the Prussians on our left."

One of Wellington's difficulties in preparing for the contest, was the motley character of some of the foreign troops placed, or offered to be placed, under his command. Some Saxon troops in particular drew from him very severe, but characteristic strictures and contempt, as appears from the subjoined documents:

To the Earl of Clancarty, G. C. B.
Brussels
May 3rd, 1815
The Saxons mutinied last night at Liege, and obliged poor old Blücher to quit the town; the cause of the mutiny was the order to divide the corps, and that the Prussian part, in which the guards were included, should take the oath of allegiance to the King of Prussia.

We hear of Bonaparte's quitting Paris, and of the march of troops to this frontier, in order to attack us. I met Blücher at Tirlemont this day, and received from him the most satisfactory assurances of support.

For an action in Belgium I can now put seventy thousand men into the field, and Blücher eighty thousand; so that, I hope, we should give a good account even of Bonaparte.

I am not satisfied with our delays.

Wellington

To Prince Hardenberg
Brussels, May 3rd, 1815
My Dear Prince,
I have received your letter of the 23rd of April, and I regret that there has been a difference of opinion about the troops to be sent to this army. I am perfectly indifferent as to whether I have many or few foreign soldiers under my orders, and as it appears that Prince Blücher and the Prussian officers are not disposed to let me be beaten by superior numbers, I am satisfied.

As to the Saxons, Your Highness will probably receive by this same opportunity the reports of their conduct yesterday evening: and as I have not enough of good troops to be able to detach any of them to watch a body of men disposed to mutiny, I think I shall do best in having nothing to do with such troops; and if they do not get out of the affair of last evening in an honourable manner, and consistently with the military character, in spite of my respect for the powers who have placed them at my disposal, I shall beg to decline taking them under my command.

Wellington

Writing to Sir Henry Hardinge, two days afterwards, the Duke observes that:

The Saxon troops, it is very obvious, will be of no use to anybody during the war; and our object must be to prevent them from doing mischief. . . . I do not think fourteen thousand men will have much weight in deciding the fate of the war. But the most fatal of all measures will be to have fourteen thousand men in the field who cannot be trusted; and who will require nearly as many more good troops to observe them.

These Saxon mutineers were, at the suggestion of the Duke, immediately sent off as prisoners, through Holland and Hanover, into Prussia, by the orders of Marshal Blücher. But for this foresight and determined maintenance of military discipline, much greater mischief would have ensued amongst certain contingents of the allied troops, who, as it was, by their doubtful attachment to the cause in which they were enlisted and un-soldierlike behaviour in the field, provoked many a hearty curse on the day of Waterloo.

CHAPTER 11

Afterword

What were Napoleon's plans, and how sanguine were his expectations, will be placed beyond all doubt by the following letter, written to the Prince de la Moskowa, the renowned Ney, who had joined the army but the day before, and by his proclamation addressed to the Belgians.

To the Prince de la Moskowa
Charleroy,
June 16th, 1815
Cousin,
I send you the present letter by my aide-de-camp, General Flahaut. The Major-General (Soult) must have already despatched orders to you, but you will receive these sooner, because my officers are faster than his. You will receive the General order of the day; but I wish to write to you in detail, because it is of the very highest importance.

I advance Marshal Grouchy with the third and fourth corps of infantry upon Sombreffe, and my guard upon Fleurus, where I shall be in person before midday. If I find the enemy there, I shall attack him, and drive everything before me as far as Gembloux. There I shall decide, according to the events of the morning, what is to be done. My decision will be made, perhaps at three o'clock, perhaps in the evening. My intention is, that the moment I have determined on my plan, you should be in readiness to march on Brussels. I will support you with the guard, which will be at Fleurus or at Sombreffe and I should like to reach Brussels tomorrow morning. You should set forward this evening, if I can form my plan in time for you to hear from me to-day, and you should march three or four leagues before night, and be in Brussels at seven tomorrow morning.

You can dispose of your troops in the following manner: One division two leagues in advance of Quatre-Bras, if there should be no obstacle: Six divisions of infantry about Quatre-Bras, and one division at Marbais, in order that I may have its assistance, should I want it, at Sombreffe; but this is not to delay your march: Count de Valmy's corps, which contains three thousand cuirassiers of elite, at the intersection of the Roman way with the Brussels road, in case I should need it; as soon as ever I have formed my plan, you will order this division to rejoin you.

I should like to have with me the division of the guard which is commanded by General Lefebvre-Desnouettes, and I send you in exchange the two divisions of Count de Valmy's corps. But, according to my plans at this moment, I prefer posting Count de Yalmy in such a manner as to have him within reach if I want him, and to avoid causing General Lefebvre-Desnouettes any false marches; for it is probable that I shall resolve upon marching with the guard this evening upon Brussels.

Nevertheless, cover Lefebvre's division by the two divisions of cavalry belonging to D'Erlon and Reille, in order to spare the guard; for if there should be any hot work with the English, it is better that it should be with our line than the guard.

I have adopted as a general principle of this campaign, to divide my army into two wings, and a reserve.

Your wing will consist of the four divisions of the first corps, of the four divisions of the second corps, of two divisions of light cavalry, and the two divisions of Count de Valmy's corps. The number of these troops cannot be much less than forty-five or fifty thousand men. Marshal Grouchy will have nearly an equal number, and will command the right wing. The guard will form the reserve, and I shall bring it up in support of the one wing or the other, according to circumstances. The Major-General will issue the most precise orders, in order to secure obedience to you, when you have a separate command: whenever I am present, the commanders of corps will receive orders directly from me. I shall draw troops, according to circumstances, from either wing, to strengthen my reserve.

You well understand the importance attached to *the taking of Brussels*. It may also produce important results; for a movement of such promptitude and daring will cut off the English troops at Mons, Ostend, etc.

I wish your measures to be so taken, that, at the first order, your eight divisions may be able to march rapidly on Brussels, without any difficulty.

Napoleon

PROCLAMATION TO THE BELGIANS AND INHABITANTS
OF THE LEFT BANK OF THE RHINE[1]

The ephemeral success of my enemies detached you for a moment from my Empire: in my exile upon a rock in the sea, I heard your complaints. The God of

---

1. A large quantity of these proclamations was found amongst the Imperial baggage.

battles has decided the fate of your beautiful provinces; Napoleon is among you. You are worthy to be Frenchmen. Rise in mass, join my invincible phalanxes, to exterminate the remainder of those barbarians, who are your enemies and mine; they fry with rage and despair in their hearts.

Napoleon

By the Emperor:

The Major-General of the army,

Count Bertrand

At the Imperial Palace of Laeken

Little comment need be made upon this letter and proclamation. They are characteristic of Napoleon. A most able plan of operations is developed with his usual recklessness of human life: we see him prepared to sacrifice his troops of the line to save his guard; and either wing, that with the other he might make a dash at Brussels.

His overweening confidence of being there even early on the 17th, and his sanguine expectations that the population would support him, are clearly shown by the above documents.

Napoleon must evidently have miscalculated the degree of energy and promptitude necessary to overcome two such Generals as Wellington and Blücher. He sadly underrated the gallant troops which he and his Marshals had to combat And when adverse writers talk so much of Wellington being taken by surprise in this campaign, we may venture to ask, was not Napoleon taken by surprise and thrown out in all his calculations by the extreme vigilance and energy which brought three corps of the Prussian army, above eighty-five thousand men, into position at Ligny by mid-day on the 16th? And but for an error in the transmission of orders, these troops would also have been joined by Bülow's corps; and had General Zieten sent information to General Müffling or to the Duke of Wellington at Brussels, when the French army in three columns was first seen in his front in advance of Charleroy, the whole allied army might have been concentrated at Quatre-Bras during the night of the 15th.

Wellington in person was at Ligny on the 16th; observing Napoleon preparing for battle, and after conferring with Blücher, he returned to Quatre-Bras in time to give a most critical check to the gallant Ney. Was it no surprise to Napoleon to find that Wellington, upon hearing of Blücher's retreat from Ligny, instead of falling back to Ostend, etc., immediately retired with ominous steadiness upon Mont-St-Jean? and there arrested the ambition of his opponent, who, instead of being at Brussels early on the 17th, as intimated to Ney, was compelled to open his eyes, on the morning of the 18th, to the fact that he was still above twelve miles from Brussels, and unable to advance a step nearer without fighting a desperate battle, and staking his empire on the result.

He did fight; the stake was lost, and, by the next morning, he found himself again at Charleroy, whence he had despatched his memorable letter to his "cousin" Ney but two days before. He must have felt an agony of *surprise* and something more, as he fled on for his very life, to escape from his enraged pursuers.

M. de Vaulabelle indeed, in his *Campaign and Battle of Waterloo*, published at Paris in 1845, (Brussels, 1849,) attributes the non-arrival of Napoleon at Brussels, to his having calculated that the Prussians would not assemble in any great force until the 17th, and further on the author says: "Napoleon's plans and arrangements were frustrated and his sanguine expectations disappointed, on finding a barrier of ninety-five thousand Prussians assembled between him and the Belgian capital." The above author also informs us, that a longer delay on the 16th, in executing his projected movements at Ligny, would have compromised his success on that day; and that on the 17th, fresh delays succeeded those of the two preceding ones.

Ney's troops, although the Marshal, it is pretended, received orders to renew the attack on Quatre-Bras at break of day, were still in bivouac at eleven o'clock. We are given to understand by M. de Vaulabelle, that similar delays occurred to different corps placed under the direct command of the Emperor and Marshal Grouchy. We are also told that "the soldiers grumbled considerably, questioned their officers, and interrogated their Generals;" in fact, to use the author's words, "All energy and activity seemed to have taken refuge in their ranks." The inhabitants of St. Amand also affirm that, on a group of Generals passing through the village, the soldiers followed them with their cries, "We made our soup at break of day in order to be sooner at the ball, and we have been four hours doing nothing; why don't we fight? There is something underhand."

In face of all these discrepant statements, and upon calm reflection and close examination of the history of the battle of Waterloo, Napoleon's disasters should not be attributed to the neglect or disobedience of his Generals, but, under Providence, to the consummate bravery of the troops, and the skill of the Generals opposed to him.

Napoleon, when at St. Helena, admitted that the tactics of his army in the Waterloo campaign had their defects; but on no occasion, to my knowledge, did he admit that he had himself committed an error. He invariably endeavoured to shift all blame, more especially the irretrievable failure at Waterloo, to other shoulders than his own, to those of his Marshals. He accused Grouchy, the well-tried soldier in many a hard-fought field, and who was banished for his attachment to the Imperial cause, of having, by neglect, delay and non-compliance with orders, occasioned his defeat at Waterloo; and Grouchy's alleged raise movement is the basis of every argument advanced by those who yet maintain the military infallibility of their idolized Napoleon.

One would imagine, from the tenor of Napoleon's order

of the day on the 14th of June, "Soldiers! we have forced marches to make, battles to fight, dangers to encounter," that he would not have allowed the precious hours of the morning of the 16th to be frittered away in inactivity, or have left his troops until near eleven o'clock in the bivouac of the night before, chiefly where they crossed the Sambre, *viz*, at Charleroy, Châtelet and Marchiennes, without making a movement to support his advanced troops at Frasnes and Fleuras. No doubt the French were fatigued and wanted rest; but, as the success of the campaign depended upon vigorously pressing forward, and making the most of the first advantages, there was no time for rest.

Again, on the 17th, after the battles of Quatre-Bras and Ligny, we find Napoleon lingering on the field of Ligny, visiting the wounded, and expressing his satisfaction at witnessing the gallantry of his troops; we find him discussing with Gérard and Grouchy subjects in no way connected with the campaign, and which should decree him Emperor or exile; we find it to be near one o'clock p. m. (17th,) before he put his own force in motion to join Ney in pursuit of us, or before he gave Grouchy his orders to pursue the Prussians.

Early in the morning, Pajol's cavalry and Teste's infantry divisions were detached towards Namur, in pursuit of the Prussians; and, strange to say, when, after capturing a Prussian battery on the Namur road, and sending it to the Imperial headquarters, they found themselves completely baffled and at fault, they returned to their bivouac of the preceding night near Mazy, and lay there till next morning, the 18th.

The Prussians, after their line had been broken at Ligny on the 16th about nine o'clock, were allowed to retreat upon Wavre unmolested; nor did Grouchy, who was subsequently ordered by Napoleon "to follow the Prussians and not to let them out of his sight, to complete their defeat by attacking them and prevent their effecting a junction with the allies," know by what route the main Prussian army had retreated, until the afternoon of the 17th; and Grouchy's advance-guard did not come up with the Prussian rear till half-past ten a. m. of the 18th, when three out of the four Prussian corps were already on their march to join us: of this Grouchy knew nothing; so far from it, he believed he had the whole Prussian army before him.

If it be objected to Grouchy, that he did not act up to the letter or the spirit of his instructions, we affirm that it was impossible for him to do so, the delay in giving him his orders having enabled the Prussians to gain fourteen hours start of him.

This fact the Marshal communicated to the Emperor, who replied that he, with the rest of his army, was about to follow the English and give them battle, should they take position in front of the forest of Soigne, directing Grouchy to communicate with him by the paved road of Quatre-Bras: but not a word about his joining in his attack on the English. Napoleon followed us by the paved road to La Belle-Alliance: Grouchy followed the Prussians by crossroads to Gembloux, about six miles, where he halted for the night, and wrote to Napoleon; receiving the following answer from Soult:

Farm of Caillot
Ten o'clock a. m. June 18th, 1815
I am directed by the Emperor, to acquaint you that he is going to attack the English who are in line of battle in front of Waterloo, near the forest of Soigne. His Majesty directs you will move upon Wavre, to be nearer to us, to report your operations, to keep up a communications etc.

Again, not one word about marching to assist the Emperor: and here we may observe that Wavre is not in the direction of Mont St. Jean. When, however, at one o'clock, Napoleon found that Wellington was not to be trifled with, and that a Prussian corps was hovering upon his right flank, he despatched another order:

Field of battle, Waterloo

One o'clock p. m. June 18th, 1815

Monsieur le Maréchal,

You wrote from Gembloux this morning at two o'clock, informing the Emperor, you were about to march to Sartlez-Walhain. His Majesty now directs you will manoeuvre in *our* direction; you must find out the point, in order to keep up the communication, and be at hand to fall upon and destroy any enemy that may attempt to attack our right. At this moment we are engaged in battle on the line of Waterloo, the enemy's centre is Mont St. Jean; so manoeuvre to join our right without loss of time.

The Adjutant-General

Duke of Dalmatia

P. S.—An intercepted letter informs us that the Prussian General Bülow is about to attack our right flank; we think we see the corps on the heights of St. Lambert; so approach us without losing an instant, and destroy Bülow, should you catch him in the fact.

The order was in itself no doubt sound and judicious; but the original vice we have already alluded to, as characterizing the movements of the French army after the passage of the Sambre, rendered obedience impossible. The letter, written at one o'clock, did not reach Grouchy until seven, before which time Napoleon's right had been attacked and driven back by Büllow's advanced brigades.

It was half-past seven o'clock a. m. on the 18th of June, when Grouchy moved from his bivouac at Gembloux, and, owing to the bad state of the roads, nearly half-past eleven, before he reached Sartlez-Walhain, a distance of about six miles.

At the latter place, the report of a heavy cannonade was distinctly heard in the direction of Waterloo: Grouchy was strongly urged by some of his Generals to march towards the firing; and for not doing so, he has been attacked at all points.

He declined the proposition of his Generals, on the ground that he did not consider it his duty to march towards the battle already raging elsewhere, but to attack, according to his instructions, the Prussians with whom he had just come up.

Grouchy has since declared, that he did not consider it his duty to follow the advice of Gérard and the other Generals, and that to have done so would have been acting contrary to his orders. To have detached a portion of his force towards the main French army would have separated his two corps by the Dyle river, whose waters were much swollen by the heavy rains, and whose banks were so swampy, that it would have been impossible for his divisions to have mutually supported each other; consequently he continued his march upon Wavre.

For argument's sake, we will suppose that Grouchy adopts the advice of his Generals, and commences his march at the time the firing was first heard, about half-past twelve o'clock. On average roads in fair condition, an army of thirty-two thousand men of all arms would take seven hours to march fifteen miles; they had already marched about six miles, as we have seen, over bad roads. From Sartlez-Walhain to Planchenois, Napoleon's right, the distance is about sixteen miles, and over bad roads; how could they have come up in time, and that, without taking into account the obstructions which they must have encountered from the Prussian corps who were scouring the whole of that part of the country? It was utterly impossible for Grouchy, after breaking up his bivouac at Gembloux at so late as half-past seven o'clock on the morning of the 18th, to prevent the three Prussian corps, who well knew his movements, from forming a junction with us, or from attacking the French right.

Had Grouchy left Gembloux at two o'clock a. m., and marched by St. Guibert and Moustier to St. Lambert, and taken position near the defiles of the Lasne and St. Lambert, he might have kept Bulow from attacking the French right, and

Napoleon might, before eight o'clock, about which time a brigade of Pirch's and part of a brigade of Zieten's corps came up, have attacked Wellington with his whole remaining force.

After the unaccountable delay on the 17th, the division of his force by Napoleon appears a false move; for a corps of cavalry would have sufficed to watch the Prussians. Grouchy, unquestionably, was dilatory, and wanting in his former energy and judgment; for though he must have known that the Prussians, or a large portion of them, would attempt their junction with us, he sent out no patrols to ascertain whether the contemplated movement was in operation, and neglected to keep up a close communication, so essential, with the main body of the French army. His whole attention appears to have been directed to his right; the events on his left he seems to have neglected.

We have stated Napoleon's anxiety to impute the blame of the failure exclusively to his two Marshals. We have endeavoured, in the fair and fearless spirit of military criticism, to examine how far such inculpation is borne out by facts in the case of Marshal Grouchy, and we now, in the same impartial manner, propose to analyze the accusation made against the gallant and daring Ney, "the bravest of the brave." The charges are twofold: delay at Quatre-Bras, and rashness at Waterloo.

Ney had been ordered by Napoleon, on the morning of the 16th, to seize Quatre-Bras, to occupy Genappe if practicable, and to be ready to march on Brussels the same evening, (16th,) or the morning of the 17th at latest, as the seizure of the capital by a *coup de main* on the 17th was the Emperor's grand object. For this purpose Ney was, if possible, to press forward three or four leagues at least, on the 16th, and to be supported by the light cavalry of the Imperial Guard.

Now, Ney is blamed by Napoleon and other military writers (French,) for not having gained possession of Quatre-Bras early on the 16th, before our force came up. Certainly no British soldier underrates the value of an early attack: (as Aroyo-de-Molinos can testify:) but was Ney justified in attempting to obtain possession of Quatre-Bras? We incline to think he was not. More than one half of his force was still in the rear: D'Erlon's corps was on the Sambre, or close to it, Girard's division of Reille's corps was near Fleurus with Grouchy, and Kellermann's cavalry had not joined. No blame to him, the gallant Ney, for *that;* he had joined the army but the evening before, (the 15th.) Notwithstanding these untoward events, he ordered forward Reille's (second) corps; but finding that heavy masses of the enemy were concentrating at St. Amand on his right, and ignorant of the force in his front, he judiciously declined to press on till D'Erlon came up as a support.

Napoleon, before he left Charleroy, sent another order to Ney to unite his force, (Reille's and D'Erlon's corps, and Kellermann's cuirassiers who were about to join him,) remarking, "With this force you ought to overwhelm any strength the enemy may oppose to you." When Ney commenced his attack on Quatre-Bras he was cautious. Napoleon had now arrived at Fleurus, and sent word to Ney, that Grouchy would attack the Prussians at half-past two o'clock; that he, Ney, was to press vigorously upon any enemy in his front, and then turn round and assist in crushing the Prussians at Ligny.

About three o'clock, Ney got another despatch, informing him that the battle of Ligny had already begun, directing him to manoeuvre *immediately,* so as to fall upon the Prussian rear with all his force, which would be utterly destroyed if he acted with vigour, adding, in his own emphatic language addressed to a heart so susceptible and patriotic as Ney's, "The fate of France is in your hands!" But that which pre-eminently characterized Napoleon's early career, that to which he almost exclusively owed his brilliant victories, that in which all men of all nations will admit his wonderful excellence—rapidity in executing his plans—here again failed him. Lightning may slumber but *time* will ceaselessly march on, heedless of the errors of heroes! The Emperor's delay enabled our noble Picton, with his gallant band, to come up from Brussels, closely followed by the Brunswickers, headed by their cherished and chivalrous Duke, who found Waterloo to be his last battlefield. Such foes occupied Ney: and Napoleon knew it not!

Observe, Napoleon (who, according to French historians, could not err,) entrusting the fate of France to a flank movement by Ney, who was unable ultimately to hold his own position! He accuses Ney of having kept Reille's and D'Erlon's corps detached, saying, "Had he united them, not an Englishman would have escaped at Quatre-Bras;" and yet it was by Napoleon's *own* order, (in a pencilled note,) conveyed by Colonel Laurent, that Ney was ordered to detach D'Erlon's corps to St. Amand! Laurent, falling in with the head of the column then marching on Frasnes, upon his own responsibility changed its direction. On inquiring for Count D'Erlon, he was informed that, as was his habit, he had gone ahead to Frasnes, preceding his column. On his arrival at the latter place, Laurent found the General, and handed over to him the pencilled note, stating, at the same time, the position in which he might find the head of his column.

At this moment General Delcambre, chief of the staff of the 1st (D'Erlon's) corps, arrived to acquaint D'Erlon of the change in the line of march. Ney, who was at this time hard pressed by Wellington himself, sent back Delcambre with peremptory orders to D'Erlon to return to Quatre-Bras: but *ere the order could reach D'Erlon,* he was close to St. Amand, and consequently at too great a distance to return *in time* to render assistance to Ney.

Could Ney therefore be made responsible for the absence of D'Erlon's corps, its change of direction, or this assumed want of vigour consequent on either?

It is evident from the tenor of the despatch from Napoleon at two o'clock on the 16th, addressed to Ney at Gosselies, that Napoleon did not imagine that the Marshal had left Gosselies *at that hour,* much less that he had attacked us. Where now was Ney's delay when, with a *fraction* of his force, (three divisions of Reille's corps,) he attacked us at Quatre-Bras?

This proves the fallacy of the assertions contained in the *Mémoires Historiques de Napoléon,* and something perhaps stronger than fallacies in Gourgaud's *Campaign of 1815.* In these Ney is assailed for not attacking us *early* in the morning of the 16th. We, however, will not leave the posthumous fame of the gallant Ney to be sacrificed to Imperial infallibility. We assert that Ney, on the 16th, did all, and attempted more at Quatre-Bras than circumstances warranted; we assert that if he failed in his attempt, (*viz.* of occupying Quatre-Bras,) his failure is to be, so far as Ney and his force are concerned, ascribed to British bayonets, and not to any want of skill, daring or rapidity on the part of Ney,[2] or to any want of gallantry, or deadly devotion on the part of the brave troops of Reille, Piré and Kellermann.

We arrive now to the different versions which have been published of the battle of Waterloo, and which issued from St. Helena. How much credit should be attached to these accounts, may be judged by the following extracts from the able work entitled *The Military Life of the Duke of Wellington:*[3]

It may perhaps be remarked, that we have attached little authority to the accounts of this campaign which emanated from St. Helena. The writer of this portion of the present work had the honour of being intimately acquainted with some of the persons composing Napoleon's suite at Longwood; and although he has reason to believe the volumes

---

2. It is notorious that Ney was one amongst the last who quitted the scene of carnage; it is also certain, we had our hands full to wrest victory from the French. Had all Napoleon's Generals acted with the same energy, gallantry and constant audacity as Ney did on his last field, our day's work would have been more troublesome, and riot so many of us left to tell the tale. As a soldier, I am sorry that both Ney and the Emperor did not die a soldier's death at. Waterloo.
3. *Military Life of the Duke of Wellington,* by Major Basil Jackson and Captain Rochport Scott; page 609, vol. II.

given to the world with the names of Generals De Montholon and Gourgaud prefixed to them to be genuine; that is, that they were prepared from Napoleon's notes and dictation; yet, he conceives, he has equal reason for rejecting them as testimony. An officer of Bonaparte's establishment told him at Longwood, that the termination of the battle of Waterloo had occasioned the utmost perplexity amongst them; and that he himself, having been employed by the ex-Emperor to write an account of the campaign, had presented no less *thaw six* distinct modes of ending the battle, all of which had been rejected.

Ab uno diêce omits.

Various accounts of the battle that subsequently emanated from St. Helena, Grouchy characterizes as containing "supposed instructions and orders, imaginary movements, etc., deductions made after the event." I will not trouble my readers with any further remarks upon accounts so destitute of truth. Gourgaud's account, dictated by Napoleon himself, is, for the most part, indignantly and completely refuted by Marshal Grouchy as a mere "military romance."

From this trait of history-making, we may judge of the rest of the accounts that were concocted in the ever fertile imagination of Napoleon. His utter disregard of truth was part of his policy; and if, for a time, it enabled him to deceive a high-minded and gallant people, amongst whom the liberty of the press had been annihilated, in the end it contributed to his ruin, nearly as much as did the bravery and perseverance of his victorious opponents. Why did we meet him at Waterloo? We were not at war with France, with its legitimate sovereign, or with the French people. But we were at war with Napoleon: he had been declared *hors la loi* (outlawed) by civilized Europe;[4] the idol indeed of a fine army, but a man devoid of truth and principle, whom no

---

4. *See* Gurwood, vol. XII, p. 852.

treaties could bind, and whose restless ambition was utterly incompatible with the peace of Europe.

His chief aim was to obtain universal dominion, and his inordinate love of glory made him conceive the chimera of a universal monarchy, of which he was to be the chief. Few have denied him to have been an able and daring commander, gifted with great military talents; and the Duke of Wellington never hesitated in affirming, that of all the chiefs of armies in the world, the one in whose presence it was most hazardous to make a false movement was Napoleon.[5]

It was against this man, and not against France, that Wellington uniformly declared he was leading his troops: in a letter dated June 4th, 1815, the Duke said:

> France has no enemies, as far as I know: I am sure that she does not deserve to have any. We are the enemies of one man only, and of his partisans, of him who has abused his influence over the French army, to overthrow the throne of the King, in order to subjugate France, and then to bring back to all of us the days of misery which we thought were gone by. . . . Our state then ought not to be called one of war with France, but of war on the part of all Europe, comprising therein France herself, against Napoleon and against his army, whose bad conduct is the cause of all the evils which are going to happen, and which we all deplore.[6]

The triumph and the vanity,
The rapture of the strife,
The earthquake voice of victory
To him the breath of life;
The sword, the sceptre and the sway,
That man seem'd born but to obey.

Lest our neighbours may think this view of Napoleon's

---

5. *Quarterly Review,* No. LXX, page 478.
6. See Gurwood, vol. XII, page 441.

character drawn by English prejudice, and as not affording sufficient reasons for the determination of Wellington to aim solely at his destruction, and with a steadiness of resolve not to be turned aside till complete success attended the efforts of the allies, I beg to record the following character of Napoleon, and his iron rule over the French people. It will be observed that this character was drawn by the pen of Frenchmen, proclaimed by French authorities, and placarded by them on all the walls of Paris, whose inhabitants knew too well the facts on which the proclamation was founded. The General and municipal Council of Paris thus addressed the people, the year before the battle of Waterloo:

You owe all the evils which overwhelm you to one man, to him who every year, by the conscription, decimates your families. Who amongst us has not lost a brother, a son, relatives, friends? And why have all these brave men fallen? For him alone, and not for the country. In what cause have they fallen? They have been immolated to the mad ambition of leaving behind him the name of the most dreadful oppressor that ever weighed on the human race. . . . It is he that has closed against us the seas of the two worlds. To him we are indebted for the hatred of the people of all nations, without having deserved it; for like them we have been the unhappy victims as well as the sad instruments of his madness. What matters it that he has sacrificed but few to his private hatred, if he has sacrificed France—we should not say, France only, but all Europe, to his boundless ambition? Look at the vast continent of Europe, everywhere strewed with the mingled bones of Frenchmen, and people with whom we had no disputes, no causes of mutual hatred, who were too distant from us to have any cause of quarrel, but whom he precipitated into all the horrors of war, solely that the earth might be filled with the noise of his name. Why boast of his past victories? What good have those dreadful triumphs brought us? The hatred of other nations, the tears of our families, our daughters forced to remain unmarried, our matrons plunged into premature widowhood, the despair of fathers and mothers, to whom there remains, out of a numerous progeny, but the hand of an infant to close their eyes: behold! these are the results of all those victories, which have brought foreign armies within our very walls. . . . In the name of our most sacred duties, we abjure all obedience to the usurper; we return to our legitimate rulers.[7]

"How just," adds a French historian, "are these accusations, although they were made by men who a little before had been prodigal of flattery and incense to the author of all these public calamities."[7]

With such a man as Napoleon is here described, whose towering military genius no one can call in question, and whose influence had so long, and so fatally fascinated the gallant French people, whose eyes were at length opened to the real character of his rule, it must not be wondered at, that we went to war; nor should our triumph over him ever be regarded as a triumph over the French nation: between that high-minded people and the rest of the civilized world, may the peace, which is already of unexampled duration, and which we bought so dearly, continue for ever!

I may here present to the reader the sentiments of a noble and distinguished writer, who had long been near Napoleon and had closely watched his career. On hearing of his arrival at St. Helena, this French statesman and scholar gave the following commentary to the world. No one who is acquainted with the writings of Chateaubriand will suspect him of any bias towards the British character: yet he wrote thus of our vanquished foe:

---

7. *Histoire de Napoléon,* par A. Gabourd, pages 345, 346.

The bloody drama of Europe is concluded, and the great tragedian, who for twenty years has made the earth his theatre, and set the world in tears, has left the stage for ever! He lifted the curtain with his sword, and filled the scenes with slaughter. His part was invented by himself, and was terribly unique. Never was there so ambitious, so restless a spirit; never so daring, so fortunate a soldier. His aim was universal dominion, and he gazed at it steadfastly with the eye of the eagle, and the appetite of the vulture.

He combined within himself all the elements of terror, nerve, malice and intellect; a heart that never trembled, a mind that never wavered from its purpose. The greatness of his plans defied speculation, and the rapidity of their execution outstripped prophecy. Civilized nations were the victims of his arts, and savages could not withstand his warfare. Sceptres crumbled in his grasp, and liberty withered in his presence. The Almighty appeared to have entrusted to him the destinies of the globe, and he used them to destroy. He shrouded the sun with the clouds of battle, and unveiled the night with his fires. His march reversed the course of nature: the flowers of the spring perished, the fruits of autumn fell; for his track was cold, and cheerless, and desolate, like the withering, wintry blast. Amid all the physical, moral and political changes which he produced, he was still the same. Always ambitious, always inexorable; no compassion assuaged, no remorse deterred, no dangers alarmed him. Like the barbarians, he conquered Italy, and rolling back to its source the deluge that overwhelmed Rome, he proved himself the Attila of the South. With Hannibal, he crossed the Alps in triumph; Africa beheld in him a second Scipio, and standing on the Pyramids of Egypt, he looked down on the fame of Alexander. He fought the Scythian in his cave, and the unconquered

Arab fled before him. He won, and divided, and ruled nearly all modern Europe. It became a large French province, where foreign kings still reigned by courtesy, or mourned in chains. The Roman pontiff was his prisoner, and he claimed dominion over the altar with the God of hosts. Even his name inspired universal terror, and the obscurity of his designs rendered him awfully mysterious. The navy of Great Britain watched him with the eye of Argus, and her coast was lined with soldiers who slept on their arms. He made war before he declared it; and peace was with him a signal for hostilities. His Mends were the first whom he assailed, and his allies he selected to plunder. There was a singular opposition between his alleged motives and his conduct. He would have enslaved the land to make the ocean free, and he wanted only power to enslave, both.

If he was arrogant, his unparalleled successes must excuse him. Who could endure the giddiness of such a mountain elevation? Who, that amid the slaughter of millions had escaped unhurt, would not suppose, that a deity had lent him armoury like Achilles? Who, that had risen from such obscurity, overcame such mighty obstacles, vanquished so many monarchs, won such extensive empires, and enjoyed so absolute a sway? Who, in the fullness of unequalled power and in the pride of exulting ambition, would not believe himself the favourite of Heaven?

He received the tribute of fear, and love, and admiration. The weight of the chains which he imposed on France was forgotten in their splendour: it was glorious to follow him, even as a conscript. The arts became servile in his praise; and genius divided with him her immortal honours. For it is mind alone that can triumph over time. Letters only yield permanent renown.

This blood-stained soldier adorned his throne with the trophies of art, and made Paris the seat of taste as well as of power. There, the old and the new world met and conversed; there, Time was seen robbed of his scythe, lingering among beauties which he could not destroy; there, the heroes and sages of every age mingled in splendid alliance, and joined in the march of fame. They will appeal to posterity to mitigate the sentence which humanity claims against the tyrant Bonaparte. Awful indeed will be that sentence; but when will posterity be a disinterested tribunal? When will the time arrive that Europe shall have put off mourning for his crimes? In what distant recess of futurity will the memory of Moscow sleep? When will Jena, Gerona, and Austerlitz, when will Jaffa, Corunna, and Waterloo be named without tears of anguish and vows of retribution? Earth can never forget, man can never forgive them.

Let him live, if he can endure life, divested of his crown, without an army, and almost without a follower. Let him live, he, who never spared his friends, if he can withstand the humiliation of owing, his life to an enemy. Let him live, and listen to the voice of conscience. He can no longer drown it in the clamorous report of war. No cuirass guards his bosom from the arrows of remorse. Now that the cares of state have ceased to distract his thoughts,, let him reflect on his miserable self; and, with the map before him, retrace his bloody career. Alas! his life is a picture of ruin, and the light that displays it in the funeral torch of nations. It exhibits one mighty sepulchre, crowded with the mangled victims of murderous ambition. Let him reflect on his enormous abuse of power, on his violated faith, and shameless disregard of all law and justice.

Let him live, and repent; let him seek to atone in humility and solitude for the sins of his political life, an example of the catastrophe of the wicked, and the vanity of false greatness. Great he unquestionably was, great in the resources of a misguided spirit, great in the conception and execution of evil; great in mischief, like the pestilence; great in desolation, like the whirlwind.

From the equivocal loyalty to the common cause of many of the troops in the allied army, and the severity of the contest, we were not so surprised as we were vexed, to see them skulk away, and make for Brussels, or seek shelter in the woods. Our numbers were greatly reduced by this sort of defection, long before the close of the battle. General Müffling estimates the runaways at ten thousand, (far below the real number.) Of course, such heroes would invent narratives and retail them in their dishonourable flight, in order to cover themselves from the reproaches and contempt richly merited by such un-soldierly behaviour. A gallant officer records a fact in point:

Having been sent before daylight, on the morning after the battle, to communicate the Duke's orders for his army to move on Nivelles. . . . I had an opportunity of witnessing how disgraceful had been the conduct of many of the foreign troops. I saw thousands making their way to the front, who had quitted their colours during the battle and fled to the forest. The commanding officer of a cavalry regiment showed me a hundred and forty men, stating that his loss in the battle had reduced it to that number. I believe this regiment was not engaged; for very nearly the original complement of eight hundred men were forthcoming a few days after! The Duke degraded it, by turning it over to the commissariat to furnish escorts.[8]

Some there were who wore the British uniform, who took advantage of the duty of carrying the wounded to the rear,

---

8. *Military Life of Wellington,* by Major Basil Jackson and Captain R. Scott, vol. II, page 604.

and did not return to their duty on the field. This circumstance has been pitiably exaggerated, and even distorted into a tale that the British Generally were flying off to Brussels when the Prussians came up.

The Duke of Wellington, in his General order, issued at Nivelles, two days after the battle, thus noticed the conduct of those who had improperly absented themselves from their colours:

> 3. The Field-Marshal has observed that several soldiers, and even officers, have quitted their ranks without leave, and have gone to Brussels, and even some to Antwerp; where, and in the country through which they have passed, they have spread a false alarm, in a manner highly unmilitary, and derogatory to the character of soldiers.
>
> 4. The Field-Marshal requests the General officers commanding divisions in the British army, and the General officers commanding the corps of each nation of which the army is composed, to report to him in writing what officers and men—the former by name—are now, or have been, absent without leave since the 16th.[9]

It may not be out of place to offer a few General remarks on some points in which the public have felt much interest, and upon which opinions have greatly differed.

It is certain that the Duke of Wellington would not have accepted battle at Waterloo, had he not been sure of the cooperation of the Prussians; and the loss which they sustained during the short time they were engaged, proves the value of that cooperation.

The diversion of the Prussians diminished the French force against us, by Count de Lobau's corps, eleven battalions of the Imperial Guard, and eighteen squadrons of cavalry, amounting to above fifteen thousand men and sixty-six guns. It is evident that the blow, which decided the fate of

---

9. See General Orders, in Gurwood's *Selections from Despatches,* page 865.

the day, was given by the Duke when he defeated the Imperial Guards, attacked the French reserves, and forced their centre: by this, D'Erlon's columns were turned on their left, and Reille's on their right: then followed the General advance of Wellington's whole line.

With the splendid light cavalry force Napoleon had at his command, and Grouchy, detached with thirty-two thousand men of all arms, it is a remarkable fact, that the first intimation Napoleon had of the advance, upon his right, of the Prussians, whom Grouchy was sent expressly to watch, was seeing them himself at St. Lambert, about one o'clock on the 18th, from his position above La Belle-Alliance.

Notwithstanding the numerous charges made by the French cavalry, not one of them was made upon our left wing; nor was their cavalry of the right wing put in motion, till the ardour of our heavy cavalry carried them upon the French position, when their lancers, cuirassiers and dragoons were let loose upon our broken and disordered cavalry, who suffered severely.

D'Erlon's infantry columns, and the last two attacking columns of the Imperial Guard were entirely unsupported by cavalry, or they never could have been so closely pursued, and so roughly handled.

The French army under Napoleon was composed almost exclusively of veterans, men inured to and whose trade was war, and whose battles equalled in number their years; all of one nation, devoted to him and his cause, most enthusiastic, and well equipped: in fact the finest army Napoleon ever brought into the field, many of whom the year before had been liberated from the English, Russian and Austrian prisons: a more gallant army, or one more complete in every respect, never stood before us.

We were, on the contrary, an army of different nations. Our foreign auxiliaries, who constituted more than half our numerical strength, with some exceptions, were little better than a raw militia: a body, but no soul; or like an inflated pillow that yields to the touch, and resumes its shape again when the pressure ceases.

It would not perhaps be out of place if we now notice an assertion of French, and even of English writers; namely, that the Duke of Wellington was taken by surprise at the commencement of this campaign.

Surely the French must laugh in their sleeves when they find English writers credulous enough to print statements which have originated in the lively imaginations of our neighbours, and to be found supporting the assertion that the Duke depended upon receiving from such a man as Fouché, information of Napoleon's arrival in Belgium, and likewise of his plan of operations. We find a very late writer quoting even Fouché, to prove what he advances. One would imagine such authors were perfectly ignorant of the contents of the Duke's twelfth volume of the *Despatches*, or of Fouché's reputation, or else that they denied His Grace the possession of common prudence, to entrust the safety of his army, and thereby the interests of Europe, to an ignoble police-spy, whose memory is justly despised by every Frenchman.

In reply to the unfounded statement that Wellington relied on any information coming from that arch traitor and lump of duplicity, it is sufficient to give the following extract from a letter in the Duke's *Despatches*, (vol. XII, page 649,) addressed to Dumouriez:

Avant mon arrivée à Paris, au mois de juillet, je n'avais jamais vu Fouché, ni eu avec lui communication quelconque, ni avec aucun de ceux qui sont liés avec lui.

(Before my arrival in Paris, in July, I had never seen Fouché, nor had I had any communication with him, nor with any one connected with him.)

Of the French movements the Duke had timely information from a very different source. I was told by Sir Hussey

Vivian, when he visited the field in 1839, that he was aware on the 13th of June, of the French being concentrated and ready to attack; and that he reported the circumstance to the Duke: this is corroborated in Siborne's history, at page 49, vol. I: these are undoubted authorities.

Those who have attentively followed the Duke in his operations during this campaign, or referred to his correspondence, will find that, for weeks before, His Grace had foreseen Napoleon's intentions and made deliberate arrangements to render them unavailing. The allied army was so cantoned by Wellington, that its divisions could be promptly united when the demonstrations of Napoleon should be sufficiently developed. The admirable organization of the allied army, effected by the Duke so shortly after he took the command, must have struck my readers: it is evident he was at once the mainspring, directing head, and very soul of the grand European coalition; and it could only be a just confidence in the admirable plan he had drawn up for the conduct of the allied troops, that dictated the letter addressed to Sir Henry Wellesley, June 2nd, 1815, and which expresses the following very remarkable anticipation of coming events:

> . . . . We have as yet done nothing here. . . . Towards the 16th, I hope we shall begin. I shall enter France with between seventy and eighty thousand men; the Prussians near me, with twice as many.[10]

This document was penned a fortnight before the action at Quatre-Bras, where we began work in earnest, as the Duke had anticipated, exactly on the 16th. This fact, of itself, should suffice to stop the mouths of those who delight in telling us that Wellington was taken by surprise. There were moments indeed, when he thought that Napoleon's ambition might be so far controlled by common prudence, as to be content with remaining within the boundaries

---

10. See Gurwood, *Despatches,* vol. XII, page 488.

of France, and leaving the odium of acting aggressively to the allied powers; and in such moments, the Duke spoke and wrote of awaiting for the combined movements of the Austrians and Prussians. But not for a single instant did he lose sight of the possibility, nay probability, that Bonaparte would begin offensive operations, rush across the borders, and make a dash to seize the person of Louis XVIII, or to get possession of the city of Brussels. Against these contingencies, how early and how ably our great chieftain provided, let facts, and not the dreams of mortified narrators, inform the world.

On the 6th, 7th, and 10th of June, the Duke despatched letters to the Prussian headquarters, informing them that the enemy was in great strength about Maubeuge, where Bonaparte was said to be on the 9th, and thence to have gone along the frontiers towards Lille; and that an attack was to be forthwith expected.[11]

With this intelligence received by Wellington, and actively circulated by him among all who were exposed to be attacked by the French, how was it possible that he should be taken by *surprise?* Every movement of the enemy was quickly known to him; and his characteristic vigilance, and matured judgment, enabled him to foretell the very time and place of the grand attack. All that depended on him was in perfect readiness, several days before fighting began. If the Prussians were unaccountably remiss in not forwarding to His Grace earlier intelligence of the descent of the enemy into Belgium, it was not for want of watchfulness on the part of the Duke; *he* was quite awake. Let the reader turn to the Appendix of this work, (No. I,) for proof that Wellington was not easily to be surprised, but that he had all his forces so well in hand on the 30th of April, that they could march at a moment's notice, and unite at any point really attacked.

In reply to the assertion made by French, and even by

---

11. See Gurwood, *Despatches,* vol. XII, pages 449, 463, 457.

Prussian official writers, that "Blücher and his troops saved the allied army," it may be observed: the battle of Waterloo must be always considered as a battle fought by the right wing of an army, for the purpose of maintaining a position until the arrival of the Prussians, its left wing, should render victory certain. The safest tactics, in the Duke's opinion, were to act entirely on the defensive, and he had, in consequence, thoroughly matured his arrangements with Blücher for mutual support. The Duke, therefore, was not only justified in receiving battle, but had every reason to expect to have been reinforced several hours before the Prussians came up, and Waterloo might have terminated with much less sacrifice of life, and as decisively at three, as it afterwards closed at eight o'clock. But even admitting, for a moment, that the arrival of the Prussians saved us at Waterloo, we undoubtedly saved them by holding our position until they came up. Had we given way before they cleared the defiles of St. Lambert, they would have been annihilated; of this they were aware, as our readers will be convinced on reference to the letters from the Prussian to the allied headquarters.[12]

But facts are stubborn things, and it is doubtful whether Napoleon could have driven the British from the ground, even if the Prussians had not arrived. The English troops had maintained their position for eight hours against the most experienced army and the ablest General ever France sent into the field; not a British regiment was broken, nor the allied army in a panic, nor, at any time, in serious danger of being penetrated. Further, even if the Prussians had not arrived, we are inclined to think that Napoleon could not, in the exhausted and dispirited condition of his troops, and the lateness of the hour, have driven the British from their ground. His cavalry was nearly annihilated: while three brigades of British infantry, one of the King's German Legion, and two brigades

12. See Appendix, No. V.

of British cavalry,[13] had, except in the loss sustained by the 27th regiment, and 12th dragoons, suffered but comparatively little; many of the foreign troops had not fired a shot: and after the arrival of Vivian and Vandeleur, the *British* cavalry were, as our readers have seen, masters of the field.

The junction of the Prussians was a part of Wellington's combinations for the battle. Their flank movement at Waterloo was similar to Desaix's from Novi to Marengo; with this no small difference, that upon Bülow's troops joining, they found the allied army firm and unbroken, and rather in advance of their position of the morning:[14] when Desaix joined Bonaparte, he was in full retreat, one wing of his army destroyed, and obliged to change his whole front to save the rest from destruction; this eventually gave him the victory. We are not astonished that the French should employ this argument as a balm to their disappointment, but it comes with a peculiar bad grace from the Prussians. Surely, in thus taking the lion's share in this glorious victory, they do not think to cover their defeat at Ligny, or their unaccountable delay in arriving on the field of Waterloo.

The roads were very bad, and the Prussians had a numerous artillery, not over-well horsed. Yet supposing them to have been put in motion at eight o'clock in the morning, (their official account says *break of day,*) they were ten or eleven hours in marching little more than a like number of miles! May we not therefore be allowed to conjecture that there was some hesitation on the part of Blücher in marching upon Waterloo, until he could feel assured of his army being in little danger from Grouchy.[15]

---

13. 4th,27th,40th,(Lambert's);52nd,71st,95th,(Adam's);14th,23rd,61st,(Mitchel's); 1st, 2nd, 3rd and 4th line of the German Legion, (Duplat's); with Vivian's 10th, 18th, and 1st hussars, and Vandeleur's 11th, 12th, and 16th light dragoons.
14. At the time the Prussians first became engaged, Duplat's Germans, a part of Halkett's Hanoverians, with Adam's brigade, altogether above five thousand bayonets, stood in their advanced position, between the orchard of Hougoumont and where the Lion now stands.
15. Jackson and Scott's *Life of the Duke of Wellington.* See Appendix, No. V.

And if true, as the Prussian official report represents, that Blücher had such a large force on the field to act, previous to, or during Napoleon's last attack upon us, why did not Blücher, to use the language of two excellent military writers, roll up the French army as Pakenham's division did at Salamanca? I have often thought that if Lord Hill, by any means, could have been transferred across the field to where Bülow debouched, with the same force of British troops as he had of Prussian (30,000) under his command, our illustrious Chiefs table that night might have been honoured by the presence of Napoleon and his chief officers, and most of the French army favoured with a free passage to England.

> There can exist no doubt whatever that, paradoxical as it may at first sight appear, the cooperation, though somewhat tardy, of the Prussians, produced, *not the defeat,* but the total rout of Bonaparte's army: for the Duke of Wellington could not, weakened as his force was at the close of the day, have hazarded an attack with his whole army, had Blücher not been at hand to support the movement. The service rendered by our brave allies was therefore most opportune, and of the highest value. . . . An error of half an hour—and men do not consult their watches during the excitement of battle—made either by the Prussians or ourselves, is sufficient to account for much of the discrepancy existing between their statements and our own.[16]

That English and Prussian writers should altogether agree as to the apportionment of the glory of the day, was not to be expected. It is clear, to the lasting honour of the two allied nations, that whatever feelings may have since grown up on this subject, none interfered at the time with the cordiality of their combined operations. The following lines, from a Prussian pen, will show that just national pride is not inconsistent with candour:

---

16. Lieutenant-Colonel B. Jackson, *Military life of Wellington,* vol. II, page 806.

Upon the question, who really fought and won the battle of the 18th, no discussion, much less contention, ought to have arisen. Without in the slightest degree impeaching the just share of Prussia in the victory, or losing sight for a moment of the fact that she bore a great share of the danger, and drew much of it from her allies and upon herself at a decisive moment, no unprejudiced person can conceal from himself that the honour of the day is due to the Anglo-Netherlandish army, and to the measures of its great leader. The struggle of Mont St. Jean was conducted with an obstinacy, ability, and foresight of which history affords few examples. The great loss of the English also speaks the merit of their services. More than seven hundred officers, among them the first of their army, whether in rank or merit, and upwards of ten thousand soldiers, fell, or retired wounded from the field.[17]

No one unacquainted with war can form the most distant idea of the weak state and disorganization to which even a victorious army is reduced by a long, trying, severe day's battle. The number of men absent from the ranks is incredible, and long continued excitement has nearly exhausted the rest.

Although we place little reliance on statements which have originated from St. Helena, yet we must be excused if we quote O'Meara, whose conversations with the Emperor have been faithfully given to the world. They contain several allusions to the battle of Waterloo, and attest the Emperor's conviction of the completeness of our victory over him, and the hopelessness of all his plans, as well as his utter despair before he quitted the field. What other honest interpretation can be given to these words:

I ought to have died at Waterloo; but, as ill luck will

---

17. *Geschichte des Preussischen Staates,* 1768-1815; Frankfort, 1880; vol. III, page 374.

have it, when you seek death you cannot meet with it. There were numbers killed close to me, before, behind, on every side of me; but there was no bullet for me!

Why should a man desire to be struck down, if, as the fond tale goes amongst some of his indiscriminate admirers, he had thrice won the battle of Waterloo? He desired death, because he saw that all his resources were gone, and that the British, notwithstanding the day's dreadful carnage, were coming on, with irresistible force, to deal the decisive blow.

The same author relates several facts connected with the battle of Waterloo, communicated to him by General Gourgaud, under Napoleon's roof. These are the General's words, as written down at the time, August 23rd, 1817:

At the close of the battle of Waterloo, and after the unsuccessful charge of the French, the English cavalry which charged in return, approached within two or three hundred yards of the spot where Napoleon was, with none about him but Soult, Drouot, Bertrand, and Gourgaud himself. At a short distance from them was a small French battalion, that had formed square. Napoleon directed General Gourgaud to order two or three field-pieces belonging to this battalion to be fired, in order to arrest the cavalry which was coming on. The order was executed, and one of the balls wounded Lord Uxbridge in the leg. Napoleon put himself at the head of the column, exclaiming, "Here we must die! we must die on the field of battle!"

Let us observe, that Napoleon must, at this moment, have felt himself beaten, and that his conquerors were the British, to whom, as the most noble of his enemies, he paid the compliment, wishing to die by our hands rather than by those of the Prussians, who were advancing on his right, ready enough to gratify his wish. But, to continue General Gourgaud's account:

At the very instant that Napoleon was desirous of making a charge with the handful of men left about him, the English light infantry was gaining ground. Labédoyère galloped round them, sword in hand, seeming to court a glorious death on the field of honour. We prevented Napoleon from rushing into the midst of the enemy. It was Soult who seized his horse by the bridle, and said, "They will not kill you: you will be taken prisoner;" and that General, with the assistance of a few others who gathered round, prevailed on Napoleon to fly from the field of battle.

We have often, throughout this discussion, quoted several of our opponents: let us now give two great authorities on every question connected with the field of Waterloo, *viz.* the Duke of Wellington and Lord Hill. It is also a conversation, but related by B. R. Haydon Esq.[18]

When Sir Walter Scott was at Paris in 1816, he was permitted to ask, and he did put the following questions, at His Grace's table, relating to Waterloo, and I repeat them as Sir Walter detailed them to me at my own:

"Suppose, Your Grace, Blücher had not come up?"

The Duke replied, "I could have kept my ground till next morning."

"Suppose Grouchy had come first?"

"Blücher would have been close behind him."

"But let us suppose, Your Grace had been compelled to retreat."

"I could have taken position in the forest of Soigne, and defied all till the allies joined."

"Was a there any part of the day when Your Grace despaired?"

"Never," was the reply.

This was the reply of the first in command. In 1833,

18. United Service Magazine, February 1844, page 281.

the writer of this letter dined at Lord Palmerston's; on his right sat Lord Hill. As His Lordship lived near the author, he offered to set him down. When alone in the carriage with Lord Hill, remembering what Sir Walter had affirmed of the Duke's confidence, he said, "Was there any part of the day at Waterloo, my Lord, you ever desponded as to the result?"

"Desponded!" replied Lord Hill, "never: there never was the least panic; we had gained rather than lost ground, by the evening. No, there was not a moment I had the least doubt of the result."

In conclusion, and as a final answer to the depredators of British valour, we offer them the speech of the celebrated Ney, uttered in the Chamber of Peers four days after the battle, and which is, perhaps, of the French accounts the most worthy of attention, and too remarkable to be omitted on the present occasion.

When the peers were assembled, Carnot gave them a flaming account of Grouchy's admirable retreat from Wavre, at the head, the minister said, of sixty thousand men; of Soult's success in collecting together twenty thousand of the old guard; of new levies from the interior, with two hundred pieces of cannon. Ney, highly incensed at these mischievous untruths, and keenly suffering from the injustice done to him in Napoleon's bulletins, started up, and declared Carnot's statement to be utterly false:

Will they dare to assert before eyewitnesses of the disastrous day of the 18th, that we have yet sixty thousand soldiers embodied? Grouchy cannot have under him above twenty or five-and-twenty thousand soldiers, at the utmost. Had he possessed a greater force, he might have covered the retreat, and the Emperor would still have been in command of an army on the frontiers. Not a man of the guard will ever rally more. I myself commanded them; I myself witnessed their total extermination, ere I left the field of battle: they are annihilated. The enemy are at Nivelles with eighty thousand men; they may, if they please, be at Paris in six days. There is no safety for France, but in instant propositions for peace.[19]

This speech opened the eyes of all Paris to the facts, and prepared the entry of the allies into France, almost without striking a blow. It was truly, like my pages, a voice from Waterloo, and is the last testimony we shall present to the reader, in refutation of the tale, that we were beaten before the arrival of the Prussians. It was not against the latter that the devoted Ney led the Imperial Guard, nor were they by the Prussians annihilated; they were defeated on no other spot but the allied position on the field of Waterloo.

19. See Ney's letter, Appendix, No. V.

Appendices

Appendix I

Secret Memorandum for:
H. R. H. the Prince of Orange,
the Earl of Uxbridge, Lord Hill and
the Quartermaster-General

Brussels
April 29th, 1815

1. Having received reports that the Imperial Guard had moved from Paris upon Beauvais, and a report having been for some days prevalent in the country that Bonaparte was about to visit the northern frontier, I deem it expedient to concentrate the cantonments of the troops, with a view to their early junction in case this country should be attacked, for which concentration the Quartermaster-General now sends orders.

2. In this case, the enemy's line of attack will be either between the Lys and the Scheldt, or between the Sambre and the Scheldt, or by both lines.

3. In the first case, I should wish the troops of the 4th division to take up the bridge on the Scheldt, near Avelghem, and with the regiment of cavalry at Courtray, to fall back

upon Audenarde, which post they are to occupy, and to inundate the country in the neighbourhood.

4. The garrison of Ghent are to inundate the country in the neighbourhood likewise, and that point is to be held at all events.

5. The cavalry in observation between Menin and Fumes are to fall back upon Ostend, those between Menin and Tournay upon Tournay, and thence to join their regiments.

6. The 1st, 2nd, and 3rd divisions of infantry are to be collected at the headquarters of the divisions, and the cavalry at the headquarters of their several brigades, and the whole to be in readiness to march at a moment's notice.

7. The troops of the Netherlands to be collected at Soignies and Nivelles.

8. In case the attack should be made between the Sambre and the Scheldt, I propose to collect the British and Hanoverians at and in the neighbourhood of Enghien, and the army of the Low Countries at and in the neighbourhood of Soignies and Braine-le-Comte.

9. In this case, the 2nd and 3rd divisions will collect at their respective headquarters, and gradually fall back towards Enghien, with the cavalry of Colonel Arentschildt's, and the Hanoverian brigade.

10. The garrisons of Mons and Tournay will stand fast; but that of Ath will be withdrawn, with the 2nd division, if the works should not have been sufficiently advanced to render the place tenable against a *coup de main.*

11. General Sir William Ponsonby's, Sir J. Vandeleur's, and Sir Hussey Vivian's brigades of cavalry, will march upon Hal.

12. The troops of the Low Countries will collect upon Soignies and Braine-le-Comte.

13. The troops of the 4th division, and the 2nd hussars, after taking up the bridge at Avelghem, will fall back

upon Audenarde, and there wait for further orders.

14. In case of the attack being directed by both lines supposed, the troops of the 4th division, and 2nd hussars, and the garrison of Ghent, will act as directed in Nos. 3 and 4 of this Memorandum; and the 2nd and 3rd divisions, and the cavalry, and the troops of the Low Countries, as directed in Nos. 8, 9, 10,11, and 12.

Wellington

MEMORANDUM FOR:
COLONEL SIR WILLIAM DE LANCEY
DEPUTY QUARTERMASTER-GENERAL

Movements of the Army

Brussels

June 15th, 1815

General Dornberg's Brigade of Cavalry, and the Cumberland Hussars, to march this night upon Vilvorde, and to bivouac on the highroad near to that town.

The Earl of Uxbridge will be pleased to collect the cavalry this night at Ninove, leaving the 2nd Hussars looking out between the Scheldt and the Lys.

The 1st division of infantry to collect this night at Ath and adjacent, and to be in readiness to move at a moment's notice.

The 3rd division to collect this night at Braine-le-Comte, and to be in readiness to move at the shortest notice.

The 4th division to be collected this night at Grammont, with the exception of the troops beyond the Scheldt, which are to be moved to Audenarde.

The 5th division, the 81st regiment, and the Hanoverian brigade of the 6th division, to be in readiness to march from Brussels at a moment's notice.

The Duke of Brunswick's Corps to collect this night on the highroad between Brussels and Vilvorde.

The Nassau troops to collect at daylight tomorrow morning on the Louvain road, and to be in readiness to move at a moment's notice.

The Hanoverian Brigade of the 5th division to collect this night at Hal, and to be in readiness at daylight tomorrow morning to move towards Brussels, and to halt on the highroad between Alost and Assche for further orders.

The Prince of Orange is requested to collect at Nivelles the 2nd and 3rd divisions of the army of the Low Countries; and, should that point have been attacked this day, to move the 3rd division of British infantry upon Nivelles, as soon as collected.

This movement is not to take place until it is quite certain that the enemy's attack is upon the right of the Prussian army, and the left of the British army.

Lord Hill will be so good as to order Prince Frederick of Orange to occupy Audenarde with five hundred men, and to collect the 1st division of the army of the Low Countries, and the Indian brigade, at Sotteghem, so as to be ready to march in the morning at daylight.

The reserve artillery to be in readiness to move at daylight.

Wellington

INSTRUCTIONS FOR THE MOVEMENT OF THE ARMY ON JUNE 16TH

Signed by Colonel Sir William De Lancey, Deputy Quarter-Master-General
To General Lord Hill
June 10th, 1816
The Duke of Wellington requests that you will move the 2nd division of infantry upon Braine-le-Comte immediately. The cavalry has been ordered likewise on Braine-le-Comte. His Grace is going to Waterloo.

To the same
June 16th, 1815
Your Lordship is requested to order Prince Frederick of Orange to move, immediately upon the receipt of this order, the 1st division of the army of the Low Countries, and the Indian brigade, from Sotteghem to Enghien, leaving five hundred men, as before directed, in Audenarde.

To the same
Genappe
June 16th, 1815
The 2nd division of infantry to move tomorrow morning at daybreak from Nivelles to Quatre-Bras.
The 4th division of infantry to move at daybreak tomorrow morning to Nivelles.

June 16th, 1815
The reserve artillery to move at daybreak tomorrow morning, the 17th, to Quatre-Bras, where it will receive further orders.

To Major-General Sir J. Lambert
June 16th, 1816
The brigade of infantry under the command of Major-General Sir J. Lambert, to march from Assche at daybreak tomorrow morning, the 17th inst., to Genappe, on the Namur road, and to remain there until further orders.

Appendix II

The reader will observe that the letters from which I make the following extracts, were written at three o'clock in the morning of the battle.

To Sir Charles Stuart

Waterloo
June 18th, 1815, three o'clock a. m
My Dear Stuart,
. . . .You will see in the letter to the Duc de Berry the real state of our case, and the only risk we run. The Prussians will be ready again in the morning for anything.

Pray keep the English (in Brussels) quiet, if you can. Let them all prepare to move, but neither be in a hurry nor a fright, as all will yet turn out well.

I have given the directions to the governor of Antwerp, to meet the *crotchets* which I find in the heads of the King's governors upon every turn. . . .
Wellington

Waterloo

June 18th, 1810, three o'clock in the morning

Sir,

I have not written to Your Royal Highness since Thursday, as I had nothing to communicate.... and I have had a great deal to do.

We had a very sanguinary battle on Friday last, near the farm of Quatre-Bras; the Prussians, about Sombreffe. I had very few troops with me, and no cavalry: I however drove the enemy back, and had considerable success. The Prussians suffered a good deal, and retreated during the night; and in consequence I retired also during the day. I saw very little yesterday of the enemy, who followed us very gently, and the Prussians not at all. The Prussians have been joined by their fourth corps, more than thirty thousand strong, and I have also nearly all my men together.

It may happen that the enemy will turn us by Hal, although the weather is terrible and the roads are in a shocking state, and although I have posted Prince Frederick's corps between Hal and Enghien. If this should happen, I beg Your Royal Highness to march on Antwerp.... and to inform His Majesty (Louis XVIII,) that I beg him to leave Ghent for Antwerp by the left of the Scheldt. He will find no difficulty in crossing at the *Tête de Flandre,*

.... I hope, and I have every reason to believe, that all will turn out well; but we must take every possible precaution, and avoid great losses. It is with this view, that I beg Your Royal Highness to follow the directions here given, and His Majesty to make for Antwerp, not upon false reports, but upon certain information that the enemy has got into Brussels, in spite of me, in turning me by Hal. ...

Wellington

The following letters, written just after the battle, will show how deeply the Duke felt the loss of his companions in arms: the renown his success would ensure was no consolation to him for the loss of friends and heroes: patriotism, and the confident expectation that an effectual stop was at length put to the horrors which had desolated Europe for more than twenty years, were the sources of such comfort as he could feel himself, or offer to others, for the expenditure of so many valuable lives.

To the Earl of Aberdeen

Brussels
June 19th, 1815
My Dear Lord,
You will readily give credit to the existence of the extreme grief with which I announce to you the death of your gallant brother, (Colonel Gordon,) in consequence of a wound received in our great battle of yesterday.

He had served me most zealously and usefully for many years, and on many trying occasions; but he had never rendered himself more useful, and had never distinguished himself more, than in our late actions.

He received the wound which occasioned his death, when rallying one of the Brunswick battalions which was shaking a little; and he lived long enough to be informed by myself of the glorious result of our actions, to which he had so much contributed by his active and zealous assistance.

I cannot express to you the regret and sorrow with which I look round me, and contemplate the loss which I have sustained, particularly in your brother. The glory resulting from such actions, so dearly bought, is no consolation to me, and I cannot suggest it as any to you and his friends; but I hope that it may be expected that this last one has been so decisive, as that no doubt remains that our exertions and our individual losses will be rewarded by the early attainment of our just object. It is then that the glory of the actions in which our friends and relations have fallen, will be some consolation for their loss.

Believe, me, etc.

Wellington

Your brother had a black horse, given to him, I believe by Lord Ashburnham, which I will keep till I hear from you what you wish should be done with it.

To the Duke of Beaufort

Brussels
June 19th, 1815
My Dear Lord,
I am very sorry to have to acquaint you that your brother Fitzroy is very severely wounded, and has lost his right arm. I have just seen him, and he is perfectly free from fever, and as well as anybody could be under such circumstances. You are aware how useful he has always been to me, and how much I shall feel the want of his assistance, and what a regard and affection I feel for him; and you will readily believe how much concerned I am for his misfortune. Indeed, the losses I have sustained have quite broken me down; and I have no feeling for the advantages we have acquired. I hope, however, that your brother will soon be able to join me again; and that he will long live to be, as he is likely to become, an honour to his country, as he is a satisfaction to his family and friends.

Believe, me, etc.

Wellington

Joncourt
June 26th, 1815

. . . . Our battle on the 18th was one of giants; and our success was most complete, as you perceive. God grant I may never see another! for I am overwhelmed with grief at the loss of my old friends and comrades.

My neighbour and fellow-labourer (Blücher) is in good health, though he suffers a little from the fall of a horse, wounded under him in the battle of the 16th. . . .
Wellington

The following extracts will prove the early and complete conviction of the Duke, that all had been decided at Waterloo.

To General Dumouriez

Nivelles
June 20th, 1815

. . . . You must have heard what I have done; and I hope you are satisfied. I never saw such a battle as the one the day before yesterday; and never before did I gain such a victory. I trust it is all over with Bonaparte. We are in hot pursuit of him. . . .
Wellington

To General the Earl of Uxbridge

Le Cateau
June 23rd, 1815

. . . . My opinion is that we have given Napoleon his death-blow. . . . He can make no head against us... *il n'a qu'à se pendre,* (he has only to hang himself). . . .
Wellington

Le Cateau
June 24th, 1815
. . . . It was I who recommended to the King (Louis XVIII,) to enter France at present, because I was aware of the extent of our success in the battle of the 18th. . . .

I enclose you, in confirmation of my opinion of the extent of our success, the *Journal de l'Empire* of the 22nd, in which you will find Bonaparte's account of the action, the truth of which, as far as it goes against himself, cannot be doubted. . . .

I conclude that you can have no scruple about joining the King forthwith, a measure which I earnestly entreat you and the other members of the King's council to adopt without loss of time.
Wellington

I may here remark, that in political foresight, the Duke was in advance of Talleyrand himself, as the letter above demonstrates.

To Marshal Lord Beresford

Gonesse
July 2nd, 1815
You will have heard of our battle of the 18th. Never did I see such a pounding match. Both were what the boxers call gluttons. Napoleon did not manoeuvre at all. He just moved forward in the old style, in columns, and was driven off in the old style. . . .

I had the infantry for some time in squares; and we had the French cavalry walking about us as if they had been our own. I never saw the British infantry behave so well. . . .
Wellington

The subjoined extracts show how steadily Wellington kept in view the sole object of the war; and that he was not to be cajoled by any diplomatic chicanery, and what pains he took to keep statesmen to the point.

To Earl Bathurst

Joncourt
June 25th, 1815
The advanced posts.... yesterday received a proposition to suspend hostilities, as it was stated that Bonaparte had abdicated in favour of his son, and has appointed a provisional government, consisting of Fouché, Carnot, Caulincourt, General Grenier, and Quinette; that these persons had sent ministers to the allied powers to treat for peace.

It appeared both to Prince Blücher and to me, that these measures were a trick....

The object of the alliance of the powers of Europe is declared by the first article of the treaty of the 25th of March, to be to force Napoleon Bonaparte to desist from his projects, and to place him in a situation in which he will no longer have it in his power to disturb the peace of the world; and, by the third article, the powers of Europe have agreed not to lay down their arms till.... it shall have been rendered impossible for Bonaparte to excite fresh troubles....

I could not consider his abdication of a usurped power in favour of his son, and his handing over the government provisionally to five persons named by himself, to be that description of security which the allies had in view, which should induce them to lay down their arms; and therefore I continue my operations....
Wellington

Headquarters
June 26th, 1815

.... Since the 15th instant, when Napoleon Bonaparte, at the head of the French armies, invaded the dominions of the King of the Netherlands, and attacked the Prussian army, the Field–Marshal has considered his sovereign, and those powers whose armies he commands, in a state of war with the government of France; and he does not consider the abdication of Napoleon Bonaparte of his usurped authority, under all the circumstances which have preceded and attended that measure, as the attainment of the object held out in the declarations and treaties of the allies, which should induce them to lay down their arms.

The Field–Marshal cannot consent therefore to any suspension of hostilities, however desirous he is of preventing the further effusion of blood. . . .

Their Excellencies. . . . will probably consider any interview with him a useless waste of their time. . . .

Wellington

It will appear, by the subjoined documents, that Wellington was tender of the life of Napoleon, who had not spared that of the Duc d'Enghien, and who had declared that he would treat in the same way, that is, put to death, any Bourbon Prince he should catch within the boundaries of his empire. Blücher was eager to put Bonaparte to death, as the guilty author of so much rapine and bloodshed; and to punish the Parisians by fines, the destruction of the bridge of Jena, and of their city itself, if they proved refractory. From this dreadful retaliation, it required all the influence of the Duke over Blücher to preserve them. Posterity should know, if the French will not pay attention to the fact, through whose intervention Napoleon's life was spared, and Paris saved from dishonour, if not pillage and utter destruction.

To Sir Charles Stuart, G. C. B.

Orvillé
June 28th, 1815
My Dear Stuart,
I send you my despatches, which will make you acquainted with the state of affairs. You may show them to Talleyrand if you choose.

General —— has been here this day to negotiate for Napoleon's passing to America, to which proposition I have answered that I have no authority. The Prussians think the Jacobins wish to give him over to me, believing that I will save his life. Blücher wishes to kill him; but I have told him that I shall remonstrate, and shall insist upon his being disposed of by common accord. I have likewise said that, as a private friend, I advised him to have nothing to do with so foul a transaction; that he and I had acted too distinguished parts in these transactions to become executioners; and that I was determined, that if the sovereigns wished to put him to death, they should appoint an executioner, which should not be me. . . .
Wellington

To Marshal Prince Blücher

Gonesse
July 2nd, 1815
Sir,
I requested General Müffling to write to Your Highness yesterday, upon the subject of the propositions which had been made to me by the French commissioners for a suspension of hostilities, upon which I have not yet had a positive answer from Your Highness. . . .

If we choose it, we can settle all our matters now, by agreeing to the proposed armistice. . . .

By adopting this measure, we provide for the quiet restoration of His Majesty to his throne; which is that result of the war which the sovereigns of all of us have always considered the most beneficial for us all, and the most likely to lead to permanent peace in Europe.

It is true we shall not have the vain triumph of entering Paris at the head of our victorious troops; but. . . . I doubt our having the means at present of succeeding in an attack upon Paris; and, if we are to wait till the arrival of Marshal Prince Wrede to make the attack, I think we shall find the sovereigns disposed, as they were last year, to spare the capital of their ally, and either not to enter the town at all, or enter it under an armistice, such as it is in your power and mine to sign this day.

I earnestly urge Your Highness. . . . to let me have your decision whether you will agree to any armistice, or not. ...

Wellington

TO THE FRENCH COMMISSIONERS

Gonesse
July 2nd, 1815

It is my duty to apprize Your Excellencies, that I have just received a letter from Marshal Prince Blücher, who expresses the greatest aversion to granting an armistice. . . .

I have written to him once more, having the greatest desire to save your capital from the danger which menaces it; and I expect his answer tonight. . . .

Wellington

Paris
July 8th, 1816, midnight
Mein Lieber Fürst,
Several reports have been brought to me during the evening and night, and some from the government, in consequence of the work carrying on by Your Highness on one of the bridges over the Seine, which it is supposed to be your intention to destroy.

As this measure will certainly create a good deal of disturbance in the town, and as the sovereigns, when they were here before, left all these bridges, etc, standing, I take the liberty of suggesting to you to delay the destruction of the bridge, at least till they shall arrive; or, at all events, till I can have the pleasure of seeing you tomorrow morning.
Wellington

The Duke of Wellington was obliged to continue his mediation with Blücher, to prevent the exasperated veteran from punishing the pockets and humbling the pride of the Parisians; and for this his generous and enlightened intervention, the Duke did not receive the gratitude that was due to him, as must appear from the following letters:

To Marshal Prince Blücher

Paris
July 9th, 1815
The subjects on which Lord Castlereagh and I conversed with Your Highness and General Comte Gneisenau this morning, *viz.* the destruction of the bridge of Jena and the levy of the contribution of one hundred millions of francs upon the city of Paris, appear to me to be so important to the allies in General,

that I cannot allow myself to omit to draw Your High-ness's attention to them again in this shape.

The destruction of the bridge of Jena is highly disa-greeable to the King and to the people, and may occa-sion disturbance in the city. It is not merely a military measure, but is one likely to attach to the character of our operations, and is of political importance. It is adopted solely because the bridge is considered a monument of the battle of Jena, notwithstanding that the government are willing to change the name of the bridge.

Considering the bridge as a monument, I beg leave to observe that its immediate destruction is inconsistent with the promise made to the commissioners on the part of the French army, during the negotiation of the con-vention; viz. that the monuments, museums, etc., should be reserved for the decision of the allied sovereigns.

All that I ask is, that the execution of the orders giv-en for the destruction of the bridge may be suspended till the sovereigns shall arrive here, when, if it should be agreed by common accord that the bridge ought to be destroyed, I shall have no objection. . . .
Wellington

To Monsieur ——

Paris
July 13th, 1815
I have received your letter of the 10th. Perhaps if you had taken the trouble to inform yourself respecting the works of the Prussian army at the bridge of Jena, and the part I have acted in this affair, you would think that I do not merit the reproaches which you with your signature, and others anonymously, have made me on this subject.

But I ascribe them to the levity with which impres-sions are received and are allowed to influence the actions of men, and the most important measures, in this country; and if the injustice you have "done me in your letter lead you to inquire and reflect before you ever again bring a charge against a public man, I pardon you.

Wellington

The pains which the Duke took to preserve the strictest discipline amongst the troops under his command, and which far surpassed the care taken by other commanders in similar circumstances, entitled him to the gratitude of the Parisians, but did not always exempt him from ill-timed and unreasonable demands. The following severe but just reply was provoked by General Count de Vaubois, who seems to have importuned the Duke for compensation for damages said to be done by the British troops to the French people.

To General Comte de Vaubois

Paris
November 10th, 1815
Monsieur,
You, who have served, must be well aware that it is not possible to give compensation to the full amount for all the damages arising from the presence of an army in a country, or the irregularities of individual soldiers, or the inevitable consequences of military occupation. It is quite true that I usually require reparation to be made for damages caused to the inhabitants by any irregularities of the troops, especially of English troops. But it is more as a means of discipline than as a full compensation to the inhabitants; and I cannot adopt in every case the same means with foreign troops, who are not so well, nor so regularly paid.

The fact is, M. le Général, that France, in carrying her arms into other countries, caused misery, devastation and ruin: I myself have been eyewitness of the destruction of property throughout whole provinces, that refused to submit to the yoke of the tyrant, and that were in consequence entirely depopulated.

Although private revenge ought never to be the motive of a man, and most assuredly it is not that of the allied sovereigns, we can hardly expect that soldiers, men taken from the poorest and most hardy ranks of society, after having seen their properties, or those of their relatives, burned, sacked, destroyed by the French, should have any very great respect for French property, when, by the fortune of war, they find themselves in France.

It is our duty, it is the interest of all of us, more even, I think, than that it is the duty of the French government, to prevent those acts of devastation; and I believe that there is no one who has endeavoured to do this duty so much as I have. But, M. le Général, you know what armies are; and I appeal to your judgment: is it possible entirely to prevent such occurrences in such an army as is under my command; particularly when the soldier is excited by the remembrance of the evils which he and his relatives have had to endure at the hands of French troops?. . . .

Wellington

To H. R. H. Prince Frederick of Orange

Paris
November 10th, 1815
I send you a letter I have just received from General Count de Vaubois, concerning the damages done by the soldiers of the Netherlands.

You will see that their officers were not present at their bivouac. . . . and that the damage done by them amounts to 30,000 francs, a sum ten times greater perhaps than the General will have to pay, as his part of the contribution to the allies, in five years. It is clearly of great importance that the allies prevent these irregularities.

Wellington

Many have been pleased to say that the Duke of Wellington both could and ought to have interposed to save Marshal Ney from being ignominiously executed. Without entering into the question, whether Ney was a perjured traitor to Louis XVIII, and if so, what was the meetest punishment for his treason, it may be confidently averred that Napoleon would have spared no man under similar circumstances. The following documents are worthy of attention.

MEMORANDUM RESPECTING MARSHAL NEY

Paris
November 19th, 1815
It is extraordinary that Madame la Maréchal Ney should have thought proper to publish in print parts of a conversation which she is supposed to have had with the Duke of Wellington; and that she has omitted to publish that which is a much better record of the Duke's opinion on the subject to which the conversation related; *viz.* the Duke's letter to the Maréchal Prince de la Moskowa, in answer to the Maréchal's note to His Grace. That letter was as follows:

November 14th, 1816
I have had the honour of receiving the note which you addressed to me on the 13th November, relating to the operation of the capitulation of Paris on your case. The capitulation of Paris of the 3rd July was made between the commanders in chief of the allied British and Prussian armies on the one part, and the Prince d'Eckmühl, Commander-in-Chief

254

of the French army, on the other; and related exclusively to the military occupation of Paris.

The object of the 12th article was to prevent the adoption of any measures of severity, under the military authority of those who made it, towards any persons in Paris on account of the offices which they had filled, or their conduct, or their political opinions. But it was never intended, and could not be intended, to prevent either the existing French government, under whose authority the French Commander-in-Chief must have acted, or any French government which should succeed to it, from acting in this respect as it might deem fit.

It is obvious from this letter that the Duke of Wellington, one of the parties to the capitulation of Paris, considers that that instrument contains nothing which can prevent the King from bringing Marshal Ney to trial in such manner as His Majesty may think proper.[1]

The contents of the capitulation fully confirm the justice of the Duke's opinion. It is made between the commanders in chief of the contending armies respectively; and the first nine articles relate solely to the mode and time of the evacuation of Paris by the French army, and of the occupation by the British and Prussian armies.

The 10th article provides that the existing authorities shall be respected by the two Commanders-in-Chief of the allies; the 11th, that public property shall be respected, and that the allies shall not interfere *en aucune manière dans leur administration, et dans leur gestion;* (in any manner, either in their administration or in their management;) and the 12th article states, *Seront pareillement respectées les personnes et les propriétés*

---

1. See the proclamation of Louis XVIII to the French people, dated Cambray, the 28th June, 1815.

particulières: les habitants, et, en général, tous les individus qui se trouvent dans la capitale, continueront à jouir de leurs droits et libertés, sans pouvoir être inquiétés, ni recherchés en rien relativement aux fonctions qu'ils occupent, o auraient occupées, à leur conduite, et à leurs opinions politiques, (The persons as well as the property of individuals, shall be equally respected; the inhabitants, and in General every individual residing in the capital, shall continue in full possession of their rights and liberties, without being molested in any manner, on account of the functions which they may have ailed, their conduct, or their political opinions.)

By whom were these private properties and persons to be respected? By the allied Generals and their troops mentioned in the 10th and 11th articles; and not by other parties to whom the convention did not relate in any manner.

The 13th article provides that *les troupes étrangères* (the foreign troops) shall not obstruct the carriage of provisions by land or water to the capital.

Thus it appears that every article in the convention relates exclusively to the operations of the different armies, or to the conduct of the allies and that of their Generals, when they should enter Paris; and, as the Duke of Wellington states in his despatch of the 4th of July, with which he transmitted the convention to England, it "decided all the military points then existing at Paris, and touched nothing political."[2]

But it appears clearly that, not only was this the Duke's opinion of the convention at the time it was signed, but likewise the opinion of Carnot, of Marshal Ney, and of every other person who had an interest in considering the subject.

---

2. See Lord Bathurst's despatch of the 7th July, and the Duke's answer of the 18th, Gurwood, vol. XII, page 567.

Carnot says, in the *Exposé de la conduite politique de M. Carnot* (page 43) : *Il fut résolu d'envoyer aux généraux anglais et prussiens une commission spéciale chargée de leur proposer une convention purement militaire, pour la remise de la ville de Paris entre leurs mains, en écartant toute question politique, puisqu'on ne pouvait préjuger quelles seraient les intentions des alliés, lorsqu'ils seraient réunis.* (It was decided to forward to the English and Prussian Generals a special commission, to the purport of proposing to them a convention, purely military, for the surrender of the city of Paris into their hands, setting aside all political questions, since it was impossible to foresee what might be the ultimate intentions of the allies, when they should be assembled.)

It appears that Marshal Ney fled from Paris in disguise, with a passport given to him by the Duc d'Otrante, under a feigned name, on the 6th of July. He could not be supposed to be ignorant of the tenor of the 12th article of the convention; and he must then have known whether it was the intention of the parties who made it, that it should protect him from the measures which the King, then at St. Denis, should think proper to adopt against him.

But if Marshal Ney could be supposed ignorant of the intention of the 12th article, the Duc d'Otrante could not, as he was at the head of the provisional government, under whose authority the Prince d'Eckmühl must have acted when he signed the convention.[3]

Would the Duc d'Otrante have given a passport under a feigned name to Marshal Ney, if he had understood the 12th article as giving the Marshal any protec-

---

3. See the Duke of Wellington's despatch to Lord Bathurst of the 8th July, (Gurwood, vol. XII, page 649,) detailing a conversation which took place with the Duc d'Otrante at Neuilly, on the night of the 5th July; the whole of which turned upon a recommendation given by the Duc d'Otrante, that the King should give a *General amnesty*.

tion, excepting against measures of seventy by the two commanders in chief?

Another proof of what was the opinion of the Duc d'Otrante, of the King's ministers, and of all the persons most interested in establishing the meaning now attempted to be given to the 12th article of the convention of the 3rd July, is the King's proclamation of the 24th July, by which nineteen persons are ordered for trial, and thirty-eight persons are ordered to quit Paris, and to reside in particular parts of France, under the observation and superintendence of the police, till the Chambers should decide upon their fate.[4]

Did the Duc d'Otrante, did any of the persons who are the objects of this proclamation, did any person on their behalf, ever then, or now, claim for them the protection of the 12th article of the convention? Certainly the convention was then understood, as it ought to be understood now, *viz.* that it was exclusively military, and was never intended to bind the then existing government of France, or any government which should succeed it.

Wellington

Extract from the Proclamation of Louis XVIII

Cambray
June 28th, 1815
. . . . In the plot which they contrived, I perceive many of my subjects to have been misled, and some guilty. I promise—I who never promised in vain, as all Europe can witness—to pardon to misled Frenchmen all that has transpired since the day I quitted Lille amidst so

---

4. "As well as the Duke of Wellington recollects, there is in the war department a letter from the Prince d'Eckmühl to Marshal St. Cyr on this subject, in which he urges every argument against the proclamation of the 28th July, excepting the 12th article of the convention of Paris."

many tears, up to the day I re-entered Cambray, amidst so many acclamations. But the blood of my people has flowed in consequence of a treason unprecedented in the annals of the world. That treason has summoned foreigners into the heart of France; every day reveals to me a new disaster. I owe it, therefore, to the dignity of my crown, to the interest of my people, and to the repose of Europe, to except from pardon the instigators and authors of this horrible plot. They shall be delivered over to the vindication of the laws by the two Chambers, which I propose forthwith to assemble. . . .

Louis

TO ——,[5] ESQ.

Paris
August 8th, 1815
My Dear Sir,
I have received your letter of the 2nd, regarding the battle of Waterloo. The object which you propose to yourself is very difficult of attainment, and, if really attained, is not a little invidious. The history of a battle is not unlike the history of a ball. Some individuals may recollect all the little events, of which the great result is the battle won or lost; but no individual can recollect the order in which, or the exact moment at which, they occurred, which makes all the difference as to their value or importance.

Then the faults or the misbehaviour of some gave occasion for the distinction of others, and perhaps were the cause of material losses; and you cannot write a true history of a battle without including the faults and misbehaviour of part at least of those engaged.

Believe me that every man you see in a military uni-

---

5. Scott.

form is not a hero; and that, although in the account given of a general action, such as that of Waterloo, many instances of individual heroism must be passed over unrelated, it is better for the general interests to leave those parts of the story untold, than to tell the whole truth.

If, however, you should still think it right to turn your attention to this subject, I am most ready to give you every assistance and information in my power. Believe me, etc.

Wellington

To the same

Paris
August 17th, 1815
My Dear Sir,
I have received your letter of the 11th, and I regret much that I have not been able to prevail upon you to relinquish your plan.

You may depend upon it you will never make it a satisfactory work.

I will get you the list of the French army, Generals, etc.

Just to show you how little reliance can be placed, even on what are supposed the best accounts of a battle, I mention that there are some circumstances mentioned in General Müffling's account which did not occur as he relates them.

He was not on the field during the whole battle, particularly not during the latter part of it.

The battle began, I believe, at eleven.

It is impossible to say when each important occurrence took place, nor in what order. We were attacked first with infantry only; then, with cavalry only; lastly, and principally, with cavalry and infantry mixed.

No houses were possessed by the enemy in Mont St. Jean, excepting the farm in front of the left of our centre,[6] on the road to Genappe, can be called one. This they got, I think, at about two o'clock, and got it from a circumstance which is to be attributed to the neglect of the officer commanding on the spot.

The French cavalry were on the plateau in the centre between the two highroads for nearly three quarters of an hour, riding about among our squares of infantry, all firing having ceased on both sides. I moved our squares forward to the guns; and our cavalry, which had been detached by Lord Uxbridge to the flanks, was brought back to the centre. The French cavalry were then driven off. After that circumstance, repeated attacks were made along the whole front of the centre of the position, by cavalry and infantry, till seven at night. How many I cannot tell.

When the enemy attacked Sir Thomas Picton I was there, and they got as far as the hedge on the crossroad, behind which the —— had been formed. The latter had run away, and our troops were on our side of the hedge. The French were driven off with immense loss. This was the first principal attack. At about two in the afternoon, as I have above said, they got possession of the farmhouse on the highroad, which defended this part of the position; and they then took possession of a small mound on the left of the highroad going from Brussels, immediately opposite the gate of the farm; and they were never removed from thence till I commenced the attack in the evening: but they never advanced farther on that side.

These are answers to all your queries; but remember, I recommend to you to leave the battle of Waterloo as it is. Believe me, etc.

Wellington

---

6. La Haye Sainte.

The fair inference is, that the Duke, on seeing the orchard and garden of La Haye Sainte in possession of the enemy about two o'clock p. m., thought the farm was also in their hands, which certainly was not the case till about five o'clock.

The farmhouse in question, La Haye Sainte, was lost from a deficiency of *proper* ammunition; its gallant defenders were riflemen. Who was to be blamed for that deficiency, it is difficult now to ascertain: the Duke, it appears, thought the officer commanding on the spot was censurable on this account. Let me be allowed to record my regret, that on this and many other occasions, valuable lives and important posts were often lost, owing to our having three different sizes for ball cartridges. If there were but one size, as I think there might be, for cavalry, infantry and rifles, the mutual supply of ammunition would be at all times practicable, and, in critical moments, of the utmost value.

To His Royal Highness the Duke of York

Orvillé
June 28th, 1815.
. . . . I would beg leave to suggest to Your Royal Highness the expediency of giving to the non-commissioned officers and soldiers engaged in the battle of Waterloo, a medal. I am convinced it would have the best effect in the army; and, if that battle should settle our concerns, they will well deserve it. . . .
Wellington

Appendix III

Summary of the rise and progress of Field-Marshal the Duke of Wellington, with the public honours and emoluments that have been conferred upon him

Born	1st May, 1769
Ensign	7th March, 1787
Lieutenant	26th December, 1787
Captain	30th June, 1791
Major	30th April, 1793
Lieutenant-Colonel	30th September, 1793
Colonel	3rd May, 1796
Major-General	29th April, 1802
Lieutenant-General	25th April, 1808
General, in Spain and Portugal	31st July, 1811
Field-Marshal	21st June, 1813
Governor of Seringapatam	6th May, 1799
The inhabitants of Calcutta vote a sword of the value of 1,000*l.* to Major-General Wellesley	21st February, 1804
The officers of his division vote to Major-General Wellesley a gold vase, which is afterwards changed to a service of plate embossed with "Assaye"	26th February, 1804
Appointed a Knight Companion of the Bath	1st September, 1804
Thanked by parliament	8th March, 1805

Returned to serve in parliament	12th April, 1806
Sworn a Privy Counsellor	8th April, 1807
Secretary to Ireland	19th April, 1807
Negotiates capitulation at Copenhagen	6th September, 1807
Thanked in parliament for the same	1st February, 1808
A piece of plate, commemorating the battle of Vimeiro, voted to Lieutenant-General Sir Arthur Wellesley by the General and field-officers who served at it	22nd August, 1808
Thanked in parliament for Vimeiro	27th January, 1809
Appointed to command the army in Portugal	2nd April, 1809
Appointed Marshal-General of the Portuguese army	6th July, 1809
Created Baron Douro of Wellesley and Viscount Wellington of Talavera	26th August, 1809
Thanks of parliament voted for Talavera	1st February, 1810
Pension of 2,000*l*. per annum, voted to him and his two succeeding male heirs	16th February, 1810
Thanks of parliament for the liberation of Portugal	26th April, 1811
License granted in the name of the King by the Prince Regent, to accept the title of Conde do Vimeiro, and the insignia of Knight Grand-Cross of the Tower and Sword from the Prince regent of Portugal	26th October, 1811
Created by the regency of Spain a Grandee, with the title of Duque de Ciudad-Rodrigo	January, 1812
Thanks of parliament for Ciudad-Rodrigo	10th February, 1812
Advanced in the British peerage by the title of Earl Wellington	18th February, 1812
Voted 2,000*l*. per annum in addition	21st February, 1812
Thanks of parliament for Badajoz	27th April, 1812
The order of the Golden Fleece conferred by the regency of Spain	July, 1812
Appointed Generalissimo of the Spanish armies	12th August, 1812
Advanced in the British peerage by the title of Marquis of Wellington	18th August, 1812
Advanced by the regent of Portugal to the title of Marquez de Torres-Vedras	12th September, 1812
Thanks of parliament for Salamanca	3rd December, 1812
A grant of 100,000*l*. from parliament, to be laid out in the purchase of lands as a reward for his services	7th December, 1812

Advanced by the regent of Portugal to the title of Duque da Victoria	18th December, 1812
Elected a Knight of the Garter	4th March, 1813
Thanks of parliament for the battle of Vittoria	8th July, 1813
The regency of Spain, on the proposition of the Cortes, offers to bestow on the Duque de Ciudad-Rodrigo, the estate of Soto-de-Roma, in Granada	22nd July, 1813
Thanks of parliament for San-Sebastian and the operations subsequent to Vittoria	8th October, 1813
The Prince Regent grants permission to the Marquis of Wellington to accept and wear the insignia of Grand-Cross of the following orders: Imperial and Royal Austrian Military order of Maria-Theresa; Imperial Russian Military order of St. George; Royal Prussian Military order of the Black Eagle; Royal Swedish Military order of the Sword	4th March, 1814
Thanks of the Prince Regent and the parliament for Orthez	24th March, 1814
Advanced in the British peerage by the titles of Marquis of Douro and Duke of Wellington	3rd May, 1814
A grant of 400,000*l.* voted by parliament, in addition to the former grants	24th June, 1814
Ambassador to France	5th July, 1814
Assists at Congress at Vienna	January, 1815
Takes command of the British forces on the continent	11th April, 1815
Battle of Waterloo	18th June, 1815
Thanks of the Prince Regent and parliament for Waterloo	22nd June, 1815
A grant of 200,000*l.* voted by parliament, in addition to the former grants	6th July, 1815
Created Prince of Waterloo by the King of the Netherlands	18th July, 1815
Commander-in-Chief of the allied armies of occupation	22nd October, 1815
Appointed Field-Marshal in the Austrian, Russian and Prussian armies	15th November, 1818
Visits Waterloo with George IV	1st October, 1821
Commander-in-Chief	22nd January, 1827
First Lord of the Treasury	14th February, 1828
Appointed Lord Warden of the Cinque Ports	20th January, 1829
Elected Chancellor of the University of Oxford	29th January, 1834

Appendix IV

The reader should be aware, that in military returns, the figures which represent the strength of regiments often greatly exceed the actual number of effective men *present*. There are always numerous casualties, not accounted for in returns, particularly before a battle. The *missing* are not all eventually *loss;* for, if not taken prisoners, most of them join after the strife. The strength of the British was of course greater on the 16th, before the action at Quatre-Bras, where the loss was particularly severe, as may be seen in the subjoined tables, in the 1st Foot-Guards, 1st Royal Scots, 32nd, 33rd, 42nd, 44th, 69th, 79th, and 92nd regiments. The officers who afterwards died of their wounds, are here returned *killed*.

Returns of the strength of officers, non-commissioned officers, drummers, trumpeters, rank and file, of the British army, on the morning of the 18th of June 1815; and of the total loss, in killed, wounded and missing, on the three days: 16th, 17th, and 18th.

STAFF

Killed—The Duke of Brunswick, Sir Thomas Picton, Sir William Ponsonby. Colonel Sir William De Lancey. Lieutenant-Colonel Currie. Captains: W. Crofton (64th Reg.), T. Smith (93rd Reg.).

Wounded—H. R. H. the Prince of Orange. Lieutenant-General Sir G. Cooke. Major-Generals: Sir E. Barnes, Sir James Kempt, Sir Colin Halkett, Sir Denis Pack, Sir Colquhoun Grant, Sir W. Dornberg, Sir F. Adam. Lieutenant-Colonels: Waters, Sir G. Berkeley (36th Reg.). Majors: A. Hamilton, Hunter Blair, Hon. G. Dawson. Captains: Hon. E. S. Erskine, E. Fitzgerald (25th Reg.), W. Murray, H. Seymour, T. Wright, H. M'Leod, J. Mitchell (25th Reg.), J. Tyler, A. Langton, H. Dumaresque. Lieutenants: W. Havelock (43rd Reg.), J. Hamilton (46th Reg.), J. Rooke, D. Hall.

Officers who were killed or wounded, serving on the staff but belonging to regiments which were on the field, are here included in the returns of their respective regiments. By adding together the figures in the first two columns opposite to any regiment on the following pages, the reader may obtain its total effective strength, at the opening of the campaign. Columns, left to right are Strength on 18th, Losses 16th/17th, Losses 18th, Officers Killed and Officers Wounded.

1st Life-Guards				
245	18	65	*Lieutenant-Colonel* Ferrior. *Captain* Lind	*Captains:* J. Whale, E. Kelly, S. Richardson, S. Cox
2nd Lifeguards				
236		155	*Lieutenant-Colonel* Fitzgerald	*Lieutenant* Waymouth
Royal Horse-Guards. (Blues)				
246	8	98	*Major* R. Packe	*Lieutenant-Colonels:* Sir J. Elley, Sir R. C. Hill, C. Hill. *Lieutenants:* C. Shawe, E. W. Bouverie

			1ST DRAGOON GUARDS	
571		246	Lieutenant-Colonel Fuller. Majors: Graham, Bringhurst. Captain Battersby. Lieutenants: Brooke, Shelver, adjutant. Cornet Hon. B. Bernard	Captains: M. Turner, P. Sweny, J. Naylor. Lieutenant D. Irvine
			1ST ROYAL DRAGOONS	
428		196	Captains: E. Windsor, 1 C. Foster. Lieutenant R. Magniac. Cornets: J. Sykes, Shepley, adjutant	Major C. Radclyffe. Captain A. Clark. Lieutenants: G. Gunning, T. Keily, S. Trafford, C. Ommaney, C. Blois, S. Goodenough, S. Wyndowe
			2ND ROYAL DRAGOONS (SCOTS GREYS)	
442		217	Lieutenant-Colonel J. Hamilton. Captain T. Reignolds. Cornets: E. Westby, J H. C. Kinchant, L. Barnard, T. Trotter, L. Shuldham	Lieutenant-Colonels: J. B. Clarke, T. P. Hankin. Major R. Vernon. Captain J. Poole. Lieutenants: J. Mills, F. Stupart, J. Carruthers, C. Wyndham
			6TH (INNISKILLING) DRAGOONS	
445		199	Lieutenants: P. Ruffe, McCluskey, adjutant	Lieutenant-Colonels: J. Muter, F. S. Miller, W. F. Browne. Captain Hon. S. Douglas. Lieutenant A. Hassard
			7TH HUSSARS	
362	46	150	Major E. Hodge. Lieutenant A. Meyers	Lieutenant-General the Earl of Uxbridge. Major W. Thornhill. Captains: W. Verner, T. W. Robbins, P. A. Heyliger, T. Wildman, J. J. Frazer, J. D. Elphinstone. Lieutenants: R. Douglas, J. R. Gordon, E. J. Peters, F. Beatty

			10TH HUSSARS	
452		94	*Major* Hon. F. Howard. *Lieutenant* G. Gunning	*Lieutenant-Colonel* G. Quentin, *Captains:* J. Grey, J. Gurwood, C. Wood. *Lieutenants:* R. Arnold, A. Bacon
			11TH LIGHT DRAGOONS	
435	3	73	*Lieutenant* E. Phelips	*Lieutenants:* F. Wood, R. Coles, J. T. Moore, R. Milligan. *Cornet* J. Schreiber
			12TH LIGHT DRAGOONS	
427		111	*Captain* E. Sandys. *Lieutenant* L. J. Bertie. *Cornet* E. Lockhart	*Lieutenant-Colonel* Hon. F. Ponsonby. *Lieutenant* W. H. Dowbiggen
			13TH LIGHT DRAGOONS	
448	1	108	*Captain* J. Gubbins	*Lieutenant-Colonel* Boyse. *Captain* J. Doherty. *Lieutenants:* G. Doherty, C. R. Bowers, J. Geale, G. Pym, J. Mill, G. H. Packe, J. E. Irving
			15TH HUSSARS	
447		79	*Major* E. Griffith. *Lieutenants:* J. Sherwood, H. Buckley.	*Lieutenant-Colonel* L. Dalrymple. *Captains:* J. Thackwell, J. Whiteford, J. Buckley. *Lieutenants:* W. Byam, E. Byam, G. F. Dawkens, R. Mansfield
			16TH LIGHT DRAGOONS	
434		32	*Captain* J. Buchanan. *Cornet* A. Hay	*Lieutenant-Colonel* J. Hay. *Captain* R. Weyland. *Lieutenants:* W. Osten, N. D. Crichton
			18TH HUSSARS	
442	2	102		*Lieutenants:* C. Hesse, H. Duperier, *adjutant*

23RD LIGHT DRAGOONS

| 341 | 6 | 72 | Lieutenant S. Coxen | Major J. M. Cutcliffe. Captains: C. W. Dance, T. Gerrard. Lieutenants: T. B. Wall, B. Disney |

1ST FOOT-GUARDS, 2ND BAT

| 781 | 285 | 153 | Lieutenant-Colonels: Sir F. D'Oyley, W. H. Milnes. Captain T. Brown. Lieutenants: Hon. T. Barrington, H. Lascelles | Colonels: Askew, R. H. Cooke. Lieutenant-Colonels: Sir H. Bradford, Sir Henry Hardinge, air T. N. Hill, Lord Fitzroy Somerset. Captains: Hon. O. Bridgeman, J. Simpson, S. Burgess. Lieutenants: G. Fludyer, T. C. Croft, F. Luttrell, C. P. Ellis |

1ST FOOT-GUARDS, 3RD BAT

| 860 | 262 | 342 | Colonels: E. Stables, C., Thomas. Captains: Lord J. Hay, E. Grose, N. Chambers. Lieutenant E. Pardoe | Colonels: Hon. W. Stewart, Hon. H. Townshend, H. D'Oyley, G. Fead. Captains; R. Adair, T. Streatfield, Hon. R. Clements. Lieutenants: R. Batty, R. Brace, W. Barton |

COLDSTREAM GUARDS, 2ND BAT

| 1,045 | | 308 | Captains: J. L. Black-man, E. Sumner, G. R. Buckley, G. H. Percival, E. Lascelles | Lieutenant-Colonels: J. Macdonnell, D. Mackinnon, Hon. A. Abercromby, C. H. Wyndham. Captain Hon. R. Moore. Lieutenants: H. Griffiths, J. Montague, H. Vane |

3RD FOOT-GUARDS, 2ND BAT

| 1,066 | 7 | 239 | Lieutenant-Colonels: Sir Alexander Gordon, C. F. Canning. Captains: S. W. Stothert, T. Crawford, J. Ashton, C. Simpson, Hon. H. Forbes | Lieutenant-Colonels: C. Dashwood, E. Bowater, C. West. Captains: R. B. Hesketh, G. Evelyn, H. Montgomerie. Lieutenants: C. Lake, D. Baird |

			1st Royal Scots, 3rd Bat	
453	218	144	*Captain* W. Buckley. *Lieutenants:* J. Armstrong, J. E. O'Neill, W. Young. *Ensigns:* Robertson, Kennedy, Anderson	*Lieutenant-Colonel* C. Campbell. *Majors:* L. Arguimbau, R, Macdonald, H. Massey. *Captain* R. Dudgeon. *Lieutenants:* A. Morrison, W. J. Rea, J. Ingram, W. Clarke, A. Cameron, *adjutant;* J. Stoyte, R. Scott, G. Lane, J. Symes, J. Alstone, J. Mann, W. Dobbs, J. F. W. Millar, G. Stewart, J. L. Black. *Ensigns:* C. Graham, T. Stephens, J. Mackay, L. M. Cooper. *Quarter-master* T. Griffiths

			4th Reg. Foot, 1st Bat	
670		134	*Lieutenant* W. Squire	*Captains:* G. D. Wilson, C. J. Edgell. *Lieutenants:* J. Browne, G. Smith, H. Boyd, A. Gerard. *Ensigns:* W. M. Mathews, B. Collins, G. Richardson

			14th Reg. Foot, 3rd Bat	
630		36		*Ensigns:* A. Cooper, A. Ormsby (24th)

			23rd Royal Welsh Fusiliers, 1st Bat	
741		104	*Lieutenant-Colonel* Sir H. W. Ellis. *Captains:* Hawtyn, C. Jolliffe, T. Fanner. *Lieutenants:* G. Fensham, J. Clyde, W. Leebody (24th)	*Captains:* H. Johnson, J. H. Hill. *Lieutenants:* A. Griffiths, Fielding. *Quarter-master* A. Sidley

			27th (Inniskilling) Regt. Foot	
750		478	*Captain* G. Holmes. *Ensign* J. Ireland	*Captains:* J. Hare, J. Tucker. *Lieutenants:* G. McDonnell, W. Henderson, R. Handcock, E. Drewe, W. Fortescne, J. Millar, C. Manley, T. Craddock. *Ensigns:* T. Handcock, T. Smith, J. Ditmas

28TH REG. FOOT

556	75	177	*Major* W. P. Meacham. *Lieutenants:* J. Clarke, C. Ingram	*Lieutenant-Colonel* Nixon. *Captains:* R. Llewellyn, R. Kelly, J. Bowks, T. English, C. Teulon. *Lieutenants:* J. Wilkinson, R. Gilbert, R. P. Eason, W. Irwin, H. Hilliard, J. Goen, C. Carrothers, J. Shelton, J. Deares. *Ensigns:* Mountsteven, P. Bridgeland, *adjutant.*

30TH REG. FOOT

635	51	228	*Major* T. Chambers. *Captain* A. M. Nabb. *Lieutenants:* H. Beere, E. Prendergast. *Ensigns:* J. James, J. Bullen	*Lieutenant-Colonel* Hamilton. *Majors:* W. Bailey, C. A. Vigoureux. *Captain* A. Gore. *Lieutenants:* R. C. Elliott, J. Rumley, R. Daniell, J. Roe, R. Hughes, P. Lockwood, J. Pratt, W. O. Warren, T. Monypenny, M. Andrews, *adjutant*

32ND REG. FOOT

503	196	174	*Captains:* J. Boyce, T. Cassan, E. Whitty	*Captains:* W. H. Toole, J. Crowe, H. Harrison, C. Wallet! *Lieutenants:* H. W. Brookes, G. Barr, M. Meighan, D. Davies, *adjutant;* J. Boase, T. R. Lewin, H. Butterworth, J. Colthurst, J. Robinson, J. Fitzgerald, T. Horan, E. Stephen, H. Quill, J. Jagoe, S. H. Lawrence. *Ensigns:* H. Metcalfe, J. Birtwhistle, A. Stewart, W. Bennett, C. Dallas, J. M. Conchy

			33rd Reg. Foot, 2nd Bat	
576	106	185	*Captain* J. Haigh. *Lieutenants:* H. Buck, J. Boyce, A. Gore, T. D. Haigh, J, Cameron, J. Hart	*Major* E. Parkinson. *Captains:* McIntyre, C. Knight, J. Harty. *Lieutenants:* T. Reid, J. Murkland, R. Westmore, J. Ogle, S. Pagan, J. Furlong. *Ensigns:* H. Bain, J. Alderson, J. A. Howard, G. Drury, W. Thain, *adjutant*

			40th Reg. Foot	
862		219	*Major* R. Heyland. *Captain* W. Fisher	*Captains:* C. Ellis, J. Barnett. *Lieutenants:* R. Moore, J. Anthony, J. Mill, T. Campbell, Hon. H. Browne. *Ensigns:* J. Robb, F. Ford, A. Clerke

			42nd Highlanders, 2nd Bat	
329	288	49	*Lieutenant-Colonel* Sir R. McAra. *Captain* G. Davidson. *Lieutenant* R. Gordon. *Ensign* G. Gerard	*Lieutenant-Colonel* R. Dick. *Major* A. Menzies. *Captains:* M. McPherson, D. McDonald, D. McIntosh, R. Boyle. *Lieutenants:* D. Chisholm, D. Stewart, D. McKenzie, H. A. Fraser, J. Malcolm, A. Dunbar, J. Brander, J. Orr, G. G. Munro. *Ensigns:* W. Fraser, A. L. Fraser, J. Young, *adjutant*. *Quartermaster* McIntosh

			44th Reg. Foot, 2nd Bat	
480	138	64	*Lieutenant* W. Tomkins. *Ensign* P. Cooke	*Lieutenant-Colonels:* Hamerton, G. O'Medley. *Captains:* A. Brugh, D. Power, W. Burney, M. Fane, J. Jessop. *Lieutenants:* R. Russell, R. Grier, W. B. Strong, J. Campbell, J. Burke, W. Hern. *Ensigns:* C. Christie, B. Whitney, T. McCann, *adjutant*; J. C. Webster, A. Wilson

51ST LIGHT INFANTRY

619		42		Captain S. Beardsley. *Lieutenant* C. W. Tyndale

53RD LIGHT INFANTRY

1,148		199	*Ensign* W. Nettles	*Lieutenant-Colonel* J. Rowan. *Captains:* W. Rowan, J. F. Love, C. Diggle. *Lieutenants:* C. Dawson, M. Anderson, G. Campbell, F. Cottingham, J. Winterbottom, *adjutant*

69TH REG. FOOT, 2ND BAT

541	155	85	*Colonel* C. Morice. *Captains:* B. Hobhouse, Hon. W. Curzon, P. Blackwood. *Lieutenant* M. Wightwick	*Captains:* J. L. Watson, H. Lindsay. *Lieutenants:* H. Anderson, J. Stewart, B. Pigot, C. Busteed. *Ensign* E. Hodder. *Volunteer* Clarke

71ST (HIGHLAND) LIGHT INFANTRY

929		202	*Captain* E. L. Estrange. *Lieutenants:* J. R. Elwes, J. Todd	*Colonel* T. Reyneel. *Major* A. Jones. *Captains:* D. Campbell, A. Grant, J. Henderson, C. Johnstone. *Lieutenants:* J. Barrallier, R. Lind, J. Roberts, C. Lewin, R. Law, J. Coote, W. Hanson, W. Anderson, *adjutant*

73RD REG. FOOT, 2ND BAT

498	56	280	*Captains:* A. Robertson, J. M. Kennedy. *Lieutenants:* J. Strachan, W. Hollis, J. Acres, Brown. *Ensigns:* W. S. Lowe, C. Page	*Colonel* G. Harris. *Major* A. J. McLean. *Captains:* A. Coane, E. T. Pirch, W. Wharton, J. Garland. *Lieutenants:* J. Mc Connell, T. Reynolds, D. Browne, J. Lloyd. *Ensigns:* R. Hesilrige, T. Deacon, W. M«Bean, C. B. Eastwood, G. D. Bridge, P. Hay, *adjutant*

			79TH HIGHLANDERS	
440	304	175	*Captains:* McKay, McRa, Neil Campbell, J. Cameron, J. Sinclair. *Lieutenants:* D. Cameron, D. McPherson, E. Kennedy, J. Kynock, *adjutant;* J. Rowling	*Lieutenant-Colonels:* N. Douglas, A. Brown, D. Cameron. *Captains:* T. Mylne, J. Campbell, N. Campbell, W. Marshall, M. Fraser, W. Bruce. *Lieutenants:* A. Cameron, T. Brown, W. Maddocks, W. Leaper, J. Fraser, D. McPhee, E. Cameron, A. Forbes, C. McArthur, J. Powling, W. A. Riach. *Ensigns:* J. Nash, J. Robertson, A. S. Crawford. *Volunteer* Cameron
			92ND HIGHLANDERS	
422	286	116	*Lieutenant-Colonel* Cameron. *Captains:* W. C. Grant, W. Little. *Lieutenants:* J. Chisholm, G. Mackie. *Ensigns:* A. Beecher, R. McPherson	*Colonel* J. Mitchell. *Captains:* G. W. Holmes, D. Campbell, P. Wilkie, A. Ferner. *Lieutenants:* R. Winchester, T. Hobbs, T. McIntosh, D. McDonald, J. Ross, R. McDonald, H. Innes, G. Logan, J. McInlay, A. McPherson, J. Hope. *Ensigns:* J. Branwell, R. Logan, A. M^conald, R. Hewit. *Assistant surgeon* J. Stewart
			95TH RIFLES, 1ST BAT	
418	64	156	*Majors:* C. Smith, C. Ecles. *Lieutenants:* J. Stilwell, E. D. Johnston	*Lieutenant-Colonel* Sir A. Barnard. *Majors:* A. Cameron, Beckwith. *Captains:* E. Chawner, W. Johnston. *Lieutenants:* J. P. Gardner, J. Fitzmaurice, W. Shenley, J. Molloy, J. Gardner, G. Simmons, A. Stewart, J. Wright, J. Church

			95TH RIFLES, 2ND BAT	
655		246	*Lieutenant* Backhouse	*Majors:* A. Norcott, G. Wilkins. *Captains:* G. Miller, J. G. McCulloch. *Lieutenants:* Humbley, D. Cameron, E. Coxon, R. Cochran, J. Fry, J. Ridge way, J. Lynam, R. Eyre, J. Walsh, P. Webb
			95TH RIFLES, TWO COMPANIES, 3RD BAT	
202		50	*Lieutenant* W. Lister	*Major* J. Ross. *Captain* J. Fullerton. *Lieutenants:* T. Worsley, G. W. Shenley
			ROYAL ARTILLERY	
4,944	28	476	*Majors:* Lloyd, N. Ramsay, Cairnes, Beane, Bolton. *Lieutenants:* W. L. Robe, M. Cromie, C. Spearman, F. Manners, F. Troughton	*Captains:* Napier, J. Parker, Bull, Whinyates, Dansey, R. Macdonald, Webber, W. Strangeway, D. Crawford, A. Macdonald. *Lieutenants:* W. Brereton, W. Smith, Barnes, Bloomfield, Barton, Forbes, W. Harvey, Foster, D. Crawford, J. Day, W. Poole, C. H. Baines, T. Harvey, J. W. Pringle. *Captain* Robt. Thomson, *Royal Engineers*

Appendix V

Marshal Blücher to Baron Müffling

Wavre
June 18th, 1815
Your Excellency will assure the Duke of Wellington from me, that, ill as I am, I shall place myself at the head of my troops, and attack the right of the French, in case they undertake anything against His Grace. If, on the other hand, the day should pass over without their making any attack, it is then my opinion that we should jointly attack them tomorrow.

I beg Your Excellency to convey to the Duke my full and firm conviction, that this is the best measure to be adopted in our present situation.
Blücher

General Count Gneisenau, the chief of the staff, felt alarmed at the tenor of the above letter, which told plainly the decided manner it was to be carried out. Fearing the Prussian army might be placed in a dangerous situation, should the allies be forced to retire before they could arrive, he wrote the following note:

General Count Gneisenau concurs with the views expressed in the enclosed letter, but entreats Your Excellency to ascertain most particularly, whether the Duke of Wellington *has really adopted the decided resolution of fighting in his present position;* or whether he only intends some demonstration, which might become very dangerous to our army.

Your Excellency will be so good as to acquaint us with the result of your observations on this point, as it is of the greatest consequence that we should be informed of the Duke's real intention.

THE PRINCE DE LA MOSKOWA TO THE DUC D'OTRANTE.

Monsieur Le Duc,
The most false and defamatory reports have been spreading for some days over the public mind, upon the conduct which I have pursued during this short and unfortunate campaign. The newspapers have reported those odious calumnies, and appear to lend them credit. After having fought for twenty-five years for my country, after having shed my blood for its glory and independence, an attempt is made to accuse me of treason; an attempt is made to mark me out to the people, and to the army itself, as the author of the disaster it has just experienced.

Forced to break silence, while it is always painful to speak of one's self, and, above all, to answer calumnies, I address myself to you, Sir, as the President of the Provisional Government, for the purpose of laying before you a faithful statement of the events I have witnessed.

On the 11th of June, I received an order from the minister of war to repair to the Imperial presence. I had no command, and no information upon the composition and strength of the army. Neither the Emperor nor his minister had given me any previous hint, from which I could anticipate that I should be employed in the present campaign; I was consequently taken by surprise, without horses, without accoutrements, and without money, and I was obliged to borrow the necessary expenses of my journey. Having arrived on the 12th at Laon, on the 13th at Avesnes, and on the 14th at Beaumont, I purchased, in this last town, two horses from the Duc de Trévise, with which I repaired, on the 15th, to Charleroy, accompanied by my first aide-de-camp, the only officer who attended me. I arrived at the moment when the enemy, attacked by our troops, was retreating upon Fleurus and Gosselies.

The Emperor ordered me immediately to put myself at the head of the 1st and 2nd corps of infantry, commanded by Lieutenant-Generals D'Erlon and Reille, of the division of light cavalry of Lieutenant-General Piré, of the division of light cavalry of the guard under the command of Lieutenant-Generals Lefebvre-Desnouettes and Colbert, and of two divisions of cavalry of Count de Valmy; forming, in all, eight divisions of infantry, and four of cavalry. With these troops, a part of which only I had as yet under my immediate command, I pursued the enemy, and forced him to evacuate Gosselies, Frasnes, Millet, Hépignies. There they took up a position for the night, with the exception of the first corps, which was still at Marchiennes, and which did not join me till the following day.

On the 16th, I received orders to attack the English in their position at Quatre-Bras. We advanced towards the enemy with an enthusiasm difficult to be described.

Nothing resisted our impetuosity. The battle became General, and victory was no longer doubtful, when, at the moment that I intended to order up the first corps of infantry, which had been left by me in reserve at Frasnes, I learned that the Emperor had disposed of it without adverting me of the circumstance, as well as of the division of Girard of the second corps, on purpose to direct them upon St. Amand, and to strengthen his left wing, which was vigorously engaged with the Prussians. The shock which this intelligence gave me, confounded me. Having no longer under me more than three divisions, instead of the eight upon which I calculated, I was obliged to renounce the hopes of victory; and, in spite of all my efforts, in spite of the intrepidity and devotion of my troops, my utmost efforts after that could only maintain me in my position till the close of the day. About nine o'clock, the first corps was sent me by the Emperor, to whom it had been of no service. Thus twenty-five or thirty thousand men were, I may say, paralyzed, and were idly paraded during the whole of the battle from the right to the left, and the left to the right, without firing a shot.

It is impossible for me, Sir, not to arrest your attention for a moment upon these details, in order to bring before your view all the consequences of this false movement, and, in general, of the bad arrangements during the whole of the day. By what fatality, for example, did the Emperor, instead of leading all his forces against Lord Wellington, who would have been attacked unawares, and could not have resisted, consider this attack as secondary? How did the Emperor, after the passage of the Sambre, conceive it possible to fight two battles on the same day? It was to oppose forces double ours, and to do what military men who were witnesses of it can scarcely yet comprehend. Instead of this, had he left a corps of observation to watch the Prussians, and marched with his most powerful masses to support me, the English army had undoubtedly been destroyed between Quatre-Bras and Genappe; and this position, which separated the two allied armies, being once in our power, would have opened for the Emperor an opportunity of advancing to the right of the Prussians, and of crushing them in their turn. The general opinion in France, and especially in the army, was, that the Emperor would have bent his whole efforts to annihilate first the English army; and circumstances were favourable for the accomplishment of such a project: but fate ordered otherwise.

On the 17th, the army marched in the direction of Mont St. Jean.

On the 18th, the battle began at one o'clock, and though the bulletin, which details it, makes no mention of me, it is not necessary for me to mention that I was engaged in it. Lieutenant-General Count Drouot has already spoken of that battle, in the House of Peers. His narration is accurate, with the exception of some important facts which he has passed over in silence, or of which he was ignorant, and which it is now my duty to declare. About seven o'clock in the evening, after the most frightful carnage which I have ever witnessed, General Labédoyère came to me with a message from the Emperor, that Marshal Grouchy had arrived on our right, and attacked the left of the English and Prussians united. This general officer, in riding along the lines, spread this intelligence among the soldiers, whose courage and devotion remained unshaken, and who gave new proofs of them at that moment, in spite of the fatigue which they experienced. Immediately after, what was my astonishment, I should rather say indignation, when I learned, that so far from Marshal Grouchy having arrived to support us, as the whole army had been assured, between forty and fifty thousand Prussians attacked our extreme right, and forced it to retire. Whether the Emperor was deceived with regard to the time when the Marshal could support him, or whether the march of the Marshal was retarded by the efforts of the enemy longer than was calculated upon, the fact is, that at the moment when his arrival was announced to us, he was only at Wavre upon the Dyle, which to us was the same as if he had been a hundred leagues from the field of battle.

A short time afterwards, I saw four regiments of the middle guard, conducted by the Emperor, arriving. With these troops, he wished to renew the attack, and to penetrate the centre of the enemy. He ordered me to lead them on: Generals, officers, and soldiers, all displayed the greatest intrepidity; but this body of troops was too weak to resist, for a long time, the forces opposed to it by the enemy, and it was soon necessary to renounce the hope which this attack had, for a few moments, inspired. General Friant had been struck with a ball by my side; and I myself had my horse killed, and fell under it. The brave men who will return from this terrible battle will, I hope, do me the justice to say, that they saw me on foot with sword in hand during the whole of the evening, and that I only quitted the scene of carnage among the last, and at the moment when retreat could no longer be prevented. At the same time, the Prussians continued their offensive movements, and our right sensibly retired; the English advanced in their turn. There remained to us still four squares of the old guard to protect the retreat. These brave grenadiers, the choice of the army, forced successively to retire, yielded ground foot by foot, till, overwhelmed by numbers, they were almost entirely annihilated. From that moment, a retrograde movement was declared, and the army formed nothing but a confused mass. There was not, however, a total rout, nor the cry of *Sauve qui peut,* as has been calumniously stated in the bulletin. As for myself, constantly in the rear-guard, which I followed on foot, having all my horses killed, worn out with fatigue, covered with contusions, and having no longer strength to march, I owe my life to a corporal who supported me on the road, and did not abandon me during the retreat. At eleven at night, I found Lieutenant-General Lefebvre-Desnouettes; and one of his officers, Major Schmidt, had the generosity to give me the only horse that remained to him. In this manner I arrived at Marchiennes-au-Pont at four o'clock in the morning, alone, without any officers of my staff, ignorant of what had become of the Emperor, who, before the end of the battle, had entirely disappeared, and who, I was allowed to believe, might be either killed or taken prisoner. General Pamphile Lacroix, chief of the staff of the second corps, whom I found in this town, having told me that the Emperor was at Charleroy, I was led to suppose that His Majesty was going to put himself at the head of Marshal Grouchy's corps, to cover the Sambre, and to facilitate to the troops the means of rallying towards Avesnes, and, with this persuasion, I went to Beaumont; but parties of cavalry following on too near, and having already intercepted the roads of Maubeuge and Philippeville, I became sensible of the total impossibility of arresting a single soldier on that point, to oppose the progress of the victorious enemy. I continued my march upon Avesnes, where I could obtain no intelligence of what had become of the Emperor.

In this state of matters, having no knowledge of His Majesty nor of the Major-General, confusion increasing every moment, and, with the exception of some fragments of regiments of the guard and of the line, every one following his own inclination, I determined immediately to go to Paris by St. Quentin, to disclose, as quickly as possible, the true state of affairs to the minister of war, that he might send to the army some fresh troops, and take the measures which circumstances rendered necessary. At my arrival at Bourget, three leagues from Paris, I learned that the Emperor had passed there at nine o'clock in the morning. Such, M. le Duc, is the history of this calamitous campaign.

Now I ask those who have survived this fine and numerous army, how I can be accused of the disasters of which it has been the victim, and of which our military annals furnish no example. I have, it is said, betrayed my country, I who, to serve it, have shown a zeal which I perhaps have carried to an extravagant height: but this calumny is supported by no fact, by no circumstance. But how can these odious reports, which spread with frightful rapidity, be arrested? If, in the researches which I could make on this subject, I did not fear almost as much to discover as to be ignorant of the truth, I would say, that all was a tendency to convince that I have been unworthily deceived, and that it is attempted to cover, with the pretence of treason, the faults and extravagancies of this campaign; faults which have not been avowed in the bulletins that have appeared, and against which I in vain raised that voice of truth which I will yet cause to resound in the House of Peers.

I expect, from the candour of Your Excellency, and from your indulgence to me, that you will cause this letter to be inserted in the *Journal,* and give it the greatest possible publicity.

Marshal Prince de la Moskowa

Paris

June 26th, 1815

Appendix VI

At a period of the battle, when the Duke was surrounded by his staff, it was evident they had become the object of the fire from a French battery. The shot fell fast around them. Their horses became restive, and Copenhagen himself (the Duke's horse,) so fidgety, that the Duke became impatient, and having reasons for remaining on the spot, said, "Gentlemen, we are rather too close together: better divide a little.»

* * * * * * * *

On one occasion Wellington rode up to Picton's division, just as a hot fire of musketry opened upon the 92nd. The staff expected every instant to see him drop, as he sat coolly watching the effect of the enemy's fire: but he remained untouched; as did also Lord Arthur Hill, who was the only officer that had accompanied him to the crest of the ground.

* * * * * * * *

During the battle, a British artillery officer rode up to the Duke of Wellington and said, "Your Grace, I have a distinct view of Napoleon, attended by his staff: my guns are well pointed in that direction, shall I open fire?"

The Duke replied, "Certainly not, I will not allow it; it is not the business of commanders to fire upon each other."

From this it is evident that circumstances alter cases, as may be seen by the following expression of the Duke: "I cannot discover the policy of not hitting one's enemy as hard as one can, and in the most vulnerable place."[1]

* * * * * * * *

Whilst the Duke was occupied intently in observing with his telescope a movement in the enemy's line, some of their skirmishers were pressing on, and the musket-balls began to whistle round His Grace in such profusion, that Colonel Gordon was induced to take the bridle of the Duke's charger, and lead him forward to a hollow, where he was in shelter; and so intent was His Grace in observing the enemy, that it was accomplished without his noticing it. Throughout this long and trying day, the Duke was always to be seen where danger threatened, or difficulties arose, fearlessly passing from point to point, and constantly exposed to the fire of the enemy, protected doubtlessly by a merciful and all-wise Providence, to add still further lustre to his name by his continued services to his country.

* * * * * * * *

During the heat of the battle, the Duke was about to pass in front of a Nassau square, the troops composing which had served Napoleon, when several of his staff requested His Grace to pass by its rear: had he rode along the front, the simple process of pulling a single trigger might have blasted all our expectations, and injured the cause of Europe more than did the whole efforts of Napoleon and his army.

The arms, clothing, and General bearing of the Nassaumen were truly French: their splendid rifle-green uniform, broad buff cross-belts, handsome white cased cap and tall black plume, produced a martial and imposing appearance.

* * * * * * * *

---

1. *Despatches,* vol. XI, page 547.

A hussar and a cuirassier had got entangled in the *mêlée,* and met in the plain, in full view of our line; the hussar was without a cap, and bleeding from a wound in the head, but that did not hinder him from attacking his steel-clad adversary. He soon proved that the strength of cavalry consists in good horsemanship, and the skilful use of the sword, and not in being clad in heavy defensive armour. The superiority of the hussar was visible the moment the swords crossed: after a few wheels a tremendous facer made the Frenchman reel in his saddle, and all his attempts to escape his more active foe became unavailing; a second blow stretched him on the ground, amidst the cheers of the light horseman's comrades, the 3rd German hussars, who were ardent spectators of the combat.

* * * * * * * *

During the cavalry charges, a man, named Gilmore, of Captain Elphinstone's troop, and belonging to my regiment, was lying under his wounded grey horse, about two hundred yards in our front. The cuirassiers were advancing; and as I was aware they spared none who fell into their hands. I sprang from my saddle, soon reached the spot, and seizing the bridle raised the horse's head; when the animal making a struggle, Gilmore was enabled to extricate himself, and to reach our line just before the enemy's cavalry came up. The pleasure I felt on this occasion will be understood by any one who has had the opportunity of saving life. Two other human beings, one, a lad, David Bale, at Clapham, in Surrey; another, a boy, named Tannis, in the village of Mont St. Jean, I was providentially enabled to rescue from drowning.

* * * * * * * *

I witnessed an encounter during the battle, between an artilleryman and a cuirassier: the former was under his gun; the latter dodging round, endeavouring to run his sword through him. At length the cuirassier's horse was shot, and the gunner, getting from his place of shelter, dealt a blow with his ramrod upon the head of his antagonist, which felled him to the ground: he then seized upon the cuirassier's sword, and collaring him, proceeded towards the rear. On passing us, the gunner gave his prisoner a kick on the hind part of his person, saying, "Be off to the rear."

* * * * * * * *

On the morning of the 18th, Colonel Ellis, of the 23rd Royal Welch fusiliers, issued an order that no man was to fall out of the ranks to assist the wounded. Upon the Colonel being severely wounded, Captain Brown ordered two men to follow and assist him to the rear; but the gallant Colonel declined their services, observing, "There are not too many bayonets in the Royal Welch, return to your post." This strict adherence to discipline, and disinterestedness, no doubt cost him his life, and deprived the service of one of its brightest ornaments.[2]

* * * * * * * *

The day before the battle of Waterloo, Captain Elphinstone, of the 7th hussars, was grievously wounded and taken prisoner. His condition was noticed by Napoleon, who immediately sent one of his surgeons to dress his wounds; and perceiving that, from loss of blood, Elphinstone had swooned away, he sent a silver goblet full of wine from his own store. On the arrival of the *Bellerophon* in England, Lord Keith presented his grateful thanks to Napoleon, for having saved the life of his nephew.

* * * * * * * *

On the 29th of May, (prior to the battle,) we had a grand review of the cavalry and horse artillery. After the review most of the superior officers breakfasted with Lord Uxbridge, at Ninove. Old Blücher was amongst them, and openly declared,

---

2. See *Despatches,* vol. XII, pages 610-11.

he had not given the world credit for containing so many fine men as he had seen that day. Our infantry, although not such fine-looking fellows, still bore away the foremost laurels of the day of battle. On parting, Blücher wished all a good day, exclaiming, "We shall soon meet again in Paris."

* * * * * * * *

In 1818, Blücher was one of a large party at Berlin, where much merriment and jesting went on from the proposal and solution of enigmas. Blücher at once absorbed the attention of all the guests, by saying, "I will do what none of you can, I will kiss my own head;" and while all were wondering how that was to be done, the old man added with the utmost assurance, "This is the way;" when rising, he approached his friend Gneisenau, whom he kissed and embraced most heartily.

* * * * * * * *

Blücher, when at dinner with the ministers of several different states of Europe, gave as a toast, "May the diplomatists not again spoil with their pens, that which the armies have with so much cost won with their swords!"

Happening to meet the Prussian minister, Prince Hardenberg, he thus boldly addressed him, "I only wish I had you gentlemen of the pen, exposed for once to a pretty smart skirmishing fire, that you might learn what it is when the soldier is obliged to repair with his life's blood the errors which you so thoughtlessly commit on paper."

The following fact shows that no personal considerations restrained him from indulging in his splenetic humour against the great diplomatist of the day:

Nearly everybody knows that, immediately after the convention of Paris, Blücher was desirous to destroy the bridge of Jena, and that he would undoubtedly have carried his intentions into effect, had it not been for the urgent representations of the Duke of Wellington.

On that occasion, Count von der Golz, formerly his aid-de-camp, and then Prussian ambassador in Paris, made a written application to him in behalf and in the name of Prince Talleyrand, beseeching the preservation of the bridge. Blücher replied in his own hand-writing, "I have resolved upon blowing up the bridge, and I cannot conceal from Your Excellency how much pleasure it would afford me, if Monsieur de Talleyrand would previously station himself upon it; and I beg you will make my wish known to him."

* * * * * * * *

When Blücher was at Oxford, in 1814, with the emperors and kings, the Prince Regent and the Duke of Wellington, he received an intimation that the heads of the University intended to confer upon him the dignity of a Doctor. Blücher, who never dreamed of becoming one of the learned, could not refrain from laughter, and jocularly remarked, "Well, if I am to be a doctor, they cannot do less than make Gneisenau an apothecary: for we both work together; and it is he who has to make up the pills, which I am in the habit of administering."[3]

* * * * * * * *

On the 15th of June, 1815, the French General Bourmont, Colonels Clouet and Villoutreys, with three Captains, deserted Napoleon, and came over to the Prussians. When Bourmont was presented to Blücher, the latter could not refrain from evincing his contempt for the faithless soldier. Some officers tried to impress him more favourably towards the General, by directing his attention to the white cockade which he wore in a conspicuous fashion: the Prince bluntly remarked, "It matters not what a man sticks in his hat for a mark; a mean-spirited scoundrel always remains the same."

* * * * * * * *

---

3. Gneisenau was the chief of the Prussian staff. He was at once the life and soul, mainspring and working head of their army.

In a private letter from Blücher to Sir Hudson Lowe, written many months anterior to Bonaparte's quitting Elba, after disavowing all desire for future triumphs, he expressed a hope, that if again called upon to act, it might be in conjunction with the General and army that had immortalized themselves in the Peninsula, when Wellington and himself would go hand in hand to victory. It was truly a prophetic epistle.

* * * * * * * *

"It has always occurred to me, however," says the Duke, (upon the battle of Leipzig,) "that if Bonaparte had not placed himself in a position that every other officer would have avoided, and had not remained in it longer than was consistent with any notions of prudence, he would have retired in such a state, that the allies could not have ventured to approach the Rhine."[4]

* * * * * * * *

It is always interesting to know what estimate great commanders have formed of one another. During the Peninsular campaign, Marshal Marmont, with about sixty thousand men, approached Wellington's position at Fuente-Guinaldo, when the iron Duke's force did not exceed two thousand five hundred horse, and two weak divisions of infantry. Still he exhibited the same coolness and imperturbable self-possession, which, in emergency, invariably marked his distinguished and successful career. On this occasion, the Spanish General Alava, whose enlightened patriotism and high military qualities had endeared him to the Duke, thus accosted him, "Here you are with a couple of weak divisions in front of the whole French army; and you seem quite at your ease! Why, it is enough to put any man in a fever!"

"I have done according to the very best of my judgment all that can be done," was the characteristic reply of the British

---

4. *Despatches,* vol. XI, page 435. At Leipzig, Napoleon selected his own position, and there he chose a field with a defile over a morass, a mile and a half bread, which probably was the principal cause of his defeat.

commander, "and therefore I care not either for the enemy in front, or for anything which they may say at home."

* * * * * * * *

Upon Marmont's being informed, that, for thirty-six hours, Wellington, with about fourteen thousand men, had lain within cannon range of him, his astonishment was unbounded; and he is said to have exclaimed, that, "Brilliant as was Napoleon's star, Wellington's was more brilliant still," Marshal Marmont's discrimination was amply proved at Waterloo.

* * * * * * * *

Lieutenant-Colonel Ponsonby, of the 12th light dragoons, gives the following account of himself on being wounded. He says: "In the *mêlée* (thick of the fight) I was almost instantly disabled in both my arms, losing first my sword, and then my rein; and, followed by a few of my men who were presently cut down, no quarter being asked or given, I was carried along by my horse, till, receiving a blow from a sabre, I fell senseless on my face to the ground. Recovering, I raised myself a little to look round, being at that time in a condition to get up and run away, when a lancer passing by, cried out, *'Tu n'es pas mort, voquint!'* and struck his lance through my back. My head dropped, the blood gushed into my mouth, a difficulty of breathing came on, and I thought all was over. Not long after, a skirmisher stopped to plunder me, threatening my life: I directed him to a small side-pocket in which he found three dollars, all I had; but he continued to threaten, tearing open my waistcoat, and leaving me in a very uneasy posture.

"But he was no sooner gone, than an officer bringing up some troops, and happening to halt where I lay, stooped down, and addressing me, said, he feared I was badly wounded. I answered that I was, and expressed a wish to be moved to the rear. He said it was against orders, to remove even their own men; but that, if they gained the day, (and he understood that the Duke of Wellington was killed, and that six of our battalions had surrendered,) every attention in his power should be shown me. I complained of thirst, and he held his brandy bottle to my lips, directing one of his soldiers to lay me straight on my side, and place a knapsack under my head: they then passed on into action, soon perhaps to want, though not to receive, the same assistance; and I shall never know to whose generosity I was indebted, as I believe, for my life.

"By and by, another skirmisher came up, a fine young man, full of ardour, loading and firing: he knelt down and fired over me many times, conversing with me very gaily all the while: at last he ran off, saying, *'Vous serez bien aise d'apprendre que nous allons nous retirer. Bonjour, mon ami.'* ('You will be pleased to learn that we are going to fall back. Good day, my friend.') It was dusk, when two squadrons of Prussian cavalry crossed the valley in full trot, lifting me from the ground, and tumbling me about cruelly.

The battle was now over, and the groans of the wounded all around me, became more and more audible: I thought the night never would end. About this time, I found a soldier lying across my legs, and his weight, his convulsive motions, his noises, and the air issuing through a wound in his side, distressed me greatly; the last circumstance most of all, as I had a wound of the same nature myself. It was not a dark night, and the Prussians were wandering about to plunder: many of them stopped to look at me as they passed; at last one of them stopped to examine me: I told him that I was a British officer, and had been already plundered. He did not however desist, and pulled me about roughly.

"An hour before midnight, I saw a man in an English uniform, coming towards me; he was, I suspected, on the same errand. I spoke instantly, telling him who I was: he belonged to the 40th, and had missed his regiment. He released me from the dying soldier, took up a sword, and stood over me as sentinel. Day broke, and at six o'clock in the morning a messenger was sent to Hervé: a cart came for me, and I was conveyed to the village of Waterloo, and laid in the bed, as I afterwards understood, from which Gordon had but just before been carried out. I had received seven wounds; a surgeon slept in my room, and I was saved by excessive bleeding."

* * * * * * * *

RELATED BY AN OFFICER

. . . . Early on the following morning, the survivors arose and hurried out to seek, amidst the dying and the dead, those comrades and friends of whose fate they were as yet ignorant.[5] But even earlier still had the wretches who hang on the skirts of every army, for the purpose of rifling the new-made corpse, been at work: the watches and purses of many were already gone; while many a brave heart, still throbbing, had received its *coup de grâce* from the hands of these merciless plunderers.

Waterloo was won; the sun set upon a scene of slaughter, and the stillness of death succeeded the roar of battle. The thunder of five hundred cannons, the roll of musketry, the shock of mail-clad horsemen, the Highland slogan, the Irish huzza, were heard no more; and the moon gleamed coldly on a field of death, whose silence was only broken by the groans of the wounded, as they lay in helpless wretchedness beside their dead companions.

While many a sufferer listened to every sound in anxious

---

5. Several ladies were on the field on the morning of the 19th, going about like ministering angels tending the wounded. How truly in this instance do Scott's lines picture the soft sex!

O woman! in our hours of ease,
Uncertain, coy, and hard to please,
And variable as the shade
By the light quivering aspen made;
When pain and anguish wring the brow,
ministering angel thou!

expectation of relief, a dropping fire was occasionally heard in the direction of Genappe, announcing that the broken army of Napoleon was fiercely followed by its conquerors.

Wearied by the unparalleled exertions of the tremendous day of Waterloo, the British pursuit gradually relaxed, and the light cavalry halted on the right of the road to Quatre-Bras; but the Prussians, less fatigued, continued to harass the flying enemy, and the mingled mass of fugitives were forced from every village where they had attempted to form bivouacs. A barrier was hastily thrown across the entrance of Genappe, to arrest the progress of the *jägers* and hussars that hung upon the rear of the guard; but it was blown down by a few discharges of a howitzer, and the French were driven from the town. Throughout the disastrous night not a moment of repose was granted to the terror-stricken. To attempt anything like serious resistance to their pursuers, where all were inextricably confused, was absurd. Officers and soldiers were mobbed together; discipline had ended: none attempted to direct, where none were found to obey; and with unrelenting fury the Prussian cavalry sabred the exhausted fugitives, till, after passing Gosselies and Charleroy, the. wreck of Napoleon's army found a temporary shelter beneath the walls of Philippeville.

That night, the British bivouac was on the same ridge which their beaten enemy had occupied on the preceding one; and as I lay upon the ground, I heard at times, and at no great distance from me, the voices of my more fortunate companions who had escaped from the slaughter, and some were roaming over the field in search of plunder. Momentarily, I expected that a friendly straggler would pass by. I must have been for a considerable period insensible; for the place where I fell, although the theatre of the final struggle between the relics of Ney's columns and the British guards, was now totally deserted by the living, and cumbered only with the dying and the dead.

I seemed as if awakening from a dream: a difficulty of respiration painfully annoyed me, and I endeavoured to rise; but a weight, too mighty to be removed, pressed me to the earth. My sight was imperfect, my eyelids felt closed. I disengaged my left hand, and raising it to my face, found that a mask of congealed blood covered it. I rubbed it away, and, prepared as I was for a sanguinary spectacle by the continuous moanings of wounded men and dying horses, I closed my eyes in horror, when the clear cold moonlight revealed the sickening scene.

Directly over me, and in the very attitude in which he had groaned his last, an officer of the old guard was stretched: our faces were nearly touching, and his open eyes had fixed their glassy stare on mine. A sword cut had divided his upper lip, and, exposing the teeth, gave to the dead man's countenance a grin so horrible and ghastly, that I who had witnessed death in every form, was glad to avert my eyes. I made a desperate effort to shake him off; but a horse's neck rested on my legs, and my feeble exertions were quite unequal to rid me of this double load.

While suffering great inconvenience of position, I felt the cold intense, and thirst intolerable. No relief was attainable; the groans of the dying were unheard, and I sullenly submitted to my fate. But morning must soon break, and then probably I should be succoured. Could I but disengage myself from the dead man who pressed me almost to suffocation, I might endure pain, cold, and thirst. I made another effort, it failed; and, in despair, I laid my head upon the ground, moistened with my own blood and that of my departed enemy. Just then a voice immediately beside me, uttered a feeble supplication for some water. I turned my head, and saw a young ensign, whose leg had been shattered by the wheels of a gun, raise himself upon his elbow, and look across the field, in hope of discovering someone who would relieve him. Nor were his cries unheard: a man dressed in the dark uniform of a Prussian *jäger*, and armed with the short sword which rifle troops carry, approached the sufferer; but, alas! he was not on the errand of mercy. Seizing the wounded man rudely, and deaf to his entreaties, he commenced his work of plunder. I heard the chinking of a purse, and a trinket, a watch, or locket, glittered in the moonlight, as he tore it from the bosom of the prostrate ensign.

'Oh! no, no, I cannot, will not part with that!' a low weak voice muttered; 'it was my mother's dying gift: I will never part with it!' A struggle ensued, but it was a short one: the ruffian, irritated at resistance, raised himself, and with a home-thrust silenced the poor youth for ever. Great God! that such a scene of death should be increased by the hand of murder!

I grew sick; I feared to breathe: my death was to be the next, for he had quickly plundered the body of his victim, and turned to the dead guardsman who lay across my breast. Suddenly he stopped, listened, and gazed suspiciously around; then sank down behind, and stretched himself upon the field.

My heart beat again. Two men came forward, and they too were plundering. But surely, all could not be so ruthless as the crouching wretch beside me! Nearer and nearer they approached; and, sounds of joy! they conversed in my native tongue. I listened with exquisite delight, and never did human voices appear so sweet as theirs. They were grenadiers of the line, and one of them wore a Sergeant's stripes. Without a moment's hesitation I addressed them; and an appeal in their native language was not disregarded, I was promptly answered in kindly tones; and while one caught the defunct Frenchman by the collar and flung him aside, his comrade extricated my legs from the dead charger, and assisted me to rise up.

I found myself in the centre of a heap of corpses; to take a second step without treading on a body was impossible; yet I scarce regarded the scene of slaughter: my eyes were riveted upon one corpse, that of the poor lad whom the crouching *jäger* had so brutally murdered.

I stood up with difficulty; a faintness overpowered me: I staggered, and would have fallen, but the Sergeant supported me, while his comrade held a canteen to my mouth. It contained brandy diluted with water, and, to one parched as I was, the draught was exquisitely grateful. My deliverers appeared anxious to move off, either to obtain fresh plunder, or secure that already acquired; and which, to judge from the size of their haversacks, must have been considerable. I begged them to assist me from the field; but they declined it, alleging that they must rejoin their regiment before daybreak. At this moment my eyes encountered those of the *jäger,* who lay as motionless behind the dead horse as any of the corpses that surrounded him. If I remained, and I could not walk without support, the chances were immense that the villain would speedily remove one who had witnessed a deed of robbery and murder, and I made a fresh appeal to my worthy countrymen:

'Sergeant, I will reward you handsomely: do not desert me.'

'I cannot remain longer, sir: morning is breaking, and you will soon have relief enough,' was the reply.

'It will never reach me: there is one within three paces, who will not permit me to look upon another sun.'

Both soldiers started.

'What do you mean?' exclaimed the Sergeant eagerly.

'Mark you that Prussian sharpshooter who skulks behind the horse?'

'What of him?' asked the grenadier.

'Yonder dead officer supplicated assistance from that scoundrel, and he answered him with curses, and commenced plundering him directly. I saw him take a purse, and tear away his epaulette. Some other article the poor fellow feebly attempted to retain; and the villain, before my eyes, stabbed him to the heart. Hearing your approach, he hid himself behind that charger: need I add, that there he lies until you leave this spot, and that I shall most probably be his next victim?'

'You shall not, by Heaven!' exclaimed the Sergeant, as he drew his sword and stepped over the dead horse. The Prussian, who had no doubt watched the conference attentively, sprang upon his feet on the first movement of the grenadier; but his fate was sealed: before the Sergeant's comrade could un-sheath his bayonet, the *jäger* was cut down, and the murderer rolled in the agonies of death beside the unfortunate youth whom but a few minutes before he had so ruthlessly slaughtered.

The corpse was speedily plundered by the grenadiers, and the spoil of the rifleman, when united to their booty, made, as I suspect, a valuable addition.

The moonlight was now yielding to the grey tint of early day, and the chief cause of my apprehensions being removed by the *jäger's* death, I found leisure to scrutinize my deliverers.

The first was a very powerful and athletic man, whose years might be set down at forty: his vigorous frame was perfectly unbroken, and his look bespoke a daring and unhesitating resolution. Indeed, his whole appearance was much above his rank; he seemed a war-worn, dissipated soldier: to him a field of battle was no novelty; and the perfect *nonchalance* with which he despatched the Prussian, betrayed a recklessness regarding human life, rather befitting a bandit than a soldier.

His companion, a very young man, was a fine strapping flanker, and in everything appeared to be wholly governed by the will of his comrade. He touched the dead, I thought, with some repugnance, and seemed of gentler heart and milkier disposition than might be expected in a midnight plunderer upon a battlefield.

'See, the dawn breaks rapidly,' said the non-commissioned officer to the young grenadier: 'we must be off, Macmanus. We leave you safe, sir; yonder black sharpshooter will never draw another trigger. Pick up a musket for the gentleman; we must not leave him without the means of keeping stragglers at a distance, should any come prowling here, before the fatigue-parties arrive to carry off the wounded. Here, sir, take another pull at the brandy-flask; nothing keeps up a sinking heart so well.'

'Thanks, my kind fellow, I owe you my life. Had you left me to yon black scoundrel, he would have served me as he did our comrade there. What are your names, your regiment? I shall take care to report your timely services to. . . .'

The elder of the grenadiers laughed: 'You are but a young soldier, sir, and this, as I suspect, your first field. I know you mean us kindly, but silence is the best service you can render us. We should have been with the advance near Genappe, instead of collecting lost property upon the plains of Waterloo. Well, we fought hard enough yesterday to allow us a right to share what no one claims, before the Flemish clowns come here by cock-crow. *Adieu!*'

As he spoke, his companion handed me a musket, after trying the barrel with a ramrod, and ascertaining from flint and pan that it was both loaded and serviceable.

'Enough; I ask no questions. But here are a few guineas.'

'Which we do not require,' said the Sergeant 'We have made a good night's work, and your money, young sir, we neither want, nor take. If we have rendered you service, it was for the sake of the old country. It is hard to shut one's ears, when the first language that we lisped in from the cradle asks pity in the field. Farewell, sir; morning comes on apace.'

'And yet,' I replied, 'I might perhaps at some time serve you. You know the fable: the mouse once cut a net, and saved a lion. I am indeed but a young soldier: but should I be able to be serviceable at any future period, ask for J—— B——, and he will remember the night of Waterloo.'

Of all the fields that ever were seen, Waterloo presented, perhaps the most bloody. The small space over which the action had been fought, rendered the scene indeed appalling: masses of dead appearing as it were piled on each other.

The field of Waterloo is twelve miles and a quarter from

Brussels; Quatre-Bras, twenty-one; and Ligny, twenty-eight miles: notwithstanding the great difference in the distances of those places, the firing at Ligny and Quatre-Bras was more distinctly heard at Brussels on the 16th, than that of Waterloo on the 18th.

Our detached force at Hall, which is about nine miles from Waterloo, heard nothing of the firing, nor did they know until the following morning, (the 19th,) how busily we had been engaged.

Appendix VII

As a tribute of the author's respectful gratitude for the information he has obtained from many officers who have visited the field, and, with all the advantages of being on the spot, have discussed the leading questions which have been raised in the United Service Journal, and so many other publications, respecting the details of the battle, their names are subjoined:

GENERALS

Lord John Hay	J B Parker
Lord Edward Somerset	D Mercer
Sir Hussey Vivian	W Mayne
Sir A Barnard	T Reynell
Sir H Ross	H Murray
Sir Colin Campbell	Thomas Hunter Blair
Sir F Adam	T W Robbins
Alexander Macdonald	J S Kennedy

COLONELS

Hon Keppell	Grey
Sir W Verner, Bart	Calvert
Sir Henry Floyd, Bart	Tinling

Sir G Hoste	Parkinson
G Gurwood	Wallace
T Wildman	Grove
Bussche	Bruce
Vigouroux	Kuhlman
Forbes	Lord Grosvenor
N Norcliffe	Lord Wellesley
Gilbourne	Bruce
Lord Douro	Hon G Cathcart

MAJORS

Turner	Fowler
Tindale	Cox
Browne	Rice
Dawson	Lloyd
Jackson	Maddox
Edward Macready	Ainsley
Belcher	Hawley

Two other officers of high rank, who served on the Duke's staff, have given me information respecting some of the most important occurrences of the day, but not permission to publish their names, as they had previously refused this favour to several writers of distinction.

The following letters are submitted to the reader as offering satisfactory evidence of the Author's competency to attempt a narration of the battle, and to act as guide to the visitors to the field, as well as of the authenticity of the spoils and relics, which anyone may inspect at his residence, Mont St. Jean.

Ems, July 23rd, 1839
Sergeant-Major Cotton,
I promised to write to you, but I have not had time to do so till now, since I saw you at Waterloo. You were desirous of having my testimony of the authenticity of the different articles collected from the field, that I saw in your house. I can have no hesitation in giving it gener-

ally. Many of the things I saw, I could speak to as having belonged to regiments of my own brigade.

It is but just also to you to say, that the account you gave me of the various occurrences of the day, was, as far as I knew, extremely correct, and by no means exaggerated, and I give you full credit for the pains you have taken to collect the details. I sincerely hope, that from the occupation you have undertaken, you will derive the means of passing the remainder of your days in competence and comfort; and thus reap the reward of your intelligence, on a field where you had, previously proved your courage.

Your friend,

Hussey Vivian

Lieutenant-General

I have seen at various times, Sergeant-Major Cotton's collection of spoils of the campaign of 1815, and I am of opinion that they are genuine relics, and such as may be relied on.

Henry Floyd, Bart.

Colonel unattached

Captain 10th hussars at Waterloo

Brussels, 1848

Brussels, October 2nd, 1845

Sergeant-Major Cotton,

I received so much satisfaction from our walk over the field of Waterloo yesterday, that I am induced to leave with you the expression of it.

Being anxious to satisfy myself regarding certain operations of the day, particularly the movements of the light brigade, (52nd, 71st, 95th,) to which I belonged, I found your exact knowledge of the ground, and the numerous details you have collected, highly instructive and interesting.

I am glad to learn that you intend publishing a memoir of the battle, and will not fail to become a purchaser as soon as it appears.

Your sincere well-wisher,

Thomas Hunter Blair

Colonel

Namur

June 29th, 1846

Sergeant-Major Cotton,

I have read your book. . . . with very great interest. . . . Thinking from our conversation on the field respecting the present condition of the ground on which Halkett's brigade acted, that you would be pleased to know the opinion of even so undistinguished a member of that body as myself, respecting your explanation of the events of the battle thereabouts. . . . I hesitate not to say that I was at once surprised and gratified to hear from you. . . . the best and most correct detail of the proceedings. . . . that I have either heard or read. . . . Further. . . . you made me far better acquainted with the details of what occurred at Hougoumont, and to its right, than I ever was before.

Hoping you may long enjoy health to pursue the interesting occupation for which your soldierly qualities and intelligence so well fit you, I remain, etc.

Edward Macready

Major unattached; of the 30th at Waterloo

The following document is to the Author, and probably it will be to not a few of his readers, deeply interesting: it from the late lamented Colonel Gurwood, whose labour in collecting and publishing the Wellington *Despatches*, whilst it rendered an invaluable, perhaps an unrequited service to his country and to civilization, broke his health, and bore down his gallant spirit:

70, Lowndes Square
London
June 18th, 1849
Sergeant-Major Cotton,
I have had a set of the *Despatches of the Duke of Wellington* packed up to be forwarded to you, which I shall endeavour to send you on the return of King Leopold to Brussels, to the care of Sir G. H. Seymour, Her Majesty's minister, to whom I shall write to inform you when they arrive.

The Marquis of Anglesey has much enhanced the value of my present to you, in writing his name in the title page at my request, and he appeared much pleased at gratifying an old soldier of his regiment.
Very faithfully yours,
J. Gurwood

A RELIC

On the 15th of May 1846, Colonel Macdonald, of the Royal Artillery, visited the author's interesting collection at Mont St. Jean, of arms, etc., spoils of the Waterloo campaign. The gallant veteran recognized his own sword of a curious workmanship, that had been lost on the field, when he was wounded. This precious relic the Colonel left with the Author, giving him the following certificate:

This sword I wore at the battle of Waterloo, and after I was wounded my servant left it on the field.
Alexander Macdonald
Colonel, Royal Horse Artillery
Waterloo, May 15th, 1846

Amongst the kind presents, which the Author has received from his countrymen, for his Waterloo Museum and library, at Mont St. Jean, he gratefully mentions the following:

Selections from Despatches, etc., of the Duke of Wellington, by Colonel Gurwood;

Presented by Lieutenant-Colonel N. Norcliffe, K. H., of Langton Hall, Yorkshire, to his fellow soldier, Sergeant Cotton, late of the 7th hussars.
July 25th, 1842

Blackheath
July 30th, 1846
Sergeant-Major Cotton,
Alderman Moon rejoiced in being able to gratify the patriotic feelings of an old Waterloo hero, and at once offered to present you with a copy of his celebrated engraving of the Waterloo Banquet, which he trusts you will frame and place in your Museum.
Francis Bennock

Mr. Billen has much pleasure. . . . in sending Sergeant-Major Cotton an engraved portrait of the brave General Sir James Kempt, and further promises, should he have the honour to engrave any other officers who took part in that eventful day, to send an impression to Sergeant-Major Cotton.
23, High Street
Camden Town
5th September, 1842

Of *the first edition* of this work, the following notice appeared in a London journal:

The author of the unpretending little volume before us is principal guide to the field of battle. This duty he is well qualified to perform from his intimate knowledge of the ground, near which he has resided during eleven years, and from his zealous endeavours to render himself master of facts, by studious research, and by communicating on the spot with military men of all ranks and nations.

The qualifications that recommend Sergeant-Major Cotton as guide, have facilitated his efforts to put in print those events which he is daily required to narrate verbally; and it is but justice to say that he has accomplished his task lucidly, impartially, and in plain, straightforward language, becoming his position and antecedents.

He states in sober and graphic terms, how the tempest first gathered and suddenly burst forth in advance of Charleroy, next upon our allies at Ligny, and our own advance corps at Quatre-Bras; he informs us of the principal incidents that led to the grand crisis, as well as of the measures adopted by the British commander to stem the torrent. The author likewise gives an intelligible sketch of the limited tactical movements executed during the battle.

Sergeant-Major Cotton shows us how the lion-hearted Glengary, with Hepburn, Saltoun, and their indomitable brother guardsmen, immortalized Hougoumont. He carries us with Hamilton and his Grey squadrons into the thick of the onslaught, where the Household Cavalry and Union brigades, the pride of English chivalry, hurled themselves upon their brave antagonists. He does not forget the "Up, guards, and make ready!" or the resistless charge that followed; nor does he pass over in silence the unflinching valour with which Baring's Hanoverians so long maintained their dangerous post. The author points out where the ardent Irish, thigh by thigh with heroic Highlanders, or knee by knee with stalwart English, bore down compactly upon advancing infantry, or with admirable coolness threw themselves into those impenetrable squares, wherein our devoted gunners found momentary shelter, when the field was swept by cuirassed hosts, more impetuous and daring than successful. We could willingly quote several interesting and graphic passages from Sergeant-Major Cotton's clear and well written narrative, from which we have risen with a more distinct acquaintance with the subject and scene, than we had hitherto derived from works of higher pretensions. But, as the whole volume merits perusal, we will content ourselves with expressing hopes that this voice from Waterloo may find an echo in public favour, and that our veteran hussar's pen may gain for him laurels more substantial than those already earned by his well-tried sabre.

Morning Chronicle, 22nd January, 1846

Extract from the Brussels Herald

We have much pleasure in reprinting, from the *Literary Gazette* of last Saturday, the following notice of Sergeant-Major Cotton's new work, A Voice from Waterloo:

The author was in the fight in the 7th hussars. He has since resided for years at Mont St. Jean, where this volume is published; and he acts as a guide to visitors when they desire to inspect this famous battlefield.

Sergeant-Major Cotton says, "Facts are stubborn things" and with the qualifications we have noticed, he is the very man to tell us all about it. And he has told us in a very circumstantial manner, separating details from masses, and altogether afforded us a better idea of this dreadful encounter than we have gathered from any other quarter. We had, by a curious coincidence, just arrived at this conclusion on reading his book, when we had an opportunity, in common with a number of leading artists and connoisseurs, of seeing Mr. Sidney Cooper's *Battle of Waterloo*, painted for the approaching exhibition in Westminster Hall. We were at once wonderfully struck with the apparent realization of the accounts which had just made such an impression on our minds. It seemed as if the artist had been present with the writer, and transferred in the most graphic and spirited manner to the canvas what he had committed with such particular effect to the paper. The chivalrous encounters, the almost single combats, the groups of cavalry slaughterings, the flight, the rally, the rush of riderless horses, the dying and the dead scattered among the trampled corn: all told the terrible tale of the last charge and effort of the French to retrieve the discomfiture of the day. Of these Mr. Cooper has made a stirring and splendid use. It is indeed a battle-piece, and upon the largest scale, such as never has been produced before by English painter, if by the greatest foreign master, in this style of art. The artist is sublime in the mysteries of moving human columns under the canopy of smoke, through which the spectator may easily imagine he hears the cannon boom. The whole is real, yet imaginative; and inspires at the same moment feelings of intense individual interest, and general awe. With regard to the author we need not add any other comment. Though he mentions that the Duke and Blücher met at La Belle-Alliance after the battle, we think he shows that this could not have been the case; and we have reason to believe that no such meeting ever took place.[6]

6. I wish I were as positive of every part of my narrative. E. C.

Sergeant-Major Cotton's
Waterloo Cabinet

THIS INTERESTING MUSEUM CONTAINS

1. The following highly finished engravings: Wellington, Napoleon, Blücher; Wellington and Napoleon at Waterloo; the Waterloo Banquet; Sir James Kempt; Battle of Waterloo; Capture of an Eagle; the Prince of Orange wounded.

2. Medallion portraits of Wellington, Napoleon, Blücher, King of the Netherlands, Lords Hill and Anglesey, Sir Thomas Picton, Count Alten, Marshals Ney and Soult; General Cambronne, or *"La garde meurt et ne se rend pas."*

3. General view of the Field (oil); View of Hougoumont.

4. Plans showing different periods of the Battles of Ligny, Quatre-Bras, Waterloo, and Wavre; map on which is indicated the distribution of the respective armies at the commencement of hostilities.

5. Autographs of the following Waterloo Commanders and Officers: Napoleon, Wellington, Field-Marshal the Marquis of Anglesey, Marshal Grouchy; Generals Vivian, Harris, Sir E. Kerrison, Hunter Blair, and Macdonald; Colonels Sir Henry Floyd, Bart., Gurwood, Hon. G. Cathcart and Muttlebury; Majors Kennedy, Macready, etc., etc.

6. An interesting collection of Relics, warranted spoils of the Waterloo campaign, a part of which are labelled for sale at moderate prices, although not so cheap as the spurious articles with which the neighbourhood abounds.

E. C. engages within three months of purchase to return the money paid for any article found not to be genuine, provided the label attached when sold accompanies it.

THE COLLECTION OF RELICS IS COMPOSED OF:

Arms
Cuirass
Casques
Caps
Clothing
Accoutrements
Military ornaments
Trappings
Gold and Silver Crosses of the Legion of honour
Prussian Crosses and Medals
etc., etc.

The most interesting is the Sword of General Alexander Macdonald, which he left on the field of battle when wounded, and recognized amongst the relics of the Waterloo Cabinet on revisiting the field in May 1846. The General's certificate is attached to the Sword,

Several pieces of Napoleon's kitchen utensils, marked with the Imperial crown, letter *N* and *Tuileries* or *Voyage*.

A Dragoon's saddlebags, with the stains of blood still visible, etc., etc., etc.

LEONAUR

ALSO FROM LEONAUR
AVAILABLE IN SOFTCOVER OR HARDCOVER WITH DUST JACKET

SEPOYS, SIEGE & STORM *by Charles John Griffiths*—The Experiences of a young officer of H.M.'s 61st Regiment at Ferozepore, Delhi ridge and at the fall of Delhi during the Indian mutiny 1857.

CAMPAIGNING IN ZULULAND *by W. E. Montague*—Experiences on campaign during the Zulu war of 1879 with the 94th Regiment.

THE STORY OF THE GUIDES *by G. J. Younghusband*—The Exploits of the Soldiers of the famous Indian Army Regiment from the northwest frontier 1847 - 1900..

ZULU: 1879 *by D.C.F. Moodie & the Leonaur Editors*—The Anglo-Zulu War of 1879 from contemporary sources: First Hand Accounts, Interviews, Dispatches, Official Documents & Newspaper Reports.

THE RECOLLECTIONS OF SKINNER OF SKINNER'S HORSE *by James Skinner*—James Skinner and his 'Yellow Boys' Irregular cavalry in the wars of India between the British, Mahratta, Rajput, Mogul, Sikh & Pindarree Forces.

TOMMY ATKINS' WAR STORIES 14 FIRST HAND ACCOUNTS—Fourteen first hand accounts from the ranks of the British Army during Queen Victoria's Empire Original & True Battle Stories Recollections of the Indian Mutiny With the 49th in the Crimea With the Guards in Egypt The Charge of the Six Hundred With Wolseley in Ashanti Alma, Inkermann and Magdala With the Gunners at Tel-el-Kebir Russian Guns and Indian Rebels Rough Work in the Crimea In the Maori Rising Facing the Zulus From Sebastopol to Lucknow Sent to Save Gordon On the March to Chitral Tommy by Rudyard Kipling

CHASSEUR OF 1914 *by Marcel Dupont*—Experiences of the twilight of the French Light Cavalry by a young officer during the early battles of the great war in Europe.

TROOP HORSE & TRENCH *by R. A. Lloyd*—The experiences of a British Lifeguardsman of the household cavalry fighting on the western front during the First World War 1914-18.

THE EAST AFRICAN MOUNTED RIFLES *by C. J. Wilson*—Experiences of the campaign in the East African bush during the First World War.

THE FIGHTING CAMELIERS *by Frank Reid*—The exploits of the Imperial Camel Corps in the desert and Palestine campaigns of the First World War.

Printed in the United Kingdom by
Lightning Source UK Ltd., Milton Keynes
141467UK00001B/254/A